Making & Using
DRIED
FOODS

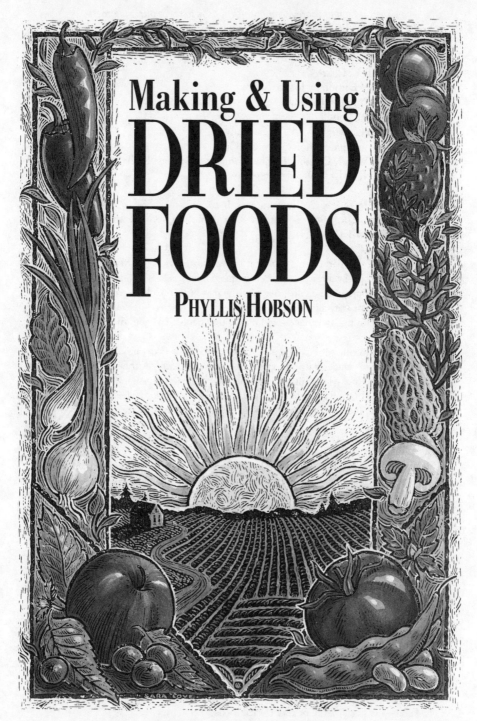

Making & Using
DRIED
FOODS

PHYLLIS HOBSON

A Garden Way Publishing Book

Storey Communications, Inc.
Schoolhouse Road
Pownal, Vermont 05261

*The mission of Storey Communications is to serve our customers
by publishing practical information that encourages personal independence
in harmony with the environment.*

Edited by Amanda R. Haar
Revised for Second Edition by Joann Tarbox
Cover design by Cindy McFarland
Text design by Greg Imhoff
Cover illustration Copyright© 1994 by Sara Love
Design assistance and production by Andrea Gray
Line drawings by Wendy Edelson, Brigita Fuhrmann, and Mary Rich
Indexed by Nan N. Badgett, Word•a•bil•i•ty

Garden Way Publishing was founded in 1973 as part of the Garden Way Incorporated Group of
Companies, dedicated to bringing gardening information and equipment to as many people as possible. Today the name "Garden Way Publishing" is licensed to Storey Communications, Inc., in
Pownal, Vermont. For a complete list of Garden Way Publishing titles call 1-800-827-8673. Garden
Way Incorporated manufactures products in Troy, New York, under the Troy-Bilt® brand including
garden tillers, chipper/shredders, mulching mowers, sicklebar mowers, and tractors. For information
on any Garden Way Incorporated product, please call 1-800-345-4454.

Printed in the United States by R. R. Donnelley
10 9 8 7 6 5 4

Library of Congress Cataloging-in-Publication Data

Hobson, Phyllis.
    Making and using dried foods / Phyllis Hobson.
        p. cm.
    Includes bibliographical references and index.
    ISBN 0-88266-615-0
    1. Food—Drying.   2. Cookery (Dried foods)   I. Title.
TX609.H58 1994
641.4'4—dc20   93-33376
    CIP

Contents

DRYING HERBS—*continued*

Introduction

W ho invented drying foods? We like to think some prehistoric hunter and his mate discarded a chunk of meat beside their cave fire, and a few days later noticed it had turned black and dry. Curious and daring, one of them chewed into it, uttered the Cro-Magnon equivalent of "Not bad," and slowly realized that here was a way to save food for the leaner days that came so regularly.

By the time records were being kept, the drying of food was widespread. Phoenicians and other fishermen were drying their catches in the open air; the Chinese were sun-drying their tea leaves.

In this country, Indians taught early settlers how to dry corn and grind it into meal; jerky was made from the meat of bear, deer, elk, and buffalo living in the forests and on the plains. The French had invented a dehydrator to dry vegetables by 1795, while American families were still using fire, sun, and smoke to dry their grapes, herbs, peppers, and meats.

Today a desire for natural, healthful, and inexpensive methods of food preservation has put dehydration in modern kitchens. People in all walks of life can dry many kinds of food in all kinds of weather at home.

The art of drying foods is a natural alternative to canning and freezing and benefits the family on a tight budget, because drying fruits, vegetables, grains, and breakfast cereals can offer a low-cost, energy-efficient way of eating for less. Drying foods benefits the hiker, the camper, the skier, or the fisherman looking for a compact food supply light enough to carry in a knapsack. It benefits the homemaker looking for delicious, healthful snacks to offer the family, and it benefits vacationers with two homes, because drying can be a safe way to store food over the winter. Drying is an ideal way of storing foods for those who live in isolated locations where electricity to operate a freezer may be undependable or nonexistent, and it is a good way to stockpile an emergency supply in a small storage area.

The goal of drying foods is to remove excess moisture, getting the water content down to 5 percent to 25 percent, so bacteria that cause decay cannot survive. Since dried foods are only one-half to one-twelfth the weight and bulk of the original food, a small, dry, cool closet will provide all the storage space needed for a winter's supply of food. If dried food is protected by airtight packaging, it will keep indefinitely.

Compared with canning, drying foods is simplicity itself. There are no complicated procedures to learn or potentially dangerous pieces of equipment to operate. You don't need a pressure canner or a hot water bath canner, nor will you have to shop for glass canning jars and boxes of canning lids. Neither will you have to have jar lifters, filling funnels, or tongs. The only special equipment manufactured for drying is a dehydrator, and it is possible to dry without one. Everything else, from oven drying trays to storage jars, you already have on hand, or you can make from castoffs.

Compared with freezing, drying is inexpensive and worry-free. Drying in the sun or with an oven pilot flame is absolutely free. It is costly to operate a food freezer, depending on the efficiency of the freezer, the amount of food it contains, and the electricity rate in your area.

Even if drying food were not simpler, less expensive and more convenient, many people might still prefer dried foods for their taste. Dried apricots, dried apple slices, and raisins compare well with fresh fruits, and honey-dipped pineapple slices, chewy, fruity leathers, and tough, tangy meat jerky have a universal appeal.

Because drying is a more natural method of preservation than canning and freezing, many people believe drying foods preserves more of the nutritional values present in raw foods, and a USDA study backs up this belief. Vitamins are lost in blanching, a pretreatment necessary for some vegetables before drying, but this nutritional loss can be kept to a minimum if the foods are steam blanched for no more than the specified time.

Almost any food can be dried by following the instructions in this book, which are aimed at preserving as much of the nutrients and the flavor of the food as possible.

Will your dried food be as good as what you can buy on the market? Commercial manufacturers have the advantage of expensive freeze-drying equipment, but you have the advantage of sweet, tree-ripened fruit and just-picked, garden-fresh vegetables. Your own homegrown fruits and vegetables, or those bought at local farmers' markets or roadside stands, should be more delicious and nutritious than those the food processors have.

CHAPTER ONE

Drying Foods Can Save You Money

If you're having trouble keeping up with the ever-increasing cost of food, a selection of dried foods on your pantry shelf can save your food budget a significant amount.

You can save the most money, of course, by drying fruits and vegetables from your own garden or foods that otherwise would go to waste. Drying is not only a safe, easy way of preserving your excess garden harvest; it also is an inexpensive method. Drying costs less than canning and freezing in equipment, energy, and storage space.

Even if you don't plant a garden, you can still save money by drying foods at home. During the harvest season, fruits and vegetables can be purchased cheaply by the bushel at the country markets and roadside stands.

Watch also for specials at the produce department of your favorite supermarket. Bananas flecked with brown, which often sell for half price, make excellent fruit leathers. Mushrooms and vegetables often are marked down because a new shipment is due.

Drying can also save you money by avoiding waste. When you have leftover cooked meat or cooked vegetables, they can be finely chopped and dried, then enjoyed another time months later. Leftover applesauce, for instance, can be pureed in the blender, dried on sheets of plastic wrap, and eaten as a leather.

Save money too by drying processed grain products. Ready-to-eat purchased breakfast cereals, noodles, and croutons are expensive not because of their ingredients, but because of the time involved in their preparation. Sometime when you have more time than money, you can make them ahead and dry them for busy days.

If there is a baby at your house, you can save money usually spent on commercially canned baby foods by cooking your own fresh fruits and vegetables (see chapters 6 and 7 for complete instructions).

At birthday and holiday time, or any time a gift is in order, save money with a very special gift:

- For your sweet-toothed friends, save your prettiest peanut butter, pickle, or jelly jars, paint the lids, decorate with ribbon bows, and fill with a mixture of dried fruits made according to the directions in chapter 6, Drying Fruits.

- For your nature-loving friends, package an assortment of dried soups and stews for their next camping trip. Directions are in chapter 14, Drying Foods for Hiking and Camping.

- For your young (and young at heart) friends, package a mixed variety of fruit leather strips in plastic wrap and tie with a big ribbon. You'll find the directions in chapter 12, Leathers.

- For your elegant friends, package several different aromatic sachets in colorful nylon nets. Tie with a matching ribbon and attach a list of the ingredients. Several recipes for sachets and potpourris are in chapter 15, Drying Flower Blossoms.

- And for your gourmet friends, fill small baby food jars with dried herbs and herb mixtures as described in chapter 8, Drying Herbs. Paste pretty labels on the jars and include a few recipes on decorative file cards.

CHAPTER TWO

How to Dry Foods

J ust as with freezing and canning, the best quality dried foods must begin with the best quality foods available. Fruits and vegetables to be dried should be picked when they are at their peak of flavor.

Most vegetables are best picked while they are still slightly immature. Harvest peas and beans when the pods are still green and succulent. Spinach and other leafy vegetables should be picked before the leaves reach full size. Most root vegetables should be pulled while still undersized. Corn should be picked before the natural sugars turn to starch, while the kernels are succulent enough to squirt out juice when punctured with the thumbnail. Cabbage family vegetables — including broccoli, cabbage, and kohlrabi — should be picked after the vegetable is well formed, but before it becomes strong tasting. Brussels sprouts are best after the first frost.

Fruits, including berries and tomatoes, should be left to ripen thoroughly before picking. Peaches, apricots, and apples are sweeter and more flavorful when tree-ripened.

In general, the faster a food is dried, the better the quality, but temperatures can't be so high that the food is cooked. Drying is speeded and quality improved if the food is as dry as possible when the process begins. Pick fruits, vegetables, and herbs in late morning when the sun has dried off the early morning dew. Drain cooked vegetables well. Wipe off washed fruit. Do not soak any food for more than 5 or 10 minutes. Most fruits and vegetables should be peeled to permit the air to penetrate the inner pulp.

Drying also is speeded if as much food surface as possible is exposed to the air. To do this, cut food pieces as small, and especially as thin as possible with a knife or in a food processor or salad maker. Some vegetables, such as onions, green peppers, and turnips, may be coarsely grated in a blender or shredded with a hand-held grater.

The foods then are ready to be pretreated according to the directions in chapter 4, To Pretreat or Not To Pretreat. Then they may be dried according to one of the three methods that follow.

After drying, foods should be cooled, tested for any sign of moisture (see chapter 5, Testing and Storing Dried Foods), then stored and labeled.

Three methods of drying are recommended for each of the foods listed in this book. Each method has its advantages and its disadvantages. The method you choose will depend upon the climate and the environment in which you live, your finances, and the amount of drying you'll be doing.

The three recommended methods are:

Dehydrator

Drying foods was once a simple procedure. The food was harvested and spread out in the sun to dry. After a few days, it was brought inside and stored for the winter. The results weren't always perfect. Sometimes the food spoiled before it dried. Dried fruits had a tendency to turn brown and hard. Sometimes dried vegetables were tough and stringy. Dried meats resembled well-tanned shoe leather. But once they were refreshed and cooked, sun-dried foods were quite acceptable, especially when good cooks came up with such dishes as *Dried Apple Pie* and *Fruitcake*.

Times have changed, however, as have our environments. Some of us live in the cities, where there are no expanses of unfiltered sunlight in which to dry foods, and where dust and chemicals and other pollutants will contaminate any foods spread out to dry. Some of us live too close to the leaded fumes of highways, to railroad tracks, and in the pathways of insecticide sprays. Some of us live in climates too sunless, too humid, or too cold. We cannot depend on the sun to dry our food.

Our tastes have changed. We have become accustomed to snowy white dried apples and bright orange dried apricots. Our palates have been educated. We no longer want our dried foods to taste like dried foods.

To accommodate our changed living conditions and our educated palates, dehydrators have been designed to dry our food with speed, efficiency, and a minimum of trouble.

To dry foods in an electric dehydrator, it is only necessary to prepare the food, fill the trays, and turn it on. The best dehydrators have thermostatically controlled heat settings and fans which blow warm air over the foods. A well-designed dehydrator will automatically control heat and air flow so that it is almost impossible to overdry or scorch the food being dried.

Many foods do not even need to be pretreated before drying in a dehydrator because the forced air dries the surface of the food before it can discolor. But with many foods, some forms of pretreatment are required for best results.

The price of a good dehydrator will vary depending on its size, the construction materials, and its design. For those who would dry a large portion of their food supply, an electric dehydrator could be a good investment, roughly equiva-

lent to the cost of a household's supply of canners, canning jars, and other equipment needed for canning.

A dehydrator should be used indoors in a dry, well-ventilated room. A
kitchen is not necessarily the best place, since the humidity often caused by
cooking hinders its operation.

To operate an electric dehydrator, just plug it into a 110-volt outlet and preheat to the desired temperature while the food is being prepared for drying.
Recommended temperatures are 115°F (46°C) for uncooked fruits, 120°F (48°C)
for vegetables and some cooked fruits, 110°F (43°C) for leaf herbs, 140°F (60°C)
for meat, and 115°F (46°C) for grains.

Estimated drying times and exact temperatures are included in the specific
drying instructions for each food in the sections that follow. All drying times listed for foods are estimates. Exact times will depend on the efficiency of your dehydrator, the humidity of the air in the room, and the amount of moisture in
the food.

As stated, some form of preparation is needed for most foods. Many must be
peeled because the drying air cannot penetrate the skin. Slicing or chopping
helps expose more surface to the warm moving air, speeding the drying process
and producing better results. Some foods must be blanched or dipped to retard
discoloration and enzyme growth, which would cause loss of flavor and nutrients.
The pretreatment of foods before drying is covered in detail in chapter 4, To
Pretreat or Not To Pretreat.

To begin the drying process, spread the prepared foods evenly over the dehydrator trays in a thin layer. Different foods may be dried at the same time, but
very moist foods should not be dried with almost-dry foods. Foods with very
strong odors or flavors should be dried alone. Foods that have been pretreated
with sulfur fumes should never be dried in a dehydrator.

Food should be examined and stirred or turned at least once while drying. At
the same time, the trays should be rotated, front to back, side to side, and top to
bottom. As the drying progresses, the food will shrink and you will be tempted
to consolidate trays and add more food to the dehydrator. You may do so, but it
will lengthen the drying time to crowd the almost-dry foods on the trays. It is
better to wait until the first batch is completely dried before adding more food to
the dehydrator.

Dehydrator drying is so trouble-free you can leave the dehydrator operating
overnight or while you're away from home. If your days are busy, you can load
the dehydrator in the morning before you leave for work and let it run all day
with complete safety. If a dryer load is almost dry at bedtime, just turn the heat
down to 105°F (41°C) or 110°F (43°C) and go to bed. By morning the food will
be ready to store.

To help you dry foods in a dehydrator, you'll need knives, a strainer, and
maybe a blender. If you want to make leather, you'll need some plastic wrap or a
special leather-making sheet. Dehydrators come complete with their own trays.

Sun

If you are blessed with clean air, low humidity, and an abundance of hot, sunny days, sun drying is the least expensive and simplest method of preserving foods. The advantages to sun drying are obvious. It's absolutely free. It does not require an outlay for electricity. There isn't even an investment in equipment. All the necessary equipment can be made at home.

If you live where sun drying is practical, by all means try it. Drying in the sun is unpredictable unless temperatures are over 100°F (38°C) and the relative humidity is low. If the temperature is too low, humidity too high, or both, spoilage (souring or molding) will occur before drying is achieved. The climate in the Northeast does not lend itself to successful sun drying. Even if your location is marginal, you can use the sun when possible, then fall back on a dehydrator or the oven to finish off a batch on those days when a sudden rainstorm or a low cloud ceiling hampers your sun-drying operation.

Because sun drying is slower and the food is exposed for a longer period of time, pretreating is more important than for drying in a dehydrator. Specific instructions are listed in chapter 4. *Sun drying is the only method recommended for fruits that have been sulfured.*

After pretreating, foods to be sun dried are spread over the drying trays and placed in a well-ventilated place in full sun. Foods that are attractive to birds and insects must be covered with a layer of cheesecloth propped up to keep it from touching the food.

Every few hours during the drying period, the food should be turned or stirred to expose all surfaces to the sun. Take trays inside at night to prevent the foods from reabsorbing moisture from dew. Any time out of the sun, of course, is "down time" and is not included in the drying time estimates.

All drying times given for sun drying under specific foods are estimates since the time required for any one food will vary depending on the temperature, the amount of sunshine, the humidity in the air, the amount of air movement, and the amount of moisture in the food.

To dry foods in the sun, you'll need a number of drying trays, preparation equipment, such as knives, a peeler, a strainer or blender, plastic wrap for making leathers, cheesecloth for covering foods, and containers for storage.

Drying trays may be cookie sheets or homemade wooden trays, but drying is speeded if air is allowed to circulate freely around the food, so trays made of fiberglass or stainless steel screening work best. **Do not use galvanized screen.** It will contaminate the food. And be careful about those wooden trays. The odors of such woods as pine and cedar will transfer to the food being dried on them. Wooden drying trays should be well sanded and sealed with mineral oil.

Unlike other drying methods, there is no capacity limit in sun drying. The only limit to the amount of food which can be dried at one time is the number of trays available.

Before storing, foods dried in the sun should be placed in an oven set at 125°F (52°C) for 30 minutes to kill any insect eggs that may have been deposited on them, or they may be stored in glass or metal containers and set in the freezer for a day or two.

Oven or Homemade Dryer

For drying small amounts of food or in an emergency when rain brings the sun-drying operation to a halt, a conventional oven may be used for drying foods.

Depending on its design and size, a homemade dryer also may be used for drying foods in large or small batches. Some homemade dryers may do the job almost as well as commercial dehydrators.

Drying foods in an oven sometimes is better than sun drying, because it is possible to have controlled, even temperatures, but it has the disadvantage of poor air circulation, and air movement is necessary for even drying. Air circulation can be improved by leaving the door ajar a few inches and placing an electric fan in front of the door, positioned so it will blow away the moist air as it accumulates.

Although commercial drying trays are available for use in an oven, homemade trays may be made of wooden frames and nylon screening. Tray sizes will depend on the oven size and must provide for circulation of air. There should be 1 inch (2.5 cm) of space on each side, 3 inches (7.5 cm) at the top and bottom, and 2½ inches (6.5 cm) between the trays.

You'll also need a thermometer that registers from 100°F (38°C) to 150°F (66°C), preparation tools, such as knives, a peeler, a strainer or blender, plastic wrap, and storage containers.

To dry foods in an oven or homemade dryer, load the trays sparsely with a thin layer of food on each tray. Different foods may be dried at the same time, but foods with different moisture content or with strong flavors or odors should not be dried together.

Using a large, easily read thermometer on the top shelf, warm the oven or dryer to the specified temperature. Place trays in the warm oven or dryer, leaving the door ajar. Set the electric fan in front of the door, as directed, to dispel moist air. Dry according to directions under each food, stirring or turning the food occasionally, and rotating trays top to bottom, front to back, and side to side every 2 to 3 hours.

Foods dried in an oven or homemade dryer must be watched more carefully than those in the sun or in a commercial dehydrator.

Microwave Oven

Microwave drying is not recommended by some oven manufacturers, as removing all of the moisture from the oven creates what's known as a "no-load" situation that can damage the machine's magnetron tube over time.

Microwave drying can also cause a "volcanic effect." That is, the food feels very hot and dry on the outside, but is still moist on the inside. If stored, this moisture can turn into mold or cause the food to become rancid. In addition, the intensity of a microwave makes it very easy to overdry foods, resulting in a burned or charred flavor. Some foods, such as herbs, may even catch on fire.

So while it is possible to dry foods in a microwave oven, it is not always wise. Be sure to consult your machine's instructions before attempting to use it to dry foods or herbs.

CHAPTER THREE

Buying a Dehydrator

Like other kitchen appliances, home food dehydrators come in an array of sizes, shapes, and colors, with a wide assortment of features. There are small-batch dehydrators styled for the apartment kitchen and floor model dehydrators big enough for the farm garden. The size of the heating element varies from 165 to 1,000 watts or more. Some are vented; some are not.

But unlike purchasing other kitchen appliances, you may have to make your choice without trying out — or even seeing — the food dehydrators available. Comparison shopping is rarely possible because most dehydrators are sold by mail, not by your hometown appliance dealer and only a few brands offer a no-risk trial period. It isn't even possible to depend on the reputation of a manufacturer you know and trust, since you may not be familiar with the companies making them.

Before you decide what to buy, write to several manufacturers and find out about the materials, the construction, the dimensions, the size and type of heating elements, and fans of several models. Specifically ask for construction details about the fan and airflow, the trays and the door. You'll get brochures, but some of them contain more adjectives than facts.

Ask for a copy of the guarantee; then, if necessary, ask for an explanation of the wording. Most mail-order dehydrators come with a limited one-year warranty against defective parts, but do not promise to pay labor costs.

To help you sort out this maze of sizes, features, and guarantees, here are some features to consider when selecting a food dehydrator.

Safety

Always look for safety, specifically the Underwriters Laboratories (UL) seal. Found on either a hang-tag or decal, the UL seal means the appliance has met the Laboratories' safety standards. It is your assurance the dehydrator is safe from fire and shock hazard.

Size

Models can weigh between 8 and 35 pounds (0.25 and 16 kg), range in size from 8 to 15 inches high (20 to 38 cm), 11 to 22 inches (28 to 56 cm) wide, and 17 to 23 inches (43 to 58 cm) deep. Some are round or oval, others rectangular with or without rounded corners. Whatever size you choose, make sure you have the space to accommodate one. A few extra inches in size may seem unimportant, but on a kitchen counter with little work space to spare, size is critical.

When choosing the size, also consider the square feet of drying space. Do you want only two trays or ten trays in the same amount of space? How much food will you be drying? As a rule of thumb, *12 square feet (1 sq m) of drying area is sufficient for a half-bushel of vegetables*.

Airflow

The key to a dryer's performance is the fan or blower used to distribute warm air evenly and to help draw off the moisture-laden air. Most models' fans tend to be side- or bottom-mounted. Side-mounted, or horizontal airflow fans tend to dry foods more evenly and require less attention than bottom-mounted styles which can require a considerable amount of tray rotation as foods closest to the fan dry faster than those at the top.

Some dryers have warm air that can be recirculated to reduce the amount of energy used by the appliance; others have the additional feature of having air recirculate or not, as you wish. If you do not want the flavors of the items you're drying (like onions and fruit leathers) to mingle, you should not use the recirculating feature.

An air vent design that allows for the escape of the moist air on one side while it pulls in dry air from the other produces excellent results in a shorter period of time. Many units have no venting systems, but rely on the escape of moist air around loosely fitting doors.

Trays

Trays vary in number and construction. They can be made completely of plastic or a combination of plastic, metal, wood, or plastic-coated fiberglass. Regardless of material, trays should have sturdy, lightweight frames. Screens of heavy plastic are safer and easier to clean than metal ones. Metal can corrode from the sulfured food, tends to hold heat, and can scorch food easily at the end of the drying process.

In their search for a lightweight, nontoxic material on which to place food, most manufacturers have settled on some form of plastic in one of two styles. The first style is made of a plastic screen embedded in a plastic or aluminum frame. The single-piece construction makes this style sturdy, but the grooves in which the screen is embedded tend to be tough to clean. These one-piece trays must also be handled with both hands when loaded with food — a difficult feat when the trays must be juggled in order to open the dryer door.

The other choice is two-piece trays. These consist of a square of plastic mesh placed on top of a plastic frame. Two-piece trays are indeed easier to clean, but their flexibility makes them hard to handle when loaded.

Regardless of what style you choose, make sure the trays are well spaced, at least 1 inch (2.5 cm) apart. They should slide in and out easily without catching, which can cause spillage when trays are full.

Most instruction sheets and books accompanying dehydrators emphasize that the rotation of trays is not necessary with their models because of advance design or a special airflow system. Results are better, however, no matter what model is used, when trays are rotated, front to back, side to side, and top to bottom, at least once during the drying period. In addition, drying is aided by stirring or turning over the pieces of food at least once or twice.

Doors

Today, not all dryers have doors, most notably stackable models. But for those that do, it is important to have a solidly constructed door that opens easily and offers unobstructed access to trays. Some styles of dryers offer doors that can be removed completely during loading and unloading. Older styles tend to be hinged and swing down from top to bottom. Regardless of style, the best doors are simple, but functional.

It is also worth noting that if it should ever be broken, the door could be replaced easily.

Controls

The drying unit should feature a clearly marked, adjustable thermostat control that indicates the temperature. Also look for a control setting to adjust the side vents for airflow control as well as an enclosed heating element. Some models also include a built-in automatic timer, a helpful feature if you don't already own a timer.

Cabinets

Outside cabinets are made from a variety of both heavy and light materials: aluminum, steel, high-impact plastic, wood, or steel with woodgrain vinyl covering. Ask yourself...is it light enough to carry around if I have to move it frequently? Is it easy to keep clean? Does it fit on my countertop? Where will I store it? How well insulated is the cabinet? (Look for double-wall construction.) Keep in mind that wood can warp, absorb odors, and harbor bacteria. Also remember that dehydrator cabinets are measured to indicate needed counter space, not food capacities.

Cost of Operation

To calculate the cost of operation of a unit, use the following formula: wattage of appliance, divided by 1,000, times the local rate per kilowatt hour. For example, a 1,050 watt dryer in an 8 cent per kilowatt hour area would cost a little over 8 cents an hour to run. Remember a three-pronged plug insures proper grounding.

Final Thoughts

Some final things to think about when buying a dehydrator include:

- Noise level may seem minor when choosing a dryer, but be aware that in a kitchen setting the additional noise of a dehydrator fan may be noticeable.
- The best temperature is not always the one recommended by the manufacturer. As a result, you may have to do some experimenting.
- In spite of the convenience of dehydrators and the quality of the food they produce, the size of the units, the constant noise of the fans, and the humidity they add to the air in an already humid room can be a little overpowering in a small kitchen. Most manufacturers' directions specify that they should not be used outdoors, but if you're buying a dehydrator, you might look for a spot on an enclosed back porch, a utility room, or even a spare bedroom. A small metal utility table on casters is ideal for holding a dryer and for moving it from one room to another.

Finally, look for an automatic shut-off device in case of overheating; at least a year's guarantee on workmanship and parts; and a nearby factory-authorized representative for repair.

CHAPTER FOUR

To Pretreat
or Not
To Pretreat

There are as many arguments for and against the need to pretreat fruits and vegetables before drying as there are foods to be dried. The truth is, some foods need pretreating; some do not.

Here are the arguments for and against pretreating, plus some opinions of my own.

For Pretreating

One of the most important substances in any fruit or vegetable is the natural enzyme. It is the catalyst that causes the plant to sprout from a seed, to develop a stem and leaves, and finally, to fruit. The enzyme causes the fruit to ripen, but the enzyme action doesn't stop then, or even when the fruit is picked. Unless it is stopped, the fruit will overmature and finally decay.

Drying foods does not stop enzymatic action. Like freezing, drying only slows it down. Some foods keep well without pretreatment, but others will continue to deteriorate in color, flavor, texture, and nutrients for months after they are dried unless they are treated. Just as in freezing, untreated vegetables tend to become tough and strong-flavored after a period of storage, and without pretreatment, some fruits — apples, bananas, peaches, and apricots — may darken considerably before and during drying, especially in sun drying. While this darkening in itself does not spoil the fruit, it is an indication that there is enzymatic action still at work on the flavor and nutritional value of the food as well as the color.

Vegetables may be pretreated before drying, just as they are before freezing, by blanching in boiling water or steam. Blanching is a method of cooking the food for a short time, just long enough to halt the natural enzymatic action. It is a form of quick, incomplete cooking.

Fruits usually are not blanched, because it spoils their fresh flavor, and their acid content makes the precaution unnecessary. Fruits may be dipped in a solution containing salt, ascorbic acid, or fruit juice to prevent darkening. Fruits also may be pretreated with sulfur fumes to keep their color bright.

Instructions for all these methods will follow.

Against Pretreating

Some people who have years of experience in drying foods claim that pretreating is unnecessary if the foods are prepared properly and dried quickly. They say that foods should be cut into small pieces to expose as much surface as possible to the air and that it is important to have good circulation of air, whether drying is done in the sun or with artificial heat.

Furthermore, they say foods retain more of their natural nutrients and digestive enzymes when they are dried without pretreatment. They argue that blanching cooks the foods and that other methods, such as dipping and sulfuring, add undesirable chemicals to the foods.

Our choice is to select from the best of both methods. Although it is a good idea to keep food drying as natural as possible, some foods require pretreating in order to keep their fresh taste and food values.

Although we do not recommend submitting fruits to sulfur fumes, we have included directions for doing so if you wish. And we agree that results are better with some fruits when they are dipped in fruit juice or an ascorbic acid solution.

Some vegetables, such as peppers and onions, retain their color and flavor best without blanching, but some, such as broccoli, Brussels sprouts, and green, leafy vegetables, fade and become strong-tasting if they are not pretreated before drying. Carrots and other root vegetables may be dried in the sun without pretreating — although they tend to become tough if they are dried in a dehydrator.

Pretreating Methods

Blanching is a method of heating the food (usually vegetables) just to the point of inactivating the enzymes without cooking the food through. Steam or water is used. Steam blanching preserves more of the vitamin and mineral values of the food, but requires a longer processing period. It also requires occasional stirring and careful watching to be sure the steam circulates around all the pieces and penetrates them to the center. Although there is more vitamin loss in water blanching, it requires less time and less special equipment.

Blanching as a pretreatment before drying is much the same as blanching as a pretreatment before freezing. After blanching, chill the food in ice water to stop the cooking action, drain, pat dry with paper towels, and place directly on the drying tray.

Steam Blanching: Bring to a boil about 2 inches (5 cm) of water in a steamer, a blanching kettle, or a deep pan with a tight-fitting lid. Place vegetables loosely in a wire basket or colander and spread out as much as possible, preferably one layer deep. Place basket in pan. Vegetables should be above water level, but steam should circulate well through the pieces.

Put a lid on the pan and keep heat high enough for water to boil rapidly. Use a timer and steam for the length of time specified for each vegetable. After blanching, cut up vegetables and chill in ice water to stop the cooking action. Drain, pat dry with paper towels, and place on drying trays. For high altitudes, add 1 minute for each 2,000 feet (607 meters) of elevation.

Water Blanching: Fill a blancher or a large pan two-thirds full of water. Use about 1 gallon (4 litres) of water to 1 pound (400 grams) of vegetables. Place vegetables in a wire basket or a cheesecloth bag or place directly in boiling water. Cover and boil for the length of time specified in the directions. Drain and cut up vegetables. Chill in ice water to stop cooking action, drain, and pat dry. Place on drying trays. For high altitudes, add 30 seconds to the time specified for each 2,000 feet (607 meters) of elevation.

Salt Water Dip: Dissolve 6 tablespoons (90 ml) flaked pickling salt in 1 gallon (4 litres) of lukewarm water. To keep fruit from darkening, slice or chop it directly into the water. Allow it to soak no more than 5 minutes or fruit will absorb too much water and acquire a salty taste. Drain before loading drying trays. This is not recommended for a low-sodium diet.

Ascorbic Acid Dip: Ascorbic acid is a form of vitamin C. Dissolve 2 tablespoons (30 ml) of ascorbic acid crystals, 2 tablespoons (30 ml) ascorbic acid powder or 5 crushed 1-gram vitamin C tablets in 1 quart (1 litre) of lukewarm water. Slice or chop fruits directly into the solution. When 1 or 2 cups (250 or 500 ml) of fruit has accumulated in the container, give it a stir and remove the fruit with a slotted spoon. Drain well before loading drying trays.

Pectin Dip: Pectin is used to prepare syrups for freezing and drying berries, cherries, and peaches. With pectin, less sugar is needed, and fresh fruit flavor, color, and texture is retained. Pectin syrups are prepared as follows: Combine 1 box of powdered pectin with 1 cup (250 ml) of water in a saucepan and stir and boil for 1 minute. Stir in ½ cup (125 ml) granulated sugar and dissolve.

Remove the saucepan from the heat and add cold water to make 2 cups (500 ml) of syrup. Chill. Put cleaned and prepared fruit in a 4- to 6-quart (4- to 6-litre) bowl and add enough pectin syrup to glaze the fruit with a thin film. Gently fold fruit to coat each piece with the syrup. Drain well before loading the drying trays.

Fruit Juice Dip: Dip peaches, apples, or banana slices into 1 quart (1 litre) undiluted pineapple juice or into 1 quart (1 litre) lukewarm water into which 1/4 cup (63 ml) lemon juice has been stirred. Let fruits remain in the dip no more than 5 to 10 minutes. Drain well before drying.

Honey Dip: Many of the commercially dried fruits sold in health food stores at fancy prices are dipped in a honey solution to retain the color of bananas, peaches, and pineapples. Surprisingly, honey-dipped fruits do not seem to be any sweeter than fruits dried without dipping, although they undoubtedly have more calories.

Prepare the dip by dissolving 1 cup (250 ml) granulated sugar in 3 cups (750 ml) hot water. Cool to lukewarm and stir in 1 cup (250 ml) honey. Dip fruit in small batches and remove with a slotted spoon. Drain well before drying.

Commercial Dip: There are several products on the market designed to be dissolved in water and used as a dip before drying fruits. The main ingredient of these powders usually is ascorbic acid or sodium sulfite or a combination of the two. Use these products according to the directions on the package, taking care not to let fruits soak for more than 5 to 10 minutes or they will absorb too much water. Drain well before drying.

Sulfuring: Although many people object to the addition of sulfur to their food, exposing fruit to sulfur fumes is the pretreatment method preferred for fruit by the U.S. Department of Agriculture. It also is the method often used in drying fruits commercially. Sulfured foods *should not* be dried in a homemade dryer or dehydrator.

The important thing to remember is that sulfuring must be done outdoors and away from the house and from livestock, pets, or valuable plant life. Although the odor eventually dissipates, *any fruit that has been sulfured must be dried outdoors in the sun.* The odor of the sulfur is too overpowering for indoor use in a dehydrator or oven.

To prepare fruit for sulfuring, slice or chop it and spread it out on slatted wood or plastic (not metal) trays. Some fruits, such as apples and peaches, which darken easily, should be dipped in fruit juice or an ascorbic acid solution to prevent darkening before the sulfuring process begins.

When the first tray is filled with fruit, set it to span two concrete or wooden blocks placed several inches apart. They should hold the tray 3 to 4 inches (8 to 10 cm) off the ground. As each tray is filled, place 1½-inch (4 cm) blocks or spools at the four corners of the previous tray and place the next tray on these to stack them with space in between. Trays may be stacked this way, keeping them 1½ inches (4 cm) apart, until the stack is four to six trays high, but still solid.

Select a cardboard box (grocery store variety) large enough to cover the stack with at least 1½ inches (4 cm) to spare. Remove the top and turn the box upside down. Using a sharp knife, cut a 6-inch (15 cm) door on one side at what is now the bottom (open end) of the box. Cut a small slash or hole at the top. Place the box, open end down, over the stack of trays filled with fruit.

Into a 1-pound (400 grams) coffee can or a disposable aluminum pie pan, measure 1 tablespoon (15 ml) flowers of sulfur for every pound (400 grams) of fruit to be sulfured. Flowers of sulfur may be purchased at most drug stores or where livestock supplies are sold. *Do not use garden dusting sulfur.* Slide the can containing flowers of sulfur through the 6-inch (15 cm) door at the bottom. Light the sulfur with a match, taking care not to leave any burned matches in the sulfur container.

As soon as the sulfur is lit, push the container away from the door to a spot directly under the trays of fruit. For the time being, keep the door and the slash at the top open.

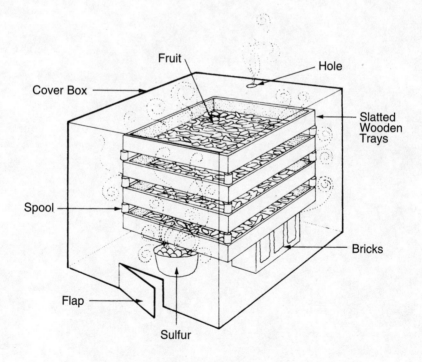

Sulfuring box.

When the sulfur has melted and is burning well, seal around the edge of the bottom of the box, piling up dirt against the box or using rags or small, washable rugs. (Remember, they will smell of sulfur when you are finished.) Leave the door and the slash open while the sulfur is burning, then close them tightly and let the fumes circulate through the trays until the fruit is bright and glistening, with a small amount of juice collected in the cavities.

Sulfuring time will depend on the size of the box and the amount of fruit to be sulfured, but most fruits are completed in 1 to 2 hours.

The fruit now is ready to be dried. Remember — sulfured fruit *must* be dried in the sun, not in an oven or dehydrator.

Testing and Storing Dried Foods

Before dried foods are stored, they should be tested to be sure enough moisture has been removed to make it impossible for mold and bacteria to grow and cause decay. Well-dried foods will vary from a moisture content of 5 percent for leafy vegetables, such as spinach, to 25 percent for juicy acid fruits, such as apricots. Percent of moisture may be checked by weighing the product before and after drying. For example, a food weighs 16 ounces (400 grams) before drying. After 8 hours of drying, the food weighs 8 ounces (200 grams). In this case you have 50 percent reduction in weight by the removal of moisture. Continue drying until there is no further reduction of weight. This will give you a fairly close estimate of the percentage of moisture in the particular food on that day. Most fruits should have about 20 percent moisture content when dried, while vegetables will have about 10 percent moisture.

All dried foods should be cooled before testing for dryness because warm foods feel more moist than when they are cooled. In general, dried foods feel dry when they are squeezed.

Root vegetables, squash, and pumpkin are dry when they are tough and leathery, still pliable, but with no moisture in the center. Cabbage, broccoli, and celery should be hard and brittle. To test, cut through the center with a knife or take a bite of it.

Green beans should be dark green with a leathery, "shoelace" appearance. Greens, such as spinach and beet tops, should be brittle enough to crumble in the hands. Corn, peas, and dry beans should be dry enough to shatter or split in half when tapped with a hammer.

Fruits are dry when leathery enough that several pieces will spring back without sticking together after being squeezed.

Fruits, such as peaches, pears, apples, and plums, should remain pliable. Others, such as berries, rhubarb, and lemon or orange peel, should be crisp and brittle. Banana slices may be crisp or slightly pliable, depending on the thickness of the slices, the method of pretreatment, and the temperature at which they were dried.

Fruit leathers are still slightly sticky to the touch when they are dried, but will pull away from the plastic wrap easily. For long-term storage, dry leathers until they are no longer sticky.

Extra care should be taken in testing all high-protein foods, particularly meats. They should be very dark colored and fibrous enough to form sharp points at the corners when bent. When dry enough for long-term storage, jerky should be so fibrous it is very hard to chew. As a compromise, many people keep dried meats and jerky tightly wrapped in the refrigerator or freezer.

Herb leaves are dry enough for storage when they are so brittle they will crumble easily in the hands.

Grains and grain products are best tested for drying by tasting. Well-dried grains will have a nutty taste and a hard, brittle texture. Grain cereals and crackers will be crisp. Noodles will be brittle enough to break in the hands.

When in doubt as to whether a food is dry, remember that it is better to overdry than to underdry.

Storing Dried Foods

Dried foods should be stored in small batches in airtight, insect-proof containers, such as a glass or plastic jar that is 8 ounces (200 grams) or less with an inner seal rim, or in pint-size (475 ml) freezer bags that are moisture and vapor proof. Dried fruits and vegetables may be stored in small glass or plastic jars, such as those in which pickles, mustard, instant coffee, and jelly are sold. After the dried food has cooled, put it inside the container and screw the lid on tightly. Don't delay this step, or the dried produce will begin to accumulate moisture. Jars are free and have the advantage of keeping the dried food visible, so it may be checked for moisture during the first few weeks of storage. Any sign of moisture beads inside the jar is a signal that the food is not dry enough for storage and should be returned to the drying trays.

If storing foods in a sealable freezer bag, watch for any signs of moisture, such as moisture beads or a foggy appearance inside the bag during the first few days of storage. If moisture appears, either the food is not dry or the bag was not properly sealed. If there are no signs of mold, return the food to the dehydrator for further drying. Molded foods should be thrown out.

Dried meats may be stored in glass or plastic jars, but the jars should be small because dried meat is a very concentrated food and is used in small amounts.

Every time the jar is opened, moisture in the air enters the jar and the food. It should be remembered, too, that dried meats, especially jerky, will keep only for a short period at room temperature because any fat on the meat will turn rancid. A refrigerator or freezer is recommended for long-term storage. Jerky should be cut in serving-size sticks, each wrapped in wax paper or plastic wrap, and sealed in jars.

Large batches of grain may be stored in metal containers, such as cookie tins, potato chip or lard cans. One to two cups (250 to 500 ml) of the grain should be sealed in plastic freezer bags or brown bags, then stacked inside the can. Different grains may be stored in one can, but don't mix packages of grains and other dried foods in one container. Also be careful not to combine packages of cabbage, onions, broccoli, fish, or any strong-flavored food with other foods, because their flavors will blend.

Fruit and vegetable leathers are rolled in plastic wrap or wax paper. Stand the rolls in a metal or glass container — clean, dry coffee or shortening cans work well — and seal with a tight-fitting lid.

Because their flavors are easily lost, herbs, herb mixtures, and herb teas are best stored separately in very small containers, such as clean, dry pill or vitamin bottles. Be certain, though, that the bottles are odor-free. Herb leaves that are to be used within a few months usually are crumbled before storing, but for the best flavor retention in long-term storage, herb leaves may be stored intact, then crumbled just before using.

Be sure to label jars and plastic packages with the name of the food and the date it was dried. One good method is to print this information on a piece of masking tape on the outside of the dried food container. Also, include on the label the number of servings in the package and — for the more involved dishes, such as soups and stews — directions for preparing the food.

For camping trips and backpacking, ready-to-cook soup mixes are best sealed in plastic freezer bags that are lightweight, disposable, and waterproof. For storage in vacation homes, where insects and predators might be a problem, store the freezer bags inside glass or metal containers with tight-fitting lids.

Although dried foods can withstand freezing temperatures without harm, they will lose color, flavor, and nutrients when exposed to light and heat. *Keep containers in a dark, dry, cool place.* This doesn't mean they need a special storage area. A closed, unheated closet anywhere in the house will serve the purpose. Lacking that, glass jars may be kept dark by inverting a cardboard box over them or covering them with a bushel basket or a sheet of black plastic. Metal containers keep their contents dark.

If You Can't Dry It Right Away

There will be times when the weather is humid, or your dryer is overloaded, or it just isn't convenient to dry foods at harvest time. When this happens, you can postpone the drying season of some foods.

Apples, pears, onions, celery, squash, pumpkins, carrots, and some other foods may be stored in a cool, dry storage room for a few weeks. Others, such as kidney and lima beans, green peppers, corn, peaches, and strawberries may be stored in the freezer until a more convenient time (see page 155 for an effective freezer wrap). Pretreat corn and peaches as you would for freezer storage, but the others need no pretreatment. For fruit leathers, puree the fruit in a blender, pour into a container, and freeze. When you're ready to dry the leathers, just thaw and spread the puree on drying trays.

Drying Fruits

Dried fruits are the oldest, the most familiar, and the most popular of dried foods. They also are the simplest to dry and the simplest to use.

For "walking around" snacks for children, dried fruits are ideal and can be a healthful substitute for candy or empty-calorie cookies. Dried apple slices, banana chips, dried apricots, and plums are favorites. Remember, however, that dried fruits are highly concentrated foods, so smaller amounts should be eaten.

For dried fruit mixtures, fruits should be chopped and dried separately, then combined. Seal dried fruits and dried fruit combinations in small packages for children. For adults, serve in a covered candy dish.

Some good dried fruit combinations are:

- Sliced strawberries, bananas, and pineapple
- Chopped apricots and bananas
- Chopped apples, cherries, and coconut
- Sliced peaches, orange peel, and bananas
- Chopped plums, bananas, and nuts

Pretreatment of fruits before drying may be as simple as a quick dip in salt water or as complicated as the sulfuring process. Pretreatment may be unnecessary when some fruits are dried in a dehydrator.

In order to preserve their fresh taste, blanching — a form of quick cooking — is not recommended for fruits although they may be dipped in fruit juice, salt water, or ascorbic acid solution to keep their color from darkening. Directions for these dips are included in chapter 4 on pretreating. (Directions for fruit leathers follow in chapter 12, Leathers.)

Directions also are included in chapter 4 for sulfuring, a method by which the fruit is subjected to sulfur fumes to preserve the bright color. Although sulfuring is not necessarily recommended, it is included for those who want to use it. Fruit that has been sulfured may be dried only by the sun drying method. Fruits that have been dipped or left untreated may be dried by any of the three methods recommended: drying in a dehydrator; drying in the sun; or drying in an oven or homemade dryer. Specific directions for each are included under each fruit.

Dried Baby Food (Fruit)

To make baby food from fresh fruit, cook fruit until just tender and then strain. Using a food mill, cone, sieve, or electric blender, puree fruit and dry as directed:

Dehydrator: Cover trays with plastic wrap and spread with ⅛-inch (3-mm) layer of fruit puree. Dry at highest heat setting for 12 to 14 hours until firm and top is hard but sticky, and puree can be pulled away from plastic wrap. Turn over, remove plastic, and discard. Dry for another 12 to 14 hours, or until hard and dry. Break into pieces and dry for another 3 to 4 hours.

Sun: Spread ⅛-inch (3-mm) layer of fruit puree over cookie sheets or trays that have been covered with plastic wrap. Dry in the hot sun until hard and brittle for 2 to 4 days, turning once. Take trays inside at night. Break into pieces and dry for another 6 to 8 hours.

Oven or Homemade Dryer: Preheat oven to 150°F (65°C). Spread fruit puree in ⅛-inch (3-mm) layer over trays lined with plastic wrap. Dry until firm, then turn over and peel off wrap. Dry for another 12 to 14 hours, or until hard and brittle. Break into pieces and dry for another 3 to 4 hours.

To Make Baby Food Powder: Pound pieces of dried puree to a fine powder using a pestle, grater, blender, or food processor. Package powder in small, one-serving portions.

To Use: Add warm water to the powder until the mixture is the desired consistency.

Apples

Use well-ripened, but still firm fruit with solid flesh and tart-sweet flavor. Wash and core. Peel or not, according to preference. Cut in wedges, then in slices ¼-inch (6.25-mm) thick or in ¼-inch (6.25-mm) crosswise rings.

Dehydrator: Slice apples directly onto trays. Spread slices one layer deep on trays, without overlapping slices. (No pretreatment is necessary if you work quickly.) As each tray is filled, place it in the dehydrator before loading the next tray. Dry at 115°F (45°C) for 6 to 8 hours, stirring or turning fruit once. After the first 6 hours, test for dryness every 2 hours until there is no moisture in the center when a slice is bitten.

Sun: Dip slices into water in which ascorbic acid or commercial dip has been dissolved. Wet slices with diluted lemon juice (¼ cup (62.5 ml) lemon juice to 1 quart (1 litre) water), full-strength pineapple juice, or sulfur for 1 hour.

Spread pretreated slices on trays. Cover with a layer of cheesecloth and place in a well-ventilated place in full sun.

Every few hours stir them to expose undried sides. Take trays inside at night. Apples will take 2 to 3 days to dry completely. Well-dried apple slices should be leathery and chewy. To test for dryness, cool a few slices and taste. There should be no crispness in the center.

Oven or Homemade Dryer: Spread apple slices — pretreated or not, according to your preference — on trays. Dry for 6 to 8 hours at 115°F (45°C), stirring slices once, then test every 2 hours until dry.

To Use: Sliced, dried apples are delicious eaten as a snack, or they may be used in almost any way cooked apples are used. One cup (250 ml) yields about 1¼ cups (315 ml) cooked or refreshed apples.

RAW APPLESAUCE

Soak 1 cup (250 ml) dried apple slices in 1 cup (250 ml) hot apple cider for 3 to 4 hours. Puree in blender and serve as you would applesauce.

COOKED APPLESAUCE

Pour 1 cup (250 ml) boiling water over 1 cup (250 ml) dried apple slices. Cover and simmer over low heat for about 30 minutes, or until apples are soft.

DRIED APPLE PIE

1½ cups (375 ml) boiling water
1½ cups (375 ml) dried apple slices
⅓ cup (75 ml) granulated sugar
½ teaspoon (2 ml) ground cinnamon

¼ teaspoon (1 ml) ground nutmeg
2 tablespoons (30 ml) butter or margarine, cut into bits
Unbaked 2-crust 9-inch (22.5 cm) pastry

Pour boiling water over dried apples and let soak for 3 to 4 hours. Add sugar, cinnamon, and nutmeg. Stir well. Fit half of the pastry into a 9-inch (22.5 cm) pie pan and pour apple mixture into pie shell. Dot with butter or margarine. Cover with remaining rolled-out pastry and bake for 45 minutes at 350°F (180°C). Makes one 9-inch (22.5 cm) pie.

DRIED APPLE COFFEE CAKE

2 cups (500 ml) dried apples
1 teaspoon (5 ml) fresh lemon juice
½ cup (125 ml) margarine
¾ cup (190 ml) granulated sugar
2 eggs
½ cup (125 ml) milk
1½ cups (375 ml) all-purpose flour

½ teaspoon (2 ml) salt
2 teaspoons (10 ml) baking powder
1 teaspoon (5 ml) pure vanilla extract

Topping
½ cup (125 ml) granulated sugar
2 teaspoons (10 ml) ground cinnamon

Place dried apples and lemon juice in a bowl. Add enough water to cover and soak for 1 hour. Cream margarine and sugar. Add eggs and milk and beat well. Sift together flour, salt, and baking powder. Add to cream mixture. Add vanilla. Beat well. Pour into two 9-inch (22.5 cm) greased and floured cake pans. Top with drained, rehydrated apple slices. For the topping, combine sugar and cinnamon and sprinkle evenly over apples. Bake at 375°F (190°C) for 35 to 40 minutes. Makes two 9-inch (22.5 cm) coffee cakes.

DRIED APPLE BREAD

1 cup (250 ml) dried apples

1 cup (250 ml) water

2 teaspoons (10 ml) baking soda

1/2 cup (125 ml) vegetable shortening

1 cup (250 ml) granulated sugar

1 egg

1 teaspoon (5 ml) ground cinnamon

1/4 teaspoon (1 ml) ground cloves

2 cups (500 ml) all-purpose flour

1/4 teaspoon (1 ml) salt

3/4 cup (190 ml) chopped dried plums

1/4 cup (62.5 ml) dried seedless grapes

1 cup (250 ml) chopped walnuts

Combine apples and water in a blender to make applesauce. Add baking soda. In a large mixing bowl, cream shortening and sugar. Add egg and mix well. In another bowl, mix together other dry ingredients and add to creamed mixture alternately with applesauce. Stir in dried plums, grapes, and nuts. Pour into greased 9 X 12-inch (22.5 X 30 cm) loaf pan. Bake in 350°F (180°C) oven for 40 to 45 minutes. Makes one 9-inch (22.5 cm) loaf.

APPLE-CHERRY BRAN MUFFINS

1 1/2 cups (375 ml) chopped dried apples

1/2 cup (125 ml) dried cherries

1 1/4 cups (315 ml) bran

2/3 cup (150 ml) milk

2 eggs

1 1/4 cups sugar (315 ml)

1/4 cup (65 ml) melted butter or margarine

1/2 teaspoon (2.5 ml) lemon or orange extract

1 cup (250 ml) all-purpose flour

2 1/2 teaspoons (15 ml) baking powder

1/4 teaspoon (1 ml) salt

1 teaspoon (5 ml) cinnamon

1 cup (250 ml) chopped pecans

Place dried apples and dried cherries in a bowl. Add enough water to cover and soak for 1 hour. Butter a 12-muffin tray. Preheat oven to 400°F (205°C). In a large bowl, combine milk and bran and let stand until most of the milk is absorbed. Add eggs, sugar, butter or margarine, and extract. Sift flour, baking powder, salt, and cinnamon into mixture. Fold in apples and pecans. Immediately pour into greased pan and bake for 25 to 30 minutes. Makes 12 muffins.

Apricots

Pick or buy apricots when perfectly ripe. Fruit should not be mushy, but green fruit does not dry well. Any size or variety will do, but choose those with a bright orange color and sweet flavor.

To simplify peeling, dip ripe apricots in boiling water for 1 minute, then in cold water for 1 minute. Skins will slip off easily.

Cut apricots in half, removing seeds. For faster drying, slice or chop. They will turn quite dark without pretreating. Dipping in ascorbic acid solution, a commercial dip, or a honey dip is recommended (see chapter 4). Sulfuring may be used if apricots are to be dried in the sun.

Dehydrator: Spread apricot halves, slices, or pieces on trays in a single layer. Dry at 115°F (45°C) until leathery, with no moisture in centers when cut. Halves will take 36 to 48 hours. Slices will take 12 to 18 hours. Chopped pieces will dry in less time, according to their size. Turn halves or stir pieces occasionally and rotate trays front to back, side to side, and top to bottom once or twice during drying.

Sun: Spread apricot halves, slices, or pieces on trays, cut side up. Cover with cheesecloth and place in full sun. Prop up cheesecloth to keep it from touching fruit. Turn or stir pieces occasionally and take trays inside at night. When top side of halves is dried, turn and flatten by mashing with the heel of the hand or by pressing with a block of wood or other flat instrument. Test for dryness before storing. The halves will take 4 or more days to dry in good weather. Peeled slices will dry in 2 days or more.

Oven or Homemade Dryer: Spread apricot halves, slices, or pieces on trays. Dry at 115°F (45°C) until leathery for 2 to 3 days for halves, less time for slices or chopped pieces, stirring pieces and turning halves every few hours. Rotate shelves once or twice a day during drying.

To Use: Eat halves and slices without refreshing, or soak, in just enough water to cover, for 3 to 4 hours or overnight. Chopped pieces may be used in fruitcake or mixed with dried banana slices for a delicious snack food. Halves may be simmered over low heat for 30 to 45 minutes and served in a fruit compote. They also may be pureed in the blender after soaking or cooking for a delicious apricot sauce. One cup (250 ml) yields about 1½ cups (375 ml) cooked fruit.

DRIED APRICOT PIE

3 cups (750 ml) dried apricots

3 cups (750 ml) boiling water

½ cup (125 ml) granulated sugar

¼ cup (62.5 ml) cornstarch

2 tablespoons (30 ml) butter or margarine

Unbaked 2-crust 9-inch (22.5 cm) pastry

Soak dried apricots in boiling water overnight or simmer in water just until tender. Do not overcook. Drain any remaining liquid into a blender and add ½ cup (125 ml) soaked or cooked apricots. Blend to a pulp. Combine sugar and cornstarch in a saucepan. Gradually add pureed apricots, stirring well to dissolve. Cook over low heat until thickened. Remove from heat, add butter or margarine, and stir until melted. Add remaining 2½ cups (625 ml) apricots and pour into unbaked pie shell. Cover with top crust or lattice strips. Bake in 350°F (176.7°C) oven for 30 to 45 minutes, or until golden brown. Makes one 9-inch (22.5 cm) pie.

Bananas

Select firm, well-ripened bananas, but flecked with brown. Peel and cut into thin slices. Dip in ascorbic acid, undiluted pineapple juice, or a mixture of ¼ cup (65 ml) lemon juice and 2 cups (500 ml) water. For crisp slices, pretreat in honey dip (see chapter 4).

Dehydrator: Spread slices on dehydrator trays one layer deep, without overlapping slices. Dry at 115°F (45°C) until leathery or at 125°F (55°C) until crisp. They will dry in 6 to 8 hours in dry weather. After 3 to 4 hours, peel slices from trays and turn over. Rotate trays front to back, side to side, and top to bottom once during drying.

Sun: Spread pretreated banana slices one layer deep on drying trays lined with cheesecloth. Top with cheesecloth propped up to keep it from touching fruit. Dry in a well-ventilated place in full sun. At the end of the day, turn slices by flipping bottom cheesecloth and take trays inside at night. They will take 2 or more days to dry.

Oven or Homemade Dryer: Spread slices in a single layer over drying trays, taking care not to overlap slices. Dry at 115°F (45°C) for 8 to 10 hours until leathery or crisp, according to preference. Turn slices and rotate trays once during drying.

To Use: Eat banana slices as a confection or combine with dried or fresh apricots, peaches, or pineapple. These slices also may be added to cake or cookie batters without being refreshed. One cup yields about 1¼ cups (310 ml) refreshed bananas or ¾ cup (190 ml) mashed bananas.

DRIED BANANA NUT BREAD

¾ cup (190 ml) boiling water

¾ cup (190 ml) dried banana slices

¼ cup (65 ml) vegetable shortening

½ cup (125 ml) granulated sugar

1 egg

1 cup (250 ml) bran cereal

1 teaspoon (5 ml) pure vanilla extract

1½ cups (375 ml) all-purpose flour

2 teaspoons (10 ml) baking powder

½ teaspoon (2 ml) salt

½ teaspoon (2 ml) baking soda

½ cup (125 ml) chopped nuts

Pour boiling water over dried banana slices. Let soak for 1 hour, then process in blender or mash with potato masher. Set aside. In a mixing bowl, cream shortening and sugar until fluffy. Add egg and beat well. Add cereal, reserved banana puree, and vanilla. Combine flour, baking powder, salt, soda, and nuts. Add to banana mixture, stirring only to blend well. Pour into greased 9 X 5-inch (22.5 X 15 cm) loaf pan and bake at 350°F (180°C) for 1 hour, or until a tester inserted in the center comes out clean. Makes one 9-inch (22.5 cm) loaf.

DRIED BANANA FRITTERS

1 cup (250 ml) dried banana slices

1½ cups (375 ml) boiling water

1 egg yolk

1 tablespoon (15 ml) vegetable oil

¼ teaspoon (1 ml) salt

½ cup (125 ml) all-purpose flour

1 tablespoon (15 ml) granulated sugar

1 egg white, stiffly beaten

Hot oil for frying, at least 2 inches (5 cm) deep

Confectioners' sugar

Cover dried banana slices with boiling water. Let soak for 1 to 2 hours, then drain, reserving any soaking liquid. In another bowl, beat egg yolk. Add oil, salt and ¼ cup (65 ml) reserved soaking liquid or water. Add flour and sugar and beat until smooth. Add slices, another ¼ cup (62.5 ml) soaking liquid or water and egg white. Drop batter by tablespoons into oil, which has been heated to 375°F (190°C). Fry until golden brown, turning once. Sprinkle with confectioners' sugar. Serves 6.

PEANUT-BANANA DROPS

3 cups (750 ml) old-fashioned rolled oats

1¼ cups (315 ml) chunk-style peanut butter

½ cup (125 ml) honey

½ cup (125 ml) butter or margarine

1 cup (250 ml) chopped dried banana slices

Spread oats over a baking sheet or jelly-roll pan in a 250°F (120°C) oven. Toast until lightly browned for 15 to 20 minutes, stirring occasionally. Meanwhile, in a heavy skillet, melt peanut butter, honey, and butter or margarine, stirring until smooth. Stir in toasted oats and dried bananas. Drop by rounded spoonfuls onto wax paper. Chill until firm. Store in refrigerator. Makes 4 dozen snacks.

Blueberries, Cranberries, and Gooseberries

Wash firm but well-ripened berries. Cut in half or drop in boiling water for 30 seconds to split skins. For added sweetening, they may be dipped in honey dip (see chapter 4).

Dehydrator: Spread in a single layer on trays and dry at 115°F (45°C) until berries are hard, but still chewy. Stir with the hands every few hours and rotate trays front to back, side to side, and top to bottom, at least once. They will dry in 12 to 24 hours.

Sun: Spread berry halves or whole berries in a thin layer over drying trays. Cover with cheesecloth propped up to keep it from touching the berries and place in full sun in a well-ventilated area. Stir with the hands occasionally to help dry uniformly. Take trays inside at night. They will dry in 2 to 4 days.

Oven or Homemade Dryer: Spread berries in a single layer on trays. Dry at 115°F (45°C) until berries are hard, but still chewy. Stir occasionally and rotate trays once or twice. They will dry in 18 to 36 hours.

To Use: These berries — plain or honey dipped — are delicious eaten as a confection, alone, or mixed with other dried or fresh fruits. They may be refreshed by soaking in an equal amount of water or fruit juice for 3 to 4 hours. Use as you would fresh berries. They may be added without soaking to muffins, cakes, and puddings. For a pureed sauce, soak or cook 1 cup (250 ml) berries in 1 cup (250 ml) boiling water. Process in a blender. Serve over pudding or ice cream.

DRIED BERRY COBBLER

Filling

2 cups (500 ml) dried blueberries, cranberries, or gooseberries

2 cups (500 ml) boiling water

1–1½ cups (250–375 ml) granulated sugar (depending on tartness of berries)

2 tablespoons (30 ml) quick-cooking tapioca

1–2 tablespoons (15–30 ml) butter or margarine (optional)

Soak berries in boiling water for 3 to 4 hours. Drain any remaining soaking-water into blender and add ½ cup (125 ml) soaked berries. Process to a fine puree. Arrange remaining berries in a shallow baking pan. Add sugar and tapioca to puree and blend. Pour over berries. Dot with butter or margarine. Cover berries with batter (see below) and bake for 30 minutes at 400°F (205°C). Serve warm, plain or with cream or whipped cream. Serves 6.

Batter

¼ cup (65 ml) butter or margarine

½ cup (125 ml) granulated sugar

1 egg, well beaten

1½ cups (375 ml) all-purpose flour

2 teaspoons (10 ml) baking powder

½ teaspoon (2 ml) salt

½ cup (125 ml) milk

Cream butter and sugar. Add egg. Sift flour with baking powder and salt. Add flour mixture, 1/2 cup (125 ml) at a time, alternately with milk.

DRIED BERRY WAFFLES

1¾ cups (440 ml) all-purpose flour
3 teaspoons (15 ml) baking powder
¼ teaspoon (1 ml) salt
2 eggs

1¼ cups (315 ml) milk
6 tablespoons (90 ml) vegetable oil
1 cup (250 ml) dried berries

Combine dry ingredients and set aside. Beat eggs with egg beater until light. Add milk and oil, then dry ingredients. Beat until smooth. Fold in dried berries and bake on a waffle iron, following manufacturer's directions. Serves 4.

CRANBERRY-CHERRY RELISH

1 cup (250 ml) dried cranberries
1 cup (250 ml) dried cherries
½ cup (125 ml) sugar
1 cup (250 ml) water

½ cup (125 ml) orange juice
2 tablespoons (30 ml) grated orange peel

In a medium saucepan, combine ingredients and heat on medium burner setting. Allow to cook, stirring regularly, until thickened. Let cool and refrigerate. Serve chilled. Serves 8–10.

CRANBERRY-ORANGE NUT BREAD

1 cup (250 ml) dried cranberries
2 cups (500 ml) all-purpose flour
1½ teaspoons (7 ml) baking powder
½ teaspoon (2 ml) salt
1 cup (250 ml) sugar

1 beaten egg
¾ cup (190 ml) orange juice
2 tablespoons (30 ml) melted butter or margarine
1 cup (250 ml) chopped walnuts

In a small bowl, soak cranberries in 2 tablespoons (30 ml) of water for 15 minutes. In a large bowl combine flour, baking powder, baking soda, salt, and sugar, mixing thoroughly. In another large bowl, blend the beaten egg, orange juice, melted butter or margarine, and soak water from cranberries. Slowly fold the flour mixture into the egg mixture. When thoroughly blended, stir in cranberries and chopped walnuts. Pour into greased loaf pan and bake at 325°F (165°C) for approximately 1 hour. Cool for 1/2 hour before removing from pan. Makes 1 loaf.

LEMON-BLUEBERRY YOGURT MUFFINS _____

1 cup (250 ml) dried blueberries	2 eggs
2 cups (500 ml) all-purpose flour	1 cup (250 ml) lemon yogurt
1 teaspoon (5 ml) baking soda	2 teaspoons (10 ml) lemon juice
1 teaspoon (5 ml) baking powder	2 tablepoons (30 ml) honey
½ teaspoon (2 ml) salt	¼ cup (65 ml) melted butter or
½ cup (125 ml) sugar	margarine

In a small bowl, soak blueberries in yogurt and lemon juice for 15 minutes. In a medium bowl, combine flour, baking powder, and baking soda. In a large bowl combine remaining ingredients and blueberry-yogurt mixture and stir well. Add dry ingredients and mix lightly. Pour into greased muffin tray and bake for 15 to 20 minutes at 375°F (190°C) or until golden brown. Makes 12 muffins.

Candied Fruit

Almost any fruit may be candied. Some of the best are pineapple, cherries, chopped apricots, watermelon rind, and lemon, orange, or grapefruit peel.

Cut pineapple, apricots, or watermelon rind into small pieces. Chop cherries or cut in halves. Remove and discard white membrane from lemon, orange, or grapefruit peel and cut into strips or small pieces.

To candy fruit, combine 1 cup (250 ml) granulated sugar, 1 cup (250 ml) honey, and 1½ cups (375 ml) water in a heavy saucepan or iron skillet. Bring to a boil over medium heat and cook to 235°F (110°C), stirring constantly. Drop in small amounts of prepared fruits or fruit peels, separately or mixed. Cook over low heat until fruit or rind is transparent, about 25 to 30 minutes. Drain and repeat until all fruit is candied.

Dehydrator: Spread candied fruit over trays in a thin layer. Dry for 12 to 18 hours at 120°F (50°C) until fruit is no longer sticky and centers have no moisture. Stir occasionally and rotate trays once or twice during drying. Sprinkle with sugar and pack in glass jars or metal tins with tight-fitting lids.

Sun: Spread a thin layer of candied fruit over cheesecloth-covered trays and cover with cheesecloth propped up to keep it from touching fruit. Dry for 1 to 2 days, stirring occasionally, until it is no longer sticky. Take trays inside at night.

Oven or Homemade Dryer: Spread candied fruit over trays. Dry at 120°F (50°C) for 18 to 24 hours, stirring occasionally and rotating trays once or twice until it is no longer sticky.

To Use: Candied dried fruit is especially popular in cookies and fruitcakes around the holidays.

HOLIDAY OATMEAL DROPS

⅔ cup (150 ml) butter or margarine

¾ cup (190 ml) firmly packed brown sugar

1 egg

1 teaspoon (5 ml) pure vanilla extract

2 cups (500 ml) all-purpose flour

2 teaspoons (10 ml) baking powder

½ teaspoon (2 ml) salt

1 cup (250 ml) uncooked rolled oats

1 cup (250 ml) mixed dried candied fruit, cut into small pieces

½ cup (125 ml) shredded coconut

¼ cup (65 ml) milk

48 pecan halves

In a large bowl, cream butter or margarine and brown sugar until fluffy. Add egg and vanilla and beat well. In another bowl, combine flour, baking powder, salt, oats, candied fruit, and coconut. Add, a little at a time alternately with milk, to creamed mixture. Blend well. Drop by teaspoonsful onto lightly greased cookie sheet. Press a pecan half into the top of each cookie. Bake for 10 to 12 minutes in 350°F (180°C) oven. Makes 4 dozen cookies.

GOLDEN FRUITCAKES

4 cups (1 litre) all-purpose flour

2 teaspoons (10 ml) baking powder

1½ teaspoons (375 ml) ground nutmeg

2 teaspoons (10 ml) ground cinnamon

½ teaspoon (2 ml) salt

2 cups (500 ml) butter or margarine

2 cups (500 ml) firmly packed brown sugar

12 eggs

1 tablespoon (15 ml) ground dried lemon peel

3 cups (750 ml) coarsely chopped pecans

4 cups (1 litre) coarsely chopped dried candied pineapple

3 cups (750 ml) halved dried candied cherries

Combine flour, baking powder, nutmeg, cinnamon, and salt. Set aside. In a large bowl, cream butter or margarine and brown sugar. Add eggs, one at a time, beating well after each addition. Gradually add ⅔ of the flour mixture, blending well. Add dried lemon peel. Add pecans and candied fruits to remaining ⅓ of flour and stir well. Add to batter, all at once.

Spoon into one large greased and floured tube cake pan or twelve greased and floured small, clean soup cans. Fill containers to within 1 inch of the top. Place a shallow pan filled with water in bottom of oven heated to 275°F (135°C). Cover large cake loosely with aluminum foil and bake for 4½ hours, uncovering last hour. Bake small cakes 1 hour, 15 minutes. With both, a tester inserted in center should come out clean when cake is done. Cool completely before removing from pans. Makes 1 large or 12 small fruitcakes.

Cherries

Wash and pit fully ripe sweet or tart cherries. May be easily pitted using the rounded end of a clean hairpin or a cherry pitter. Drain well. Cut in half, chop, or leave whole.

Dehydrator: Spread cut or whole cherries over dehydrator trays and dry at 115°F (45°C), stirring occasionally and rotating trays front to back, side to side, and top to bottom at least once during drying. When dry, cherries should be chewy. Whole cherries will take 24 hours or more. Cut cherries will dry in less time.

Sun: Spread cut or whole cherries thinly over trays. Cover with cheesecloth propped up to keep from touching cherries. Dry in hot sun in a well-ventilated area, stirring occasionally. Cut cherries will dry in 1 to 2 days. Whole cherries will take 4 to 5 days. Take trays inside at night.

Oven or Homemade Dryer: Spread cut or whole cherries over trays. Dry at 115°F (45°C), stirring occasionally and rotating trays once or twice a day, until cherries are chewy and dried through. Whole cherries will dry in 24 to 36 hours.

To Use: Dried sweet or tart cherries are delicious eaten like raisins. They also add taste and eye appeal when used in any recipe for cookies, cakes, breads, or puddings in place of raisins. To refresh dried cherries, soak overnight in an equal amount of water. One cup yields about 1¼ cups (315 ml) refreshed fruit.

DRIED CHERRY DUMPLINGS

Sauce

1 cup (250 ml) dried tart cherries
3½ cups (875 ml) boiling water
½ cup (125 ml) granulated sugar

2 tablespoons (30 ml) butter or margarine
½ teaspoon (2 ml) pure almond extract (optional)

Combine all ingredients in heavy skillet or electric frying pan. Bring mixture to a boil, reduce heat, and simmer for 20 to 30 minutes, or until cherries are tender.

Dumplings

1 cup (250 ml) all-purpose flour
1½ (7 ml) teaspoons baking powder
¼ teaspoon (1 ml) salt
¼ cup (65 ml) granulated sugar

1–2 tablespoons (15–30 ml) butter or margarine (optional)
½ teaspoon (2 ml) pure vanilla or almond extract
½ cup (125 ml) milk

Combine dry ingredients. Cut in butter or margarine with two knives or pastry blender until mixture is crumbly. Add vanilla and milk and stir only enough to moisten flour. Drop by spoonsful into boiling sauce. Simmer over low heat, uncovered, for 5 minutes, then cover and steam gently for 15 minutes more. Serve warm with sauce. Serves 4.

DRIED CHERRY MARMALADE

2 cups (500 ml) dried sweet cherries

2 cups (500 ml) boiling water

1 orange, finely chopped

1 package powdered pectin

3½ cups (875 ml) granulated sugar

2 tablespoons (30 ml) dried lemon peel

In a large pan, combine dried cherries, water, and chopped orange (remove any seeds, but chop or grind peel with orange). Cook over low heat for 30 minutes. Remove from heat and add pectin, sugar, and lemon peel. Bring to a boil over low heat, stirring until sugar and pectin are dissolved. Bring to a full, rolling boil and cook for 2 minutes, stirring frequently. Pour into hot, sterilized jars and process for 10 minutes to seal. Makes about 2 pints (950 ml).

CHERRY CHICKEN SALAD

1 pound (400 grams) boneless
chicken, cooked and cubed

¾ cups (190 ml) cherries

½ cup (125 ml) sliced celery

⅓ cup (75 ml) chopped scallion greens

½ cup (125 ml) chopped fresh
mint leaves

5–6 lettuce leaves

Dressing

½ cup (125 ml) sunflower oil

2 tablespoons (30 ml) raspberry
vinegar

1 tablespoon (15 ml) dijon mustard

Salt and pepper to taste

Combine cooked chicken cubes, cherries, celery, scallions, and mint in a large bowl. Add dressing and toss lightly. Serve on bed of lettuce.

Currants

Select red ripe currants at their sweetest. Wash and drain well. Drop in boiling water for 30 seconds to split skins. Drain well. Pat dry with paper towels.

Dehydrator: Spread whole currants on trays. Dry at 115°F (45°C) until shriveled and chewy with no moisture in the centers. Stir occasionally during drying and rotate trays. Currants will dry in 18 to 24 hours.

Sun: Spread whole currants thinly on drying trays and cover with cheesecloth propped up so it will not touch the currants. Place trays in a well-ventilated area in full sun. Dry until chewy, stirring occasionally with the hands. Take trays inside at night. Currants will take 2 to 3 days to dry.

Oven or Homemade Dryer: Spread currants in a thin layer over drying trays. Dry at 115°F (45°C), stirring occasionally and rotating trays until currants are hard and chewy. Drying will take 24 hours or more.

To Use: Use currants as you would raisins or dried figs, in fruit cakes or in any baking. They cannot be refreshed, but should be used in the dry form.

DRIED CURRANT JELLY

3 cups (750 ml) boiling water　　1 package powdered pectin
4 cups (1 litre) dried currants　　3 cups (750 ml) granulated sugar

Pour boiling water over dried currants and let set for 1 hour. Crush currants with a potato masher and bring slowly to a boil in the soaking water. Simmer for 20 minutes. Strain juice through jelly bag or three thicknesses of cheesecloth. Discard berries and measure juice. Add water to make 4 cups. Combine with pectin in a jelly kettle or large pan. Bring to a boil and boil hard for 1 minute, stirring to dissolve pectin. Bring to a full, rolling boil that cannot be stirred down. Add sugar and stir until dissolved. Bring to a full, rolling boil again and cook, stirring constantly for 1 minute. Remove from heat, skim off foam, and pour into hot, sterilized jelly glasses. Process for 5 minutes in hot water bath to seal immediately. Makes five 6-ounce (150-gram) glasses.

DRIED CURRANT BARS

2 cups (500 ml) all-purpose flour　　⅔ cup (150 ml) vegetable shortening
¼ teaspoon (1 ml) baking soda　　⅓ cup (75 ml) packed brown sugar
½ teaspoon (2 ml) salt　　¼ cup (65 ml) light molasses
1 teaspoon (5 ml) ground cinnamon　　1 egg
½ teaspoon (2 ml) ground nutmeg　　2 tablespoons (30 ml) water
½ teaspoon (2 ml) ground allspice　　1 tablespoon (15 ml) white vinegar
½ teaspoon (2 ml) ground ginger　　1½ cups (375 ml) dried currants
¼ teaspoon (1 ml) ground cloves　　¾ cup (190 ml) chopped nuts

Combine flour, baking soda, salt, and spices. Set aside. In another bowl, cream shortening and brown sugar. Add molasses and egg. Stir in water and vinegar. Blend in dry ingredients, currants, and nuts. Spread in greased 10 X 15-inch (25 X 40 cm) shallow baking pan and bake in 350°F (180°C) oven for about 20 minutes, or until lightly browned. Cool slightly, then mark off into 2 X 3-inch (5 X 7.5 cm) bars. While still warm, drizzle with thin confectioners' sugar icing. Cool and cut into bars. Makes 20 cookies.

Figs

Figs should be soft and greenish yellow or purple in color when ripe. They soften and bruise easily, so they should be dried soon after picking. Wash in cold water and drain until dry. For whole figs, blanch in boiling water for 30 seconds to check the skins, then drain and blot dry. Or skins may be pierced a few times with a fork. For faster drying, cut figs in half or finely chop. Figs may be steam blanched, dipped in honey dip, candied, or dried without pretreating.

Candied Figs: Make syrup by combining 1 cup (250 ml) granulated sugar and 1 cup (250 ml) water. Bring to a boil, stirring well to dissolve sugar. Drop whole figs gradually into syrup without stopping the boiling. Cook over low heat until they look transparent, about 40 to 50 minutes. Stir occasionally to keep from sticking. Drain well.

Dehydrator: Thinly spread whole fruit or pieces — untreated, pretreated, or candied — over dehydrator trays. Preheat dehydrator to 120°F (50°C). Dry, stirring fruit occasionally and rotating trays, until figs are chewy and dried through. Pieces take 10 to 12 hours. Whole figs take 36 to 48 hours.

Sun: Spread figs — whole or cut-up, pretreated or not — thinly over drying trays. Cover with cheesecloth propped up and place in a well-ventilated area in full sun. Drying takes 1 to 6 days, depending on the weather and the size of the pieces. Stir occasionally and take trays inside at night.

Oven or Homemade Dryer: Spread whole or cut-up figs over trays. Dry at 115°F (45°C) until chewy and dry in center, stirring occasionally and rotating trays once or twice a day. Drying will take 2 to 3 days.

To Use: Try dried figs as a confection, in dried fruit mixes, or as an ingredient in any recipe calling for figs. Cut-up figs are an excellent substitute for raisins in many recipes.

STUFFED DRIED FIGS

Steam dried figs over hot water for 15 minutes. Drain and blot with a paper towel to dry. Split down one side. Stuff with nuts, dried pineapple bits, or marshmallows. Chill for 1 hour or more. Dip in melted chocolate or melted caramel. Chill again. Serve as a candy.

DRIED FIG BARS

1 cup (250 ml) boiling water

1 cup (250 ml) chopped dried figs, stems removed

1½ cups (375 ml) all-purpose flour

½ teaspoon (2 ml) baking powder

½ teaspoon (2 ml) baking soda

½ teaspoon (2 ml) salt

2 egg yolks

1 cup (250 ml) granulated sugar

1 teaspoon (5 ml) pure vanilla extract

½ cup (125 ml) buttermilk

½ cup (125 ml) chopped nuts

2 egg whites, stiffly beaten

Pour boiling water over chopped figs. Let stand for 10 minutes. Drain. In a small bowl, combine flour, baking powder, baking soda, and salt. In a large mixing bowl, beat egg yolks and add sugar gradually, beating until light. Add vanilla. Add mixed dry ingredients alternately with buttermilk. Stir in reserved figs and nuts. Fold in egg whites. Spread in greased 8 X 12-inch (20 X 30-cm) baking pan and bake in 375°F (190°C) oven for 25 minutes. Cut into 48 bars.

Grapes (Raisins)

Any variety of grapes is excellent dried, but should be left on the vine until well ripened. They may be left whole or cut in half for faster drying. Any seeds may be removed as they are cut in half; no pretreatment is necessary for grapes cut in half. Whole seedless grapes should be dipped in boiling water for 30 seconds to split the skins.

Dehydrator: Spread grapes over trays and dry at 115°F (45°C) until dry through to the center, stirring occasionally and rotating trays once or twice. Drying time will vary from 24 to 48 hours.

Sun: Spread grapes on trays and dry in the sun in a well-ventilated place until wrinkled and dried through. Stir often during the day and take trays inside at night. If birds or insects are a problem, cover with a layer of cheesecloth propped up so it does not touch the fruit. They will take 3 to 5 days to dry.

Oven or Homemade Dryer: Spread whole or halved grapes thinly over trays. Dry for 48 to 72 hours at 115°F (45°C), stirring occasionally and rotating trays, until wrinkled and dry to the center.

To Use: Dried grapes are a nutritious snack food when eaten alone or combined with any dried fruit mixture. Add them to cookie dough, spice cake, or rice pudding. Like any raisins, they may be plumped by soaking or cooking in boiling water, but dried grapes cannot be returned to the fresh grape form.

DRIED GRAPE COFFEE CAKE

2 cups (500 ml) all-purpose flour

3 teaspoons (15 ml) baking powder

¾ teaspoon (3 ml) salt

⅓ cup (75 ml) granulated sugar

1 teaspoon (5 ml) ground cinnamon

⅓ cup (75 ml) vegetable shortening

1 egg

½ cup (125 ml) milk

½ cup (125 ml) seeded and chopped dried grapes

1 tablespoon (15 ml) butter or margarine, melted

Combine flour, baking powder, salt, sugar, and cinnamon. Cut in shortening with pastry blender or two knives. Combine egg and milk in a cup and add, all at once, to mixture. Add dried grapes and blend. Spread evenly over bottom of well-greased 8-inch (20 cm) square baking pan and brush with melted butter or margarine. Sprinkle with Crumb Topping and bake for 25 to 30 minutes in a 375°F (190°C) oven. Serve hot or cold. Makes 8 servings.

Crumb Topping

3 tablespoons (45 ml) butter or margarine

¼ cup (65 m) granulated sugar

¾ teaspoon (3 ml) ground cinnamon

3 tablespoons (45 ml) all-purpose flour

Cream butter or margarine and sugar until fluffy. Add remaining ingredients and blend well. Brown sugar may be substituted for granular sugar.

DRIED GRAPE SAUCE

1 cup (250 ml) firmly packed
   brown sugar

½ cup (125 ml) boiling water

1 cup (250 ml) seeded dried grapes

2 tablespoons (30 ml) butter or
   margarine

4 tablespoons (60 ml) white vinegar

1½ teaspoons (7 ml) Worcestershire
   sauce

½ teaspoon (2 ml) salt

¼ teaspoon (1 ml) ground cloves

Add brown sugar to water in saucepan. Simmer for 5 minutes, stirring to dissolve sugar. Add remaining ingredients and cook over low heat for 10 minutes. Serve as a meat sauce. Especially good with ham. Makes 2 cups (500 ml).

Lemon or Orange Peel

Wash lemon or orange peel in hot water and cut into ½-inch (1.25 cm) strips. Scrape and discard white membrane from inside of peel. Cut peel into pieces. No pretreatment is necessary.

Dehydrator: Spread small pieces of peeling on trays and dry at 115°F (45°C) for 6 to 8 hours until crisp, stirring occasionally. Grate by running through a blender or food mill and store in small bottles.

Sun: Spread small pieces of peeling on trays and dry in full sun in a well-ventilated place, stirring occasionally. They should be crisp after 1 day of good drying weather. Grate by processing in a blender or food mill and store in small bottles.

Oven or Homemade Dryer: Spread small pieces of peeling on trays. Dry at 115°F (45°C), stirring occasionally, until peel is crisp, about 8 to 12 hours. Grate by processing in blender or food mill. Store in small bottles.

To Use: These peels may be used as a substitute for fresh lemon or orange juice in many cookie or cake recipes. They add an interesting touch when sprinkled over fruit salads and whipped cream toppings. One-half teaspoon (2 ml) dried lemon peel replaces 1 tablespoon (15 ml) lemon juice in most recipes.

DRIED ORANGE SUGAR COOKIES

¾ cup (190 ml) granulated sugar

½ cup (125 ml) vegetable oil

2 eggs, well beaten

3 tablespoons (45 ml) grated dried
   orange peel

2 cups (500 ml) all-purpose flour

2 teaspoons (10 ml) baking powder

½ teaspoon (2 ml) salt

Granulated sugar to sprinkle on tops

Blend sugar and oil. Stir in eggs and orange peel. In another bowl, combine flour, baking powder, and salt. Add gradually to sugar-oil mixture, mixing well after each addition. Chill for 3 to 4 hours or overnight. On a lightly floured surface, roll out thinly and cut with cookie cutter. Arrange 2 inches (5 cm) apart on greased cookie sheet and sprinkle tops with sugar. Bake in 350°F (180°C) oven for 10 to 12 minutes, or until golden brown around the edges. Makes 2 dozen cookies.

DRIED LEMON PUDDING

½ cup (125 ml) granulated sugar

5 tablespoons (75 ml) all-purpose flour

¼ teaspoon (1 ml) baking powder

⅛ teaspoon (½ ml) salt

2 egg yolks

1 cup (250 ml) milk

3 teaspoons (15 ml) grated dried lemon peel

1½ tablespoons (25 ml) butter or margarine, melted

2 egg whites, stiffly beaten

Combine ¼ cup (65 ml) sugar, flour, baking powder, and salt. In another bowl, beat egg yolks until light. Add milk, lemon peel, and melted butter or margarine. Beat well. Stir in dry ingredients and beat until smooth. Fold remaining ¼ cup (65 ml) sugar into stiffly beaten egg whites. Fold egg white mixture into batter and pour into a greased 1-quart (1-litre) casserole. Set in a pan of warm water and bake in a 350°F (180°C) oven for 45 minutes, or until firm and lightly browned. Pudding will have a cake-like layer on top and a lemon sauce on bottom. Cool before serving. Serves 4.

Peaches

Peel completely ripened peaches by dipping in boiling water for 1 minute, then in cold water. Skins will slip off. Cut peaches in half and remove stones. Leave in halves, slice, or chop into small pieces. Pretreat with one of the dips in chapter 4 to keep fruit from darkening. If you prefer and the peaches are to be dried in the sun, they may be sulfured according to directions in chapter 4.

To speed drying, spread halves, skin-side down, on trays and dry until they begin to wrinkle. Turn halves over and flatten with the hand, a spatula, or a block of wood. Continue drying until completely dry to the center.

Dehydrator: Spread halves, slices, or pieces of peaches over trays. Dry at 115°F (45°C) until leathery with no hint of moisture when cut or bitten. Dry halves for 24 to 36 hours, slices for 10 to 12 hours, and small pieces for 8 to 12 hours, stirring or turning occasionally and rotating trays once or twice a day. Test before storing.

Sun: Spread peach halves, slices, or pieces over trays and cover with cheesecloth propped up to not touch fruit. Dry in a well-ventilated place in full sun, stirring occasionally and taking trays inside at night. When dry, fruit should be leathery and almost stiff with no hint of moisture in the center. Halves will take 4 to 6 days, slices 2 to 3 days, and pieces 1 to 2 days, depending on the weather.

Oven or Homemade Dryer: Spread peach halves, slices, or small pieces over trays. Dry at 115°F (45°C) until leathery and almost stiff with no moisture inside. Stir occasionally and rotate trays during the drying period, 10 to 14 hours for pieces, 12 to 16 hours for slices, and 36 to 48 hours for halves.

To Use: Peaches are delicious eaten dry as a snack. They may be mixed with other dried fruits or refreshed by soaking overnight in an equal amount of boiling water. They also may be simmered for 20 to 30 minutes in boiling water to cover. It is not necessary to add sugar, but you may if you wish. One cup yields about 1¼ cups (315 ml) refreshed or cooked peaches.

They may be combined with fresh or canned fruit as a compote. Just mix the fruits, add 1–2 cups (250–500 ml) of the juice, and let set in the refrigerator for 3 to 4 hours or overnight before serving.

DRIED PEACH UPSIDE-DOWN CAKE

1 cup (250 ml) boiling water

9 dried peach halves or 1½ cups (375 ml) dried peach slices

2 tablespoons (30 ml) butter or margarine

¼ cup (65 ml) firmly packed brown sugar

¼ cup (65 ml) vegetable shortening

¾ cup (190 ml) granulated sugar

1 egg, beaten

1 teaspoon (5 ml) pure vanilla extract

1¼ cups (315 ml) all-purpose flour

1½ teaspoons (7 ml) baking powder

¼ teaspoon (1 ml) salt

Pour boiling water over dried peaches and let soak for 3 to 4 hours or simmer for 20 to 30 minutes, or until tender. Drain, reserving any soaking or cooking liquid. Melt butter or margarine in an 8-inch (20-cm) square baking pan and sprinkle with brown sugar. Arrange drained peach halves or slices over brown sugar. Set aside. In a mixing bowl, cream shortening and granulated sugar until fluffy. Add egg and vanilla and beat well. Combine dry ingredients and gradually add, alternately with ½ cup (125 ml) soaking or cooking liquid or water, beating until smooth after each addition. Pour over peaches in pan and spread out evenly. Bake in 350°F (180°C) oven for 35 to 40 minutes, or until a tester inserted in the center comes out clean. While still hot, invert onto a serving plate, fruit-side up. Cut into nine squares. Serve warm. Makes 9 bars.

DRIED PEACH RICE PUDDING

½ cup (125 ml) uncooked white rice

½ cup (125 ml) granulated sugar

1 cup (250 ml) finely chopped dried peaches

4 cups (1 litre) milk

¼ teaspoon (1 ml) ground ginger

¼ teaspoon (1 ml) salt

Combine all ingredients in a 2-quart (2-litre) casserole. Bake, uncovered, in a 325°F (165°C) oven for 2½ hours, or until rice is tender. Stir occasionally as it cooks. Cool. Pudding thickens and becomes creamy as it cools. Serves 6.

Pears

Peel and slice or chop ripe pears, which have been softened by wrapping in paper and storing for 2 to 3 weeks. They should be pretreated according to the directions for dips in chapter 4 or will darken badly during drying.

Dehydrator: Spread pear slices or pieces on trays. Dry for 12 to 18 hours at 115°F (45°C), or until slices are leathery with no moisture in the centers when cut. Stir or turn pieces occasionally and rotate trays once or twice during drying.

Sun: Spread pretreated slices or pieces on cheesecloth-covered trays. Cover with cheesecloth propped up to keep from touching fruit. Dry in a well-ventilated place in full sun until pieces and slices are leathery with no moisture in the centers. Pears will dry in 2 to 3 days. At the end of each day, flip bottom cheesecloth to turn pieces over and take trays inside at night. Cheesecloth cover can be removed after first day.

Oven or Homemade Dryer: Spread pear slices or pieces in a thin layer over trays. Dry at 115°F (45°C), stirring pieces occasionally and rotating trays at least once, for 18 to 24 hours, or until pieces are leathery with no moisture inside.

To Use: These slices may be eaten as a snack or may be refreshed and used in salads and desserts as you would canned pears. One cup yields about 1¼ cups (315 ml) refreshed or cooked pears.

STEWED DRIED PEARS

2 cups (500 ml) boiling water
1 cup (250 ml) dried pear slices
3 tablespoons (45 ml) granulated sugar

1 teaspoon (5 ml) grated dried lemon peel
3 whole cloves

Pour boiling water over dried pear slices. Add sugar, lemon peel, and cloves and cover. Simmer over low heat for 20 to 30 minutes, or until pears are tender. Serves 4.

BAKED DRIED PEAR SLICES

2½ cups (625 ml) boiling water
1½ cups (375 ml) dried pear slices
½ cup (125 ml) granulated sugar

2 teaspoons (10 ml) grated dried orange peel
¼ cup (65 ml) frozen orange juice concentrate

Pour boiling water over dried pear slices, sugar, and grated orange peel in a 1½-quart (1½-litre) casserole. Cover and bake for 30 to 45 minutes in a 400°F (205°C) oven. Add frozen orange juice concentrate and stir until blended. Chill. Serves 6.

Persimmons

If soft varieties of persimmons are used, dry while still firm. Use riper fruits of round, drier varieties. Peel and cut with stainless steel knife. Cut into ¼-inch (0.65-cm) slices. No pretreatment is necessary.

Dehydrator: Spread slices on trays without overlapping. Dry for 18 to 24 hours at 115°F (45°C) until chewy with no moisture in center. Stir or turn once or twice during drying and rotate trays.

Sun: Spread slices on trays thinly, covering with a layer of cheesecloth propped up so it does not touch fruit. Dry in a well-ventilated area in hot sun. Persimmon slices will dry in 3 to 5 days, depending on the humidity in the air. Stir occasionally and take trays inside at night. When dry, they will be brown and leathery, but not sticky.

Oven or Homemade Dryer: Spread persimmon slices in a thin layer over trays. Dry at 115°F (45°C) for 24 to 36 hours, or until leathery with no moisture in the centers. Stir or turn occasionally during drying and rotate trays once or twice.

To Use: Because of their extreme sweetness, dried persimmons are used as a confection, in place of candy, or mixed with other dried fruits, such as plums, cherries, and apricots. They may be cut into fine pieces and dried until hard and crisp, then pulverized to a sugar in a blender. Use as you would sugar on cereal or fruit. Use refreshed as you would fresh fruit in puddings, or in cookies in place of dates. One cup (250 ml) yields about ½ cup (125 ml) sugar or 1 cup (250 ml) refreshed fruit.

Dried Persimmon Pudding

½ cup (125 ml) boiling water

½ cup (125 ml) dried persimmon slices

2 eggs, well beaten

1 cup (250 ml) milk

1½ tablespoons (25 ml) butter or margarine, melted

1 cup (250 ml) all-purpose flour

½ teaspoon (2 ml) baking soda

¾ cup (190 ml) granulated sugar

½ teaspoon (2 ml) salt

¼ teaspoon (1 ml) ground cinnamon

¼ teaspoon (1 ml) ground nutmeg

½ cup (125 ml) dried grapes

½ cup (125 ml) chopped nuts

Pour boiling water over dried persimmon slices. Soak for 3 to 4 hours or overnight until softened. Process in a blender or food mill to a smooth pulp. Add eggs, milk, melted butter or margarine and beat well. In another bowl, combine flour, baking soda, sugar, salt, and spices. Blend into first mixture and beat to a soft batter. Add dried grapes and nuts. Pour into a greased 8-inch (20-cm) square baking pan or casserole dish and bake for 30 to 40 minutes in a 350°F (180°C) oven. Serve with whipped cream or nondairy whipped topping. Serves 6.

DRIED FRUIT BARS

1 cup (250 ml) dried persimmon slices

½ cup (125 ml) dried apricot slices

½ cup (125 ml) dried figs

½ cup (125 ml) halved dried candied cherries

⅔ cup (150 ml) all-purpose flour

1 teaspoon (5 ml) baking powder

¼ teaspoon (1 ml) salt

1 cup (250 ml) chopped walnuts or pecans

½ cup (125 ml) soft butter or margarine

1 cup (250 ml) granulated sugar

2 eggs

1 teaspoon (5 ml) pure vanilla extract

Confectioners' sugar

Cut dried persimmons, apricots, and figs into small pieces. Combine with cherries, flour, baking powder, salt, and chopped nuts. Set aside. In a large bowl, cream butter or margarine and sugar until fluffy. Add eggs and vanilla and blend well. Add fruit-flour mixture, 1 cup (250 ml) at a time, beating with a spoon after each addition. Spread batter in a greased 9-inch (22.5-cm) square baking pan. Bake for 45 minutes in a 350°F (180°C) oven. Cool completely in pan before cutting into 1 X 3-inch (25 X 75-mm) bars. Roll each bar in confectioners' sugar. Makes 27 bars.

Pineapple

Cut whole, ripe pineapples into ¼-inch (6-mm) slices. Peel and core each slice. Dry slices whole or cut each slice into wedges or small bits. No pretreatment is necessary, but slices treated in honey dip are a delicacy (see chapter 4).

Dehydrator: Spread slices, wedges, or bits on trays in a thin layer. Dry at 115°F (45°C) until chewy and dried through, about 24 to 36 hours. Well-dried pineapple pieces will not stick together when squeezed. Turn slices occasionally or stir pieces once or twice a day. Rotate trays once or twice during drying.

Sun: Spread slices, wedges, or bits on trays and cover with cheesecloth. Dry in a well-ventilated place in hot sun, turning or stirring once or twice a day and taking trays inside at night. Bits will dry in 1 to 2 days, wedges will take 2 to 3 days, and slices will dry in 4 to 5 days.

Oven or Homemade Dryer: Spread slices, wedges, or bits on drying trays. Dry at 115°F (45°C) until chewy and no longer sticky, about 36 to 48 hours. Stir or turn pieces occasionally and rotate trays once or twice a day.

To Use: Slices may be refreshed by combining with canned or fresh peaches or pears or by incorporating into gelatin or whipped cream salads. Let set overnight in refrigerator before serving. They may be used in the dry state by adding cut-up bits to cookie or raisin bread dough or by adding to any pudding recipe before cooking. One cup (250 ml) yields about 1¼ cups (310 ml) refreshed pineapple.

DRIED PINEAPPLE SAUCE

2 cups (500 ml) boiling water
1 cup (250 ml) dried pineapple bits
¼ cup (65 ml) granulated sugar
1 tablespoon (15 ml) cornstarch

1 tablespoon (15 ml) butter or margarine
¼ teaspoon (1 ml) salt

Pour boiling water over dried pineapple bits in a bowl. Let cool. In a saucepan, combine sugar and cornstarch. Gradually stir in cooled water with pineapple, stirring well to dissolve. Cook over low heat, stirring constantly, until thickened. Add butter or margarine and salt, cover, and cook over very low heat for 10 to 15 minutes longer, stirring occasionally. Serve hot over bread pudding or plain cake. Makes about 2 cups (500 ml) sauce.

DRIED FRUIT MEDLEY

1 cup (250 ml) dried pineapple slices
½ cup (125 ml) dried banana slices

½ cup (125 ml) dried peach slices
½ cup (125 ml) large flaked coconut

Combine all ingredients. Serve as a finger snack, or top with yogurt or fold into whipped cream and serve in pudding cups. Serves 6.

Plums (Prunes)

Blue Stanley plums usually are dried commercially for prunes, but any variety of plums is delicious when dried. To dry whole plums, wash and dip 1 to 1½ minutes in boiling water to crack skins. Or, if you prefer, pierce each plum several times with a fork. Do not peel.

For faster drying and for use in dried fruit mixtures, desserts, cookies, and cereals, slice and seed plums and cut into small pieces. Plums also may be halved and seeded, partially dried on one side, then mashed with the heel of the hand or a block of wood. The mashed plums are turned over and the drying is completed.

Dehydrator: Spread plums — whole, halved, or cut up — on trays and dry at 115°F (45°C), stirring pieces and turning whole or half plums every few hours. Rotate trays every 3 to 4 hours. Pieces will dry in 8 to 12 hours, halves will take 18 to 24 hours, whole plums will take 36 to 48 hours or more.

Sun: Spread plums — whole, halved, or cut up — on trays in the sun in an area with good air circulation. Stir or turn 2 or 3 times a day. Take trays inside at night. Whole plums will take 4 to 5 days in good weather. Halves will take 3 to 4 days. Slices and pieces will dry in 2 to 3 days.

Oven or Homemade Dryer: Spread plums — whole, halved, or cut up — over trays in a thin layer. Dry at 115°F (45°C) until hard and chewy, stirring or turning pieces occasionally and rotating trays once or twice a day. Whole plums will take 2 to 3 days, halves from 24 to 35 hours, and pieces 18 to 24 hours.

To Use: Eat cut-up plums as a snack alone or mixed with dried peaches, bananas, apricots, or other cut-up dried fruits. Whole or halved dried plums may be refreshed by soaking overnight in water to cover (the process may be speeded up by starting with boiling water) or by simmering for 20 to 30 minutes in water to cover. Either cut-up or whole dried plums may be chopped and used in any recipe calling for prunes or raisins. One cup (250 ml) yields about 1½ cups (375 ml) cooked plums.

DRIED PLUM DROPS

3½ cups (875 ml) all-purpose flour
1 teaspoon (5 ml) baking soda
1 teaspoon (5 ml) salt
1 cup (250 ml) vegetable shortening

2 cups (500 ml) packed brown sugar
2 eggs
½ cup (125 ml) buttermilk or sour milk
¾ cup chopped dried plums

Combine flour, baking soda, and salt. Set aside. In a large bowl, cream shortening and brown sugar. Add eggs. Stir in buttermilk. Gradually add flour mixture and beat well. Stir in chopped plums. Chill for 1 hour. Drop by teaspoonsful (5 ml) about 2 inches (5 cm) apart on a greased cookie sheet. Bake in 400°F (200°C) oven for 8 to 10 minutes. Makes about 6 dozen cookies.

DRIED PLUM DESSERT

1½ cups (375 ml) boiling water
2 cups (500 ml) chopped dried plums
2 cups (500 ml) uncooked rolled oats
1 cup (250 ml) all-purpose flour
1 cup (250 ml) firmly packed brown sugar
¾ cup (190 ml) butter or margarine, melted

1 tablespoon (15 ml) all-purpose flour
½ cup (125 ml) granulated sugar
2 tablespoons (30 ml) grated dried lemon peel
⅛ teaspoon (½ ml) salt

Pour boiling water over dried plums and let soak for 3 to 4 hours or overnight. In another bowl, combine oats, 1 cup (250 ml) flour, and brown sugar. Add melted butter or margarine and mix well. Line bottom of an 8-inch (20-cm) square baking pan with oat mixture, reserving about ½ cup (125 ml) for topping. In a saucepan, combine soaked plums and soaking water, 1 tablespoon (15 ml) flour, granulated sugar, lemon peel, and salt. Simmer for about 5 minutes, stirring frequently. Remove from heat and pour over oat mixture. Sprinkle with reserved topping. Bake for 45 minutes in a 350°F (180°C) oven. Serve with whipped cream or nondairy whipped topping. Serves 6 to 8.

Raspberries and Blackberries

Treatment also applies to Boysenberries, Blackberries, and Dewberries, Loganberries, and Youngberries.

Wash and dry. No pretreatment is necessary.

Dehydrator: Spread berries in a single layer over trays and dry at 115°F (45°C) until brittle, stirring berries and rotating trays once or twice during drying. They will dry in 24 to 48 hours.

Sun: Spread berries thinly on trays and place in a well-ventilated area in full sun. Cover with cheesecloth if birds or insects are a problem. Stir once or twice a day and take trays inside at night. They will be brittle and well dried in 3 to 4 days.

Oven or Homemade Dryer: Spread berries in a thin layer over trays. Dry at 115°F (45°C) until they are brittle, stirring occasionally and rotating trays every few hours. Drying will take 2 to 3 days.

To Use: Refresh berries by pouring 1 cup (250 ml) boiling water over 1 cup (250 ml) dried berries. Let set for 3 to 4 hours or overnight in the refrigerator. For a quick berry sauce, the soaked berries and soaking water may be processed in a blender. Refreshed berries may be used in any way the fresh berries would be used in pies, sauces, and puddings. Dried berries may be added without refreshing to muffin or cake batter or cookie dough. One cup (250 ml) yields about 1½ cups (375 ml) refreshed berries.

DRIED BLACKBERRY TAPIOCA

2 cups (500 ml) boiling water
½ cup (125 ml) dried blackberries
½ cup (125 ml) granulated sugar
¼ cup (65 ml) quick-cooking tapioca

⅛ teaspoon (½ ml) salt
1 teaspoon (5 ml) grated dried lemon peel
Cream

Pour boiling water over dried blackberries in a saucepan. Cover and soak for 3 to 4 hours or overnight in the refrigerator. Add sugar, tapioca, and salt. Cover and cook for 10 to 12 minutes, stirring constantly, until tapioca is cooked. Remove from heat and add lemon peel. Chill. Serve with cream. Serves 4.

DRIED RASPBERRY CAKE TOPPING

⅓ cup (75 ml) boiling water
⅓ cup (75 ml) dried raspberries
2 egg whites
1⅓ cups (325 ml) granulated sugar

1 teaspoon (5 ml) grated dried lemon peel
1 white or yellow cake, baked in an 8 X 12-inch (20 X 30.5-cm) pan

Pour boiling water over dried raspberries. Let soak for 3 to 4 hours or overnight in refrigerator. Add remaining ingredients in a deep bowl and beat with hand beater or electric mixer until light and stiff enough to stand in peaks. Spread over top of cooled cake. Especially good on plain white cake and angel food cake. Serve immediately. Serves 12.

Rhubarb

Thinly slice or chop tender, rosy red rhubarb stalks. Do not peel. No pretreatment is necessary before drying rhubarb that will be used in pies or sauce. For rhubarb to be used as a snack or in dried fruit mixtures, glaze slices with honey dip before drying (see chapter 4).

Dehydrator: Spread slices or pieces — plain or honey dipped — thinly over trays. Dry until hard, about 8 to 12 hours at 115°F (45°C). Pieces should be stirred occasionally and trays rotated at least once during drying.

Sun: Spread thin slices or pieces in a single layer over trays and place in a well-ventilated place in full sun. Honey-dipped slices should be covered with cheesecloth propped up to keep it from touching the fruit. Dry until hard, about 1 to 2 days in good weather. Take trays inside at night.

Oven or Homemade Dryer: Spread cut up rhubarb in a thin layer over drying trays. Dry at 115°F (45°C) until hard, stirring fruit and rotating trays occasionally. Drying will take 12 to 18 hours.

To Use: Refresh rhubarb by adding 1 cup (250 ml) boiling water to 1 cup (250 ml) dried pieces. Let set for 3 to 4 hours or overnight. To make rhubarb sauce, add ¾ cup (190 ml) granulated sugar and cook over low heat until fruit is soft. One cup (250 ml) yields about 2 cups (500 ml) cooked or refreshed rhubarb.

DRIED RHUBARB PIE

2 cups (500 ml) boiling water

1½ cups (375 ml) dried rhubarb slices

Unbaked 2-crust pie 9-inch (22.5-cm) pastry

2 eggs

1½ cups (375 ml) granulated sugar

¼ cup (65 ml) all-purpose flour

¼ teaspoon (1 ml) salt

Butter or margarine

Pour boiling water over dried rhubarb slices and soak overnight. Line a pie pan with one half of pastry dough and roll out remainder and cut into strips. To assemble pie, combine eggs, sugar, flour, and salt. Add refreshed rhubarb and mix well. Pour into pie shell and dot with butter or margarine. Top with pastry strips woven into a lattice design. Bake for 15 minutes in a 450°F (230°C) oven. Lower heat to 350°F (180°C) and bake for 30 minutes more, or until lightly browned.

DRIED RHUBARB BETTY

1½ cups (375 ml) boiling water

1½ cups (375 ml) dried rhubarb

3 cups (750 ml) soft bread crumbs

1 teaspoon (5 ml) grated dried orange
   peel

3 tablespoons (45 ml) orange juice

¼ cup (65 ml) honey

½ cup (125 ml) granulated sugar

Pour boiling water over dried rhubarb pieces and soak overnight. Place 1 cup (250 ml) bread crumbs in 1½-quart (1½-litre) casserole. In layers, add one-half rhubarb, one-half orange peel and orange juice, and all the honey. Top with 1 cup (250 ml) crumbs and cover with remaining rhubarb, orange peel, and juice, then sugar, in that order. Top with remaining 1 cup (250 ml) crumbs. Cover and bake for 45 minutes in 350°F (180°C) oven. Serves 4.

Strawberries

Pick strawberries at the peak of flavor, when they are well ripened, but still firm. Slice. No pretreatment is necessary for drying, but slices may be glazed with honey dip for a delicious confection (see chapter 4).

Dehydrator: Spread slices thinly over trays and dry at 115°F (45°C), turning slices after the first 4 hours and rotating trays after 6 to 8 hours. They will dry in 12 to 18 hours and should be hard when dry.

Sun: Spread slices on trays and cover with cheesecloth propped up to keep it from touching fruit. Place in a well-ventilated area in full sun and dry until slices are hard with no moisture in the center when cut. Turn slices occasionally and take trays inside at night. Will dry in 1 to 2 days.

Oven or Homemade Dryer: Spread slices thinly over drying trays. Dry at 115°F (45°C) for 18 to 24 hours until hard, stirring occasionally and rotating trays once or twice.

To Use: These berries, plain or honey dipped, are delicious eaten as a confection, alone, or mixed with other dried fruits, such as bananas and pineapple. Dried strawberries may be refreshed and used in any dish in place of fresh strawberries. Chopped, dried strawberries may be added to cookie and cake batters, puddings, and muffins. A strawberry sauce may be made by processing refreshed strawberries in the blender. One cup yields about 1¼ cups (315 ml) refreshed berries.

DRIED STRAWBERRY TOPPING

1 cup (250 ml) boiling water

1 cup (250 ml) dried strawberries

1 small package strawberry gelatin

½ cup (125 ml) whipped cream or
   nondairy whipped topping

Pour boiling water over dried strawberries and soak for 3 to 4 hours or overnight in the refrigerator. Drain, reserving both berries and any remaining soaking liquid. Add water to liquid to make 2 cups (500 ml). Add gelatin and heat until gelatin is dissolved. Add refreshed strawberries and chill until almost set. Fold in whipped cream or nondairy whipped topping and serve on squares of cake. Especially good on angel food cake.

DRIED STRAWBERRY SHERBET

¾ cup (190 ml) boiling water

¾ cup (190 ml) dried strawberries

10 ounces (250 grams) sweetened
    condensed milk

2 tablespoons (30 ml) lemon juice

2 egg whites, stiffly beaten

Pour boiling water over dried strawberries and simmer, covered, over low heat for 20 to 30 minutes, or until strawberries are soft. Press through a sieve, discarding strawberry pulp and seeds and reserving liquid. To the juice, add condensed milk and lemon juice. Chill. Fold in stiffly beaten egg whites. Freeze until firm in ice cube trays. A great summer snack. Serves 4.

CHAPTER SEVEN

Drying Vegetables

To obtain the best flavor and nutrition in dried vegetables, pick or buy the crispest, most flavorful fresh vegetables. Drying can preserve much of the nutrition and good taste of vegetables, but it cannot improve on the original food.

Vegetables may be dried by any of the three methods recommended for fruits. Artificial heat should not go above 120°F (50°C). More care must be taken in pretreating and drying vegetables, because low-acid vegetables are more susceptible to spoilage than acid fruits. Blanching is necessary to keep most vegetables from overmaturing during storage. Careful drying and inspection before storing is also necessary. During storage, dried vegetables should be checked for moisture once or twice a week the first few weeks. One small piece still moist inside can cause the entire batch to mold. This is why vegetables should be stored in small batches.

Most dried vegetables are best cooked without soaking in order to restore their fresh taste and texture. No salt should be added to the cooking or soaking water, however, since salt retards the water absorption of the vegetable. Exceptions are beans and sprouts. Beans usually are soaked before cooking. Sprouts are enjoyed for their dried crispness. Sliced parsnips, tomatoes, turnips, and zucchini are delicious eaten in the dry form as snacks in addition to their use as a cooked vegetable.

Dried Baby Food (Vegetable)

To make baby food from fresh vegetables, cook vegetable until just tender and then strain. Using a food mill, cone, sieve, or blender, puree vegetable and dry as directed.

Dehydrator: Cover trays with plastic wrap and spread with ⅛-inch (3-mm) layer of vegetable puree. Dry at highest heat setting for about 12 to 14 hours, or until firm, and top is hard but sticky, and puree can be pulled away from plastic wrap. Turn over, remove plastic, and discard. Dry for another 12 to 14 hours, or until hard and dry. Break into pieces and dry for another 3 to 4 hours.

Sun: Spread ⅛-inch (3-mm) layer of vegetable puree over cookie sheets or drying trays that have been covered with plastic wrap. Dry in hot sun until hard and brittle for 2 to 4 days, turning once. Take trays inside at night. Break into pieces and dry for another 6 to 8 hours.

Oven or Homemade Dryer: Preheat oven to 150°F (65°C). Spread vegetable puree in ⅛-inch (3-mm) layer over trays lined with plastic wrap. Dry until firm, then turn over and peel off wrap. Dry for another 12 to 14 hours, or until hard and brittle. Break into pieces and dry for another 3 to 4 hours.

To Make Baby Food Powder: Pound pieces of dried puree to a fine powder using a pestle, grater, blender, or food processor. Package powder in small, one-serving portions.

To Use: Add warm water to the powder until the mixture is desired consistency.

Asparagus

Asparagus spears should snap off easily at ground level when ready to pick. During warm spring weather they may have to be picked twice a day or more to keep them from growing too tall. Dry as soon after picking as possible. Wash, drain dry, and cut into ½-inch (12.5 mm) slices or split lengthwise down the middle. Steam blanch for 5 minutes or water blanch for 3 minutes. Chill in ice water to stop cooking process and retain more color, flavor, and nutrients. Dry immediately on paper towels.

Dehydrator: Spread slices or halves thinly over dehydrator trays. Dry at 120°F (50°C) for 4 to 6 hours. Stir pieces and turn over halves. Rotate trays. Continue drying until brittle. Will dry in 8 to 10 hours, depending on thickness of pieces.

Sun: Spread pieces or split spears on trays. Dry for 1 to 2 days in a well-ventilated area in hot sun until brittle, stirring occasionally and taking trays inside at night.

Oven or Homemade Dryer: Spread pieces or halves on drying trays. Dry at 120°F (50°C) for 10 to 12 hours, stirring or turning pieces, until brittle and dried through.

To Use: Small pieces give excellent flavor to soups. Add to simmering stock without refreshing. To cook as a vegetable, pour 1 cup (250 ml) boiling water over 1 cup (250 ml) asparagus spears or pieces. Cover and simmer for 30 to 40 minutes, or until tender. One cup (250 ml) yields about 1½ cups (375 ml) cooked asparagus.

SCALLOPED DRIED ASPARAGUS

1 cup (250 ml) boiling water

1 cup (250 ml) dried asparagus pieces

1 tablespoon (15 ml) diced dried pimiento

3 tablespoons (45 ml) butter or margarine

3 tablespoons (45 ml) all-purpose flour

½ teaspoon (2 ml) salt

1 cup (250 ml) milk

2 hard-cooked eggs, shelled and sliced

¼ cup (65 ml) grated dried cheese

Pour boiling water over dried asparagus pieces and diced pimiento. Simmer for 30 to 40 minutes, or until tender. Drain, reserving liquid. In another saucepan, melt butter or margarine and blend in flour and salt. Gradually stir in milk and cooking liquid. There should be 1½ cups (375 ml) liquid in all. Cook over low heat, stirring constantly until smooth and thickened. Carefully stir in drained asparagus and pimiento and hard-cooked egg slices. Sprinkle top with grated dried cheese. Bake for 30 to 45 minutes in 350°F (180°C) oven until lightly browned. Serves 4 to 6.

Marinated Dried Asparagus

½ cup (125 ml) vegetable oil

4 tablespoons (60 ml) lemon juice

1 tablespoon (15 ml) minced dried celery

½ teaspoon (2 ml) minced dried chives

1 dried bay leaf

1 sprig dried thyme

½ teaspoon (2 ml) salt

½ teaspoon (2 ml) ground paprika

12–18 dried split asparagus spears

Combine all ingredients, except asparagus in a jar. Shake until well blended. Pour over dried asparagus in serving dish and refrigerate overnight. Remove bay leaf and thyme before serving. Serves 4 to 6.

Beans
(Navy, Kidney, Butter, Great Northern, Lima, Lentils or Soybeans)

Wet beans, shelled from green pods, are difficult to dry satisfactorily and should not be attempted by the beginner. Leave bean pods on the vine in the garden until the beans inside rattle. When vines and pods are dry and shriveled, pick and shell beans. No pretreatment is necessary. After drying, place beans in freezer for 48 hours or in 125°F (50°C) oven for 30 minutes to kill any insect eggs.

Dehydrator: Spread partially dried beans in a single layer on trays. Stirring every few hours, dry at 120°F (50°C) until so dry they will split when tapped with a hammer.

Sun: Spread partially dried beans in a thin layer over trays and place in a well-ventilated place in hot sun. Dry for 1 to 2 days, or until dry enough to split when tapped with a hammer. Stir occasionally and take trays inside at night. To destroy any insect eggs that may have been deposited during drying, heat in 125°F (50°C) oven for 30 minutes before storing. Or store sealed containers in the freezer for 2 to 3 days.

Oven or Homemade Dryer: Spread partially dried beans over trays. Dry at 120°F (50°C) until they can be split with a hammer, stirring occasionally and rotating trays once or twice.

To Use: These may be refreshed before cooking by soaking for 3 to 4 hours or overnight in water to cover. To speed the soaking process, start with boiling water. To reduce the gas-producing properties of beans, drain soaking water and pour fresh water to cover the soaked beans. Cover and bring to a boil over medium heat. Simmer over low heat for 30 minutes and drain again. Cook until tender in fresh water. One cup (250 ml) yields about 2 cups (500 ml) cooked beans

BAKED DRIED LIMA BEANS

3 cups (750 ml) boiling water

1½ cups (375 ml) dried lima beans

4 slices bacon, chopped

2 tablespoons (30 ml) all-purpose flour

1½ cups (375 ml) canned tomatoes

3 tablespoons (45 ml) chopped dried celery

¼ cup (65 ml) minced dried onion

2 tablespoons (30 ml) diced dried green bell pepper

¼ teaspoon (1 ml) minced dried garlic

2 teaspoons (10 ml) salt

Dash black pepper

Pour boiling water over dried beans and let set for 1 hour to plump. Cover and cook until tender, about 2 to 3 hours in a saucepan. (Beans also may be cooked by soaking overnight in the water, then cooking for 8 to 10 hours in a slow cooker.) Drain, reserving liquid to use in soup. Place beans in a 1½-quart (1½-litre) casserole. Sauté chopped bacon in a small skillet. Stir in flour. Add tomatoes, celery, onion, green pepper, garlic, salt, and pepper. Cook over low heat, stirring constantly until thickened, about 15 to 20 minutes. Pour over cooked beans. Cover and bake in 300°F (150°C) oven for 1 hour. Serves 4.

DRIED KIDNEY BEAN SALAD

3 cups (750 ml) boiling water

1½ cups (375 ml) dried kidney beans

1 peeled clove garlic

3 tablespoons (45 ml) white vinegar

2 teaspoons (10 ml) salt

1 teaspoon dry (5 ml) mustard

¼ teaspoon (1 ml) granulated sugar

¼ teaspoon (1 ml) ground paprika

Black pepper to taste

½ cup (125 ml) vegetable oil

Lettuce

Pour boiling water over dried beans, let set for 1 hour to plump up. Cover and cook until tender, about 2 to 3 hours. Drain, saving liquid for soups. Chill beans in refrigerator. Meanwhile, crush garlic with a fork in a wooden bowl. Add vinegar and let set for 10 minutes. Remove garlic and add salt, mustard, sugar, paprika, pepper, and oil. Beat until blended. Add chilled, cooked kidney beans and mix lightly. Cover and chill for several hours, tossing occasionally with a fork. Serve on lettuce leaves. Serves 6.

QUICK-SOAK METHOD

The quick-soak method is good to use when time is limited or when you haven't planned ahead to soak dried beans or peas overnight.

In a large soup pot, cover the beans or peas with water. Bring to a boil and cook, covered, for 2 minutes. Remove the pot from the heat and let stand for 1 to 2 hours. This is equivalent to as much as 15 hours of soaking time.

BOSTON BAKED BEANS

2 cups (500 ml) small white beans
6 cups (1½ litre) water
½ teaspoon (2 ml) salt
¾ cup (190 ml) salt pork cubes

¼ cup (62.5 ml) packed brown sugar
¼ cup (62.5 ml) molasses
½ teaspoon (2 ml) dry mustard

Soak beans overnight. Place beans in a kettle with 6 cups (1½ litres) soaking water or fresh water. Add salt. Bring to a boil, reduce heat, cover, and simmer until tender, about 2 hours.

Mix beans and all cooking water in a baking dish with salt pork, brown sugar, molasses, and dry mustard. Cover and bake beans at 225°F (110°C) for 6 to 8 hours or more. Check occasionally to see if you need to add more water. You may raise the heat and shorten the baking time, but the long, slow cooking produces tastier beans. Serves 8 to 10.

EIGHT BEAN SOUP

¼ cup (65 ml) each: red kidney
   beans, green split peas, yellow split
   peas, lentils, black-eyed peas, navy
   beans, lima beans, and pinto beans
2 tablespoons (30 ml) barley
Water to cover
2 quarts (2 litres) water
1 ham bone or ham hock
1 bay leaf

2 cloves garlic
1 cup (250 ml) chopped onion
1 large can tomatoes, pureed in
   blender
1 tablespoon (15 ml) chili powder
2 tablespoons (30 ml) lemon juice
½ teaspoon (2 ml) dried thyme
1 teaspoon (5 ml) dried savory

Wash beans and barley thoroughly. Place in a soup kettle, cover with water, and soak overnight. In the morning, drain off water and place beans and barley back in kettle. Add 2 quarts (2 litres) water, ham bone, bay leaf, and garlic. Simmer gently for 2½ – 3 hours.

Add remaining ingredients and simmer for an additional 30 minutes. Remove bay leaf and the ham bone and serve. Season at the table with freshly ground pepper and a little salt, if desired. Serves 8.

LOUISIANA RED BEANS AND RICE

2⅓ cups (575 ml) or 1 pound (400 grams) red kidney beans

3 cups (750 ml) water

½ teaspoon (2 ml) salt

2–3 ham hocks

1 medium onion, chopped

1 minced clove garlic

1 chopped celery stalk with leaves

1 bay leaf

1 pound (400 grams) bulk sausage

2 cups (500 ml) cooked brown rice

Chopped green onion

Grated cheddar cheese

Soak beans overnight. Drain and place in a kettle with 3 cups (750 ml) fresh water. Bring to a boil, reduce heat, cover, and simmer for about 30 minutes. Add salt, ham hocks, onion, garlic, celery, and bay leaf. Simmer for 2 hours or more. Add water if mixture gets too thick. Beans will be tender in 2 hours, but longer simmering makes the flavor richer.

About 30 minutes before serving, remove ham hocks and cool until you can remove meat from bones. Cut meat into small pieces and return meat to kettle. Meanwhile, cut sausage into small pieces and fry until brown. Drain off fat and stir sausage into beans. Simmer over very low heat to blend the flavors.

To serve, spoon beans over rice on a large platter and garnish with generous amounts of chopped green onion and grated cheddar cheese. Serves 8 to 10.

LENTIL RICE STEW

¼ cup (65 ml) olive oil

1 sliced large onion

½ cup (125 ml) uncooked long-grain brown rice

2 cups (500 ml) lentils

½ teaspoon (2 ml) salt

6 cups (1½ litres) water

1 cup (250 ml) canned tomatoes

6 cups (1½ litres) coarsely chopped Swiss chard

Coarsely ground black pepper

White vinegar

Yogurt or sour cream

Heat olive oil in a heavy saucepan or Dutch oven. Sauté onion and rice in oil over medium-high heat until onions are golden and rice grains are coated with oil and look translucent. Add lentils, salt, and water. Bring to a boil, reduce heat, cover, and simmer until rice is done, about 45 minutes. By then lentils should be tender, too; if not, simmer for about 20 minutes more. Add water if mixture becomes too thick.

When everything is tender, add tomatoes and cook for 10 minutes more. About 5 minutes before serving, stir in the chopped chard and steam with lid on just until greens are wilted. Season with pepper and vinegar, and top with yogurt or sour cream. Serves 8.

BLACK BEAN SOUP

1 cup (250 ml) dried black beans

4 cups (1 litre) water

½ teaspoon (2 ml) salt

1 chopped celery stalk with leaves

1 chopped medium onion

1 chopped leek (white part only)

2 ham hocks

1 bay leaf

½ teaspoon (2 ml) dried thyme

2 tablespoons (30 ml) dry sherry

2 hard-cooked eggs

Soak beans overnight. Drain beans and place in a kettle with 4 cups (1 litre) fresh water. Add all remaining ingredients, except sherry and eggs. Bring to a boil, reduce heat, cover, and simmer until beans are tender and meat is falling off ham hocks, about 3 hours.

Remove ham hocks and set aside to cool. Scoop out about ½ cup (125 ml) of cooked beans and puree remaining beans in a blender, food processor, or food mill. Return puree to kettle, add reserved beans and all meat you can pick off ham bones. If soup seems too thick, thin with a little hot water or stock. Bring almost to a boil, then stir in sherry. Serve garnished with thin slices of hard-cooked eggs. Serves 6.

MINESTRONE

¾ cup (190 ml) dried beans

3 cups (750 ml) water

½ teaspoon (2 ml) salt

2 tablespoons (30 ml) chopped fresh parsley

1 chopped leek (white part only)

1 chopped medium onion

2 chopped celery stalks with leaves

2 minced cloves garlic

3 tablespoons (45 ml) olive oil

6 cups (1½ litres) water or stock

2 cups (500 ml) chopped fresh or canned tomatoes

2 cups (500 ml) coarsely chopped mixed raw vegetables

1 cup (250 ml) uncooked macaroni

Salt and pepper to taste

Dried oregano or basil (optional)

Soak beans overnight. Place in a kettle with 3 cups (750 ml) soaking water or use fresh water. Add salt. Bring to a boil, reduce heat, cover, and simmer until beans are tender, about 2½ hours.

Place chopped parsley, leek, onion, celery, and garlic together on a cutting board and chop everything together until all ingredients are finely minced, almost to a paste. Heat olive oil in another kettle and sauté minced ingredients until they begin to soften. Add water or stock and tomatoes and bring to a boil. Add coarsely chopped vegetables, macaroni, and cooked beans with liquid. Simmer for about 20 minutes, or until vegetables and macaroni are tender. Season to taste with salt, pepper, and oregano or basil. Serves 8 to 10.

BUTTER BEANS

1 cup (250 ml) large dried limas

3 cups (750 ml) water

½ teaspoon (2 ml) salt

1 tablespoon (15 ml) brown sugar

1 tablespoon (15 ml) butter

1 cup (250 ml) water

¼–½ (65–125 ml) cup cream

Soak beans overnight or use the quick-soak method. Put beans in a saucepan with 3 cups (750 ml) of soaking water or fresh water. Add salt. Bring to a boil, reduce heat, and cover pan. Simmer for about 2 hours, adding water from time to time if necessary, until beans are tender. Turn beans and cooking liquid into a baking dish. Mix in brown sugar and butter. Bake in 225°F (105°C) oven, uncovered, for about 6 hours, adding water as needed to keep beans covered. As limas cook at the low temperature, the liquid will become thick like gravy.

Just before serving, remove beans from oven and stir in enough cream to thin gravy to desired consistency. Serves 6.

SPLIT PEA SOUP

1 pound (400 grams) (about 2¼ cups (565 ml) green or yellow split peas

6 cups (1½ litres) chicken or vegetable stock

2 tablespoons (30 ml) butter

1 teaspoon (5 ml) salt

1 whole clove

1 medium onion, chopped

1 chopped celery stalk with leaves

1 minced small clove garlic

1 chopped medium carrot

1 unpeeled and diced small potato

1 cup (250 ml) cooked diced chicken or turkey (optional)

Wash and sort split peas. Place in a 6-quart (1½-litre) kettle with remaining ingredients, except chicken or turkey. Bring to a boil, reduce heat, cover, and simmer for 2 to 3 hours, stirring occasionally to keep peas from sticking to bottom of pan. Peas and vegetables should be very soft and begin to fall apart. The thicker part of soup will tend to sink to bottom of pan and should be stirred before serving, or you can puree soup before serving. Stir in chicken or turkey about 5 minutes before serving. Grated Parmesan cheese makes a good garnish. Serves 6 to 8.

Beets

Wash whole beets and cut off tops, leaving 1-inch (25 mm) stubs. Cook in water to cover just until skins slip off, about 30 to 35 minutes in a saucepan or 10 to 15 minutes in a pressure cooker. Cut off tops and roots and slip off skins. Chop, grate, or cut into ⅛-inch (3-mm) slices.

Dehydrator: Spread beets sparsely over trays. Dry at 120°F (50°C) until hard, about 8 to 10 hours for slices, 4 to 6 hours for chopped and grated pieces. Turn slices or stir pieces occasionally during drying and rotate trays at least once.

Sun: Spread sliced, chopped, or grated beets over trays. Place in a well-ventilated area in hot sun. Dry, stirring occasionally, and take trays inside at night. In dry weather, slices will dry in 2 to 3 days, pieces in 1 to 2 days. Cover with cheesecloth if birds are a problem, but this will lengthen drying time.

Oven or Homemade Dryer: Spread beets in a thin layer over trays. Dry at 120°F (50°C) until hard, about 10 to 12 hours for slices, 6 to 8 hours for chopped or grated pieces. Stir occasionally and rotate shelves once or twice during drying.

To Use: These slices may be eaten as a snack alone or with a cheese dip. For a cooked vegetable, cook slices in boiling water for 30 to 40 minutes, add butter or margarine, and serve hot. Chopped or grated beets may be cooked in boiling water for 20 to 30 minutes over low heat. One cup (250 ml) yields about 2 cups (500 ml) cooked vegetables.

DRIED HARVARD BEETS

1 cup (250 ml) boiling water

1 cup (250 ml) chopped dried beets

⅓ cup (75 ml) granulated sugar

½ teaspoon (2 ml) salt

1 tablespoon (15 ml) cornstarch

½ cup (125 ml) white vinegar

2 tablespoons (30 ml) butter or margarine

1 teaspoon (5 ml) minced dried onion

Pour boiling water over dried beets in a saucepan. Cover and cook over low heat for 30 to 40 minutes, or until tender. Meanwhile, blend sugar, salt, and cornstarch in a saucepan. Add vinegar and stir until well mixed. Cook over very low heat until smooth and thickened, stirring constantly. Add butter or margarine, onion, and beets. Cook over very low heat for 15 to 20 minutes to blend flavors, stirring frequently. Serves 6.

Broccoli

Pick or buy crisp, dark green broccoli with small and tightly closed buds. Do not attempt to dry any that have grown limp or on which the buds have begun to open. Trim stalks, wash thoroughly, and soak in salt water (1 teaspoon (5 ml) salt to 1 quart (1 litre) water) for 10 minutes to remove any insects or insect eggs. Rinse again. Split stalks lengthwise in pieces no more than ½ inch (15 mm) thick and blanch in boiling water for 2 minutes or in steam for 3½ minutes. Plunge into cold water to stop cooking process and to retain color and flavor. Pat dry with paper towels for 2 or more minutes, then cut into 2- to 3-inch (5 to 7.5-cm) pieces or chop.

Dehydrator: Spread pieces over trays in a thin layer. Dry at 120°F (50°C) for 12 to 18 hours, or until crisp, stirring small pieces and turning over large pieces. Rotate trays at least once during drying. Check for moisture in the center by cutting a cooled piece in the middle.

Sun: Spread pieces over trays and dry in a well-ventilated area in full sun. Stir and turn pieces every few hours. Dry for 1 to 2 days, taking trays inside at night. Test for moisture in the center before storing by cutting a cooled piece in the middle.

Oven or Homemade Dryer: Spread broccoli over trays. Dry at 120°F (50°C) until crisp, about 18 to 24 hours, turning pieces and rotating trays occasionally during drying.

To Use: Pour 1 cup (250 ml) boiling water over 1 cup (250 ml) broccoli. Cover and cook just until tender. Serve as you would fresh. One cup (250 ml) yields about 2 cups (500 ml) cooked broccoli.

BROCCOLI SOUFFLÉ

1 cup (250 ml) boiling water

1 cup (250 ml) chopped dried broccoli pieces

2 tablespoons (30 ml) butter or margarine

4 tablespoons (60 ml) all-purpose flour

½ teaspoon (2 ml) salt

1 cup (250 ml) milk

3 eggs, separated

Pour boiling water over dried broccoli. Cover and cook over low heat for 30 to 40 minutes, or until tender. Drain, reserving liquid for soups. In a saucepan, melt butter or margarine and stir in flour and salt. Gradually add milk, stirring well. Cook over low heat, stirring constantly until well thickened. Beat egg yolks until thick and lemon colored. Stir into thickened mixture. Add chopped, well-drained, cooked broccoli. Beat egg whites until stiff and fold in. Pour mixture into ungreased casserole. Bake in 325°F (165°C) oven for 30 to 45 minutes. Serves 4 to 6.

DRIED VEGETABLE TRIO

2 cups (500 ml) boiling water

½ cup (125 ml) dried broccoli pieces

½ cup (125 ml) sliced dried carrots

6–8 dried cauliflower pieces

½ teaspoon (2 ml) salt

2 tablespoons (30 ml) butter or margarine

Pour boiling water over broccoli, carrots, and cauliflower. Cover and cook until vegetables are tender, about 30 to 40 minutes. Lift vegetables out of liquid onto a serving dish. Add salt and butter or margarine to liquid and cook until butter or margarine is melted and liquid has cooked down to ½ cup (125 ml). Pour over vegetables. Serves 6.

Brussels Sprouts

Cut Brussels sprouts in half. Steam blanch for 6 to 7 minutes or blanch in water for 3 to 5 minutes. Drain, chill in cold water, drain again, and pat dry with paper towels.

Dehydrator: Spread halves, cut-side up, on trays in a single layer. Dry at 120°F (50°C) for 8 to 9 hours. Turn halves over. Rotate trays. Continue drying for another 8 to 9 hours. Check for moisture by cooling and cutting through the center with a knife. They should be brittle.

Sun: Spread halves over trays, cut-side up. Dry for 2 to 3 days in full sun, turning once a day and taking trays inside at night. Dry until brittle and dry to the center. Check for moisture by cutting a cooled piece through the center. If there is any moisture, dry for 1 more day.

Oven or Homemade Dryer: Spread halves over drying trays, cut-side up. Dry at 120°F (50°C) until crisp, turning pieces occasionally and rotating trays. Drying will take 18 to 24 hours.

To Use: Pour 1½ cups (375 ml) boiling water over 1 cup (250 ml) sprouts. Cover and simmer over low heat for 30 to 40 minutes, or until tender. Use as you would fresh or frozen sprouts. One cup (250 ml) dried yields about 2 cups (500 ml) cooked vegetable.

FRENCH-FRIED BRUSSELS SPROUTS

1 cup (250 ml) boiling water

1 cup (250 ml) dried Brussels sprouts

1 egg, well beaten

½ cup (125 ml) dried bread crumbs

¼ teaspoon (1 ml) salt

1–2 tablespoons (15–30 ml) hot oil for frying

Pour boiling water over Brussels sprouts in a saucepan. Cover and cook over low heat for 30 to 40 minutes, or until tender. Drain, reserving any liquid for soup. Dip cooked Brussels sprouts first in beaten egg, then in combined bread crumbs and salt. Sauté in hot oil until lightly browned, about 3 minutes. Serves 4 to 6.

SCALLOPED BRUSSELS SPROUTS

1 cup (250 ml) boiling water

1 cup (250 ml) dried Brussels sprouts

4 tablespoons (60 ml) butter or margarine, melted

3 tablespoons (45 ml) all-purpose flour

¼ teaspoon (1 ml) salt

1 cup (250 ml) milk

½ cup (125 ml) dried bread crumbs

Pour boiling water over Brussels sprouts. Cover and cook over low heat for 30 to 40 minutes. Drain, reserving liquid. In another pan, melt 2 tablespoons (30 ml) butter or margarine. Blend in flour and salt and gradually stir in milk and reserved cooking liquid. Cook, stirring constantly, until smooth and thickened. Put cooked Brussels sprouts into casserole and pour sauce over. Top with bread crumbs that have been mixed with remaining 2 tablespoons (30 ml) butter or margarine. Bake in 350°F (180°C) oven until lightly browned, about 25 minutes. Serves 4 to 6.

Cabbage

Select solid, heavy cabbage heads with fresh, green color. Remove any tough outer leaves and cut heads into quarters. Core each quarter and shred by cutting into strips lengthwise. Blanch in steam for 2 to 3 minutes or in boiling water for 1½ to 2 minutes. Chill in cold water. Drain well. Pat dry.

Dehydrator: Spread shreds thinly over trays. Dry for 12 to 15 hours at 120°F (50°C), or until brittle. Every 3 to 4 hours stir with the hands and rotate trays.

Sun: Spread shreds thinly over trays and place in hot sun where there is good circulation. Dry for 2 to 3 days, or until crisp, stirring occasionally, and taking trays inside at night.

Oven or Homemade Dryer: Spread shreds in a thin layer over trays. Dry at 120°F (50°C) for 18 to 24 hours, stirring occasionally and rotating trays once or twice. Dried cabbage should be brittle.

To Use: Drop shreds into boiling soup and allow to cook as the soup simmers. To use as a vegetable, pour 1 cup (250 ml) boiling water over 1 cup (250 ml) shreds and simmer for 40 minutes, or until tender. One cup (250 ml) yields about 1½ cups (375 ml) cooked vegetable.

SWEET AND SOUR DRIED CABBAGE

2 cups (500 ml) dried cabbage

1 cup dried (250 ml) apple slices

2 tablespoons (30 ml) butter or margarine, melted

2 cups (500 ml) boiling water

2 tablespoons (30 ml) all-purpose flour

1½ teaspoons (7 ml) grated dried lemon peel

4 tablespoons (60 ml) brown sugar

Salt and pepper

Add dried cabbage and apple slices to melted butter or margarine in a skillet. Add boiling water, cover, and simmer until cabbage and apples are tender, about 30 to 40 minutes. Sprinkle with flour. Add lemon peel and brown sugar and stir well. Salt and pepper to taste. Cover and simmer for 5 minutes more. Serves 6.

DEVILED DRIED CABBAGE

2 cups (500 ml) boiling water

2 cups (500 ml) dried cabbage

1 teaspoon (5 ml) prepared mustard

½ teaspoon (2 ml) salt

1 teaspoon (5 ml) granulated sugar

3 tablespoons (45 ml) butter or margarine

1 tablespoon (15 ml) lemon juice

Pour boiling water over dried cabbage in a saucepan. Cover and cook for 30 to 40 minutes, or until tender. Mix remaining ingredients in another saucepan. Heat slowly, stirring to blend. Pour over hot cabbage, mixing lightly. Serves 6.

Carrots

Select dry young, tender carrots. Scrape or scrub with a stiff vegetable brush. Cut off tops. Cut into ⅛-inch (3-mm) slices or chop into small pieces. Steam blanch for 3 to 4 minutes or water blanch for 2 to 3 minutes. Drain. Chill in ice water, drain again, and pat dry.

Dehydrator: Spread slices or pieces one layer deep over trays. Dry for 12 to 18 hours at 120°F (50°C) until tough and leathery with no moisture in the centers. Stir pieces and rotate trays occasionally.

Sun: Spread slices or pieces in a thin layer over trays. Place in a well-ventilated area in hot sun and dry for 2 to 3 days, stirring occasionally and taking trays inside at night. Dried carrots should be leathery and pliable.

Oven or Homemade Dryer: Spread pieces thinly over trays. Dry at 120°F (50°C) for 18 to 24 hours, or until pieces are leathery and pliable, stirring occasionally and rotating trays 2 or 3 times.

To Use: Add 1 cup (250 ml) boiling water to 1 cup (250 ml) slices or pieces and simmer for 35 to 45 minutes, or until tender. Serve buttered or creamed. One cup (250 ml) yields about 1¼ cups (315 ml) cooked carrots.

DRIED CARROT PATTIES

2 cups (500 ml) chopped dried carrots

2 cups (500 ml) boiling water

2 tablespoons (30 ml) butter of margarine

1 egg, well beaten

½ teaspoon (2 ml) ground nutmeg

½ teaspoon (2 ml) salt

1 cup (250 ml) dried bread crumbs

1–2 tablespoons (15–30 ml) hot oil for frying

Cook carrots in boiling water for 35 to 40 minutes, or until tender. Drain. Add butter, egg, nutmeg, and salt to cooked carrots. Combine well and mash with potato masher or electric mixer. Shape into patties and coat with bread crumbs. Chill thoroughly. Sauté in hot oil until golden brown. Serves 6 to 8.

DRIED CARROT RING

1 cup (250 ml) boiling water

1 cup (250 ml) dried carrots

1 teaspoon (5 ml) minced dried onion

2 tablespoons (30 ml) butter or
    margarine, melted

2 eggs, well beaten

1 tablespoon (15 ml) all-purpose flour

1 cup (250 ml) light cream or
    evaporated skim milk

Salt and pepper to taste

Pour boiling water over dried carrots and dried onion in a saucepan. Cover and cook until tender, about 35 to 45 minutes. Mash with potato masher or process in a blender until smooth. Add remaining ingredients, one at a time, beating well after each addition. Pour into buttered ring mold and place in a shallow pan of hot water. Bake for 40 to 50 minutes in 350°F (180°C) oven until set. Unmold and serve filled with a green vegetable. Serves 6.

CARROT-OAT COOKIES

1 cup (250 ml) packed brown sugar

½ cup (125 ml) vegetable shortening

3 eggs

⅔ cup (150 ml) milk

1 cup (250 ml) grated dried carrots

2 cups (500 ml) all-purpose flour

1 teaspoon (5 ml) baking powder

½ teaspoon (2 ml) salt

½ teaspoon (2 ml) baking soda

½ teaspoon (2 ml) ground cinnamon

1½ cups (375 ml) rolled oats

1½ cups (375 ml) dried seedless grapes
    or chopped dried plums

½ cup (125 ml) chopped nuts

1 tablespoon (15 ml) grated dried
    orange peel

Mix together brown sugar, shortening, eggs, milk, and carrots. Let stand for 10 minutes. Meanwhile, combine dry ingredients. Mix with dried fruit, nuts, and dried orange peel. Drop by spoonsful on greased cookie sheet. Bake for 10 to 12 minutes in 350°F (180°C) oven. Makes 4 dozen cookies.

Cauliflower

Select firm, white heads of cauliflower with tight, well-formed florets. Soak for 10 minutes in a solution of 1 teaspoon (5 ml) salt to 1 quart (1 litre) water to remove insects. Cut in half, slice, or chop. Blanch halves in boiling water for 3 to 4 minutes or steam blanch for 5 minutes. Slices or pieces should be water-blanched for 1 to 2 minutes or steam-blanched for 3 minutes. Drain, chill in cold water. Pat dry with paper towels.

Dehydrator: Spread florets or pieces on trays and dry at 120°F (50°C) until pieces are crisp and halves are leathery and dry to the center. Turn halves and stir pieces once or twice during the drying period, about 12 to 15 hours for small pieces and 18 to 24 hours for halves.

Sun: Spread cauliflower halves or pieces on trays. Place in full sun where there is good air circulation. Dry for 1 to 2 days for small pieces, 2 to 3 days for halves, turning halves and stirring pieces every few hours. Take trays inside at night. When dry, small pieces should be crisp, and larger ones should be leathery.

Oven or Homemade Dryer: Spread pieces over trays. Dry at 120°F (50°C) for 18 to 24 hours for small pieces and for 24 to 36 hours for halves, or until pieces are crisp and halves are leathery. Stir occasionally and rotate trays, front to back, side to side and top to bottom, every 4 to 6 hours.

To Use: Cover pieces with boiling water, place over medium heat and bring to a boil. Cover and cook for 45 to 50 minutes until tender. Or drop thin slices or small pieces in boiling water or soup broth and cook for 20 to 30 minutes. One cup (250 ml) yields about 1½ cups (375 ml) cooked vegetable.

DRIED CAULIFLOWER IN TOMATO SAUCE

1½ cups (375 ml) dried cauliflower pieces

1½ cups (375 ml) boiling water

2 tablespoons (30 ml) butter or margarine

2 tablespoons (30 ml) all-purpose flour

½ teaspoon (2 ml) salt

1½ tablespoons (25 ml) minced dried onion

1½ cups (375 ml) water

1½ cups (375 ml) dried tomatoes

Cook cauliflower in boiling water until tender, about 45 to 50 minutes. Meanwhile, melt butter or margarine in a saucepan. Stir in flour and add salt, dried onion, 1½ cups (375 ml) water, and dried tomatoes. Cook, stirring constantly, until thickened, then cover and cook over very low heat until tomatoes and onions are tender and sauce is smooth. Add cooked cauliflower and serve. Serves 6.

FRENCH-FRIED CAULIFLOWER

1½ cups (375 ml) boiling water

1½ cups (375 ml) dried cauliflower floret halves

8 ounces (200 grams) American cheese

1 cup (250 ml) milk

5 cups (1 litre 250 ml) corn flakes

2 eggs, well beaten

2 tablespoons (30 ml) cold water

1–2 tablespoons (15–30 ml) hot oil for frying

Pour boiling water over dried cauliflower. Cover and cook for 45 to 50 minutes, or until tender. Drain. Melt cheese in top of a double boiler. Gradually add milk, stirring constantly until smooth. Keep hot. Meanwhile, crush corn flakes into fine crumbs (or use dried bread crumbs). Combine eggs and 2 tablespoons (30 ml) cold water. Roll cauliflower halves in crumbs, then dip in egg mixture, then back in crumbs again. Sauté in hot oil until lightly browned. Drain. Serve with hot cheese sauce. Serves 6.

Celery

Wash and trim celery stalks. Cut off leaves and dry leaves according to instructions in chapter 8. Cut stalks into very thin slices. Do not blanch.

Dehydrator: Spread slices in a thin layer over trays and dry for 12 to 18 hours at 120°F (50°C), or until crisp. Cool. Test by cutting through center to be sure there is no moisture. Celery is especially susceptible to mold unless it is perfectly dry to the center. While drying, stir slices occasionally and rotate trays once or twice.

Sun: Spread slices sparsely over trays and place in full sun where there is good air circulation. Dry for 2 to 3 days, stirring occasionally and taking trays inside at night. Test for moisture before storing.

Oven or Homemade Dryer: Spread a thin layer of slices over trays. Dry at 120°F (50°C) until crisp, about 18 to 24 hours. Stir slices and rotate trays occasionally during drying.

To Use: Drop slices into simmering soup stock and cook with soup. To use as a vegetable, pour 1 cup (250 ml) boiling water over 1 cup (250 ml) dried celery and simmer for 20 to 30 minutes in a covered saucepan. One cup (250 ml) yields about 1½ cups (375 ml) cooked celery.

DRIED CELERY AU GRATIN

1½ cups (375 ml) boiling water

1½ cups (375 ml) dried celery slices

2 tablespoons (30 ml) butter or margarine

3 tablespoons (45 ml) all-purpose flour

1 cup (250 ml) milk

½ teaspoon (2 ml) salt

¾ cup (90 ml) shredded American cheese

Pour boiling water over celery in a saucepan. Cover and cook for 20 to 30 minutes until tender. Drain, reserving liquid. In another pan, melt butter or margarine. Stir in flour and blend well. Gradually add milk, stirring constantly. Add salt and cheese. Cook over low heat, stirring constantly, until smooth and thickened. Arrange alternate layers of celery and cheese sauce in casserole. Top with a layer of cheese sauce. Bake in 350°F (180°C) oven for 20 minutes until lightly browned. Serves 6.

DRIED CELERY AND GREEN BEANS

½ cup (125 ml) boiling water

½ cup (125 ml) dried celery

2 cups (500 ml) cooked or canned green beans

½ teaspoon (2 ml) salt

1 tablespoon (15 ml) butter or margarine

Pour boiling water over celery. Cover and cook for 20 to 30 minutes until tender. Add remaining ingredients and cook for 20 minutes more. Serves 6.

Corn

Husk and trim sweet, immature ears of corn. Steam or water blanch until kernels are no longer milky, about 1½ to 3 minutes. Drain and chill in cold water. Drain again and cut kernels from cob.

Dehydrator: Spread kernels over trays. Dry at 120°F (50°C), stirring corn and rotating trays every 4 hours. Dry for 8 to 12 hours until kernels are shriveled and dry inside.

Sun: Spread kernels over cheesecloth-covered trays and dry for 1 to 2 days in full sun, stirring occasionally and taking trays inside at night. When dry, corn should be hard and brittle and should rattle in the storage jar.

Oven or Homemade Dryer: Spread kernels in a thin layer over trays. Dry at 120°F (50°C), stirring occasionally and rotating trays once or twice until corn is hard and brittle, about 12 to 18 hours.

To Use: Pour 2 cups (500 ml) boiling water over 1 cup (250 ml) corn and simmer, covered, for about 50 minutes until corn is tender. One cup yields approximately 2 cups (500 ml) cooked corn.

DRIED CORN FRITTERS

1 cup (250 ml) boiling water	2 eggs
1 cup (250 ml) dried corn	¼ cup (65 ml) milk
1 cup (250 ml) all-purpose flour	1 tablespoon (15 ml) butter or margarine, melted
½ teaspoon (2 ml) salt	
1 teaspoon (5 ml) baking powder	Hot oil for frying

Pour boiling water over dried corn in a saucepan. Cover and cook for 40 to 50 minutes until tender. Drain. Combine flour, salt, and baking powder in a bowl. Mix eggs with milk and add melted butter or margarine and corn. Combine two mixtures lightly. Drop by teaspoonsful into deep, hot oil. Fry until golden and cooked to center, about 4 to 5 minutes. Drain on paper towels. Serves 4 to 6.

SCALLOPED DRIED CORN

3 cups (750 ml) boiling water	½ teaspoon (2 ml) salt
1½ cups (375 ml) dried corn	Dash black pepper
2 teaspoons (10 ml) chopped dried pimiento	2 eggs, beaten
4 tablespoons (60 ml) butter or margarine	½ cup (125 ml) dried bread crumbs
2 tablespoons (30 ml) all-purpose flour	Dash ground paprika

Pour boiling water over dried corn and pimiento in a saucepan. Cover and cook over low heat until tender, about 50 minutes. Drain, reserving liquid in a measuring cup. Add water to liquid to make 1 cup (250 ml). In another saucepan, melt 2 tablespoons (30 ml) butter or margarine and blend in flour. Gradually stir in 1 cup (250 ml) cooking liquid. Cook over low heat, stirring constantly, until thickened. Season with salt and pepper. Remove from heat and add eggs, stirring constantly. Mix in drained corn and pimiento. Pour into greased casserole. Melt remaining 2 tablespoons (30 ml) butter or margarine and stir in dried bread crumbs. Sprinkle over top of casserole. Add paprika. Set in a shallow pan of water and bake in a 350°F (180°C) oven for 45 to 50 minutes. Serves 4 to 6.

Cucumbers

Wash slender, dark green cucumbers in which seeds have not yet developed. Slice, without peeling, into ⅛-inch (3-mm) slices.

Dehydrator: Spread slices in a single layer over trays without overlapping. Dry at 120°F (50°C) for 4 to 5 hours. Turn slices and rotate trays. Continue drying for another 5 to 6 hours, or until slices are crisp enough to snap in half.

Sun: Spread slices on trays and place in full sun where there is good air circulation. Dry for 2 to 3 days, turning slices every day and taking trays inside at night. Dry until very brittle.

Oven or Homemade Dryer: Spread cucumber slices in a single layer over trays. Dry at 120°F (50°C) until crisp, turning occasionally and rotating trays once or twice. Will dry in 12 to 18 hours.

To Use: Eat crisp slices as a snack, with or without a cheese dip. Break or cut into pieces and add to salads just before serving. Dried cucumbers have an excellent flavor and texture and are best eaten when dry, because they tend to become limp when refreshed.

Eggplant

Peel whole eggplant and cut into ¼-inch (6-mm) slices. Leave slices whole, cut into ½-inch (12-mm) strips, or cut into 1-inch (25-mm) squares. Steam blanch for 4 minutes for larger pieces, 3 minutes for smaller pieces. Do not water blanch.

Dehydrator: Spread slices or pieces over trays. Dry at 120°F (50°C) for 18 to 24 hours or until leathery with no moisture in the center. Turn slices or stir pieces occasionally and rotate trays once or twice.

Sun: Spread slices or pieces over drying trays without overlapping. Dry in full sun in an area with good air circulation for 2 to 3 days, or until dry and leathery. Turn slices or stir pieces occasionally and take trays inside at night.

Oven or Homemade Dryer: Spread slices or pieces over drying trays. Dry at 120°F (50°C) for 24 to 36 hours, stirring or turning every few hours and rotating trays 2 or 3 times.

To Use: Refresh slices by soaking for 3 to 4 hours or overnight in the refrigerator. Prepare as you would fresh eggplant slices by frying or using in casseroles. Pieces may be soaked for 1 to 2 hours before cooking or may be cooked without soaking. One cup (250 ml) yields about 1¼ cups (315 ml) cooked eggplant.

DRIED EGGPLANT CASSEROLE

12 dried eggplant slices

2 cups (500 ml) boiling water

1 egg, beaten

⅓ cup (75 ml) milk

¼ teaspoon (1 ml) salt

3 tablespoons (45 ml) vegetable oil, heated in skillet

½ pound (200 grams) mozzarella cheese, sliced

3 medium tomatoes, sliced

½ teaspoon (2 ml) dried oregano

1 tablespoon (15 ml) olive oil

Soak eggplant slices in boiling water for 3 to 4 hours or overnight in refrigerator. In a small bowl, combine egg, milk, and salt. Dip eggplant slices in egg mixture and lightly brown in skillet in oil. As slices are browned, arrange in a casserole. On top of slices, place slices of cheese and tomatoes. Repeat layers, ending with cheese. Add oregano. Brush cheese with olive oil. Bake in 350°F (180°C) oven for 30 minutes. Serves 6.

MARINATED DRIED EGGPLANT

Marinate dried eggplant slices in French dressing for 2 to 3 hours in the refrigerator. Lift slices from dressing into a casserole. Dot with butter or margarine and bake in 400°F (205°C) oven for 20 to 25 minutes.

Green Beans

Pick green beans while still immature, before beans have developed inside the pods. Wash and trim. Cut French-style (lengthwise), snap in half, or leave whole. Steam blanch for 4 minutes or water blanch for 2 minutes. Chill in cold water. Drain. Pat dry.

Dehydrator: Spread beans in a single layer over trays. Dry at 120°F (50°C) stirring once or twice and rotating trays. Dry for 8 to 14 hours, or until leathery and greenish black in color. Whole beans will take much longer to dry than cut beans.

Sun: Spread cut or whole beans on trays and place in a well-ventilated place in full sun. Dry, stirring occasionally, until leathery and dark colored, about 2 to 3 days. Take trays inside at night.

Oven or Homemade Dryer: Spread cut or whole beans over trays in a thin layer. Dry at 120°F (50°C) for 18 to 24 hours, or until leathery and dark colored. Stir occasionally and rotate trays once or twice.

To Use: Pour 2 cups (500 ml) boiling water over 1 cup (250 ml) beans. Cover and simmer over low heat until beans are plump and tender, about 45 minutes. One cup (250 ml) yields about 2½ cups (625 ml) cooked beans.

DRIED GREEN BEANS TARRAGON

2 cups (500 ml) boiling water

¾ cup (190 ml) dried green beans

2 tablespoons (30 ml) minced dried onion

4 slices bacon, diced

½ teaspoon (2 ml) salt

1 tablespoon (15 ml) tarragon vinegar

Pour boiling water over dried green beans and onion in a saucepan. Cover and cook over low heat for 45 minutes until plump and tender. Meanwhile, sauté diced bacon in a small skillet until brown. Add drained bacon and seasonings to cooked green beans. Mix lightly and serve. Serves 4 to 6.

DRIED GREEN BEANS IN MUSTARD SAUCE

2 cups (500 ml) boiling water

1 cup (250 ml) dried green beans, cut French style

2 tablespoons (30 ml) minced dried onion

1 tablespoon (15 ml) prepared mustard

2½ teaspoons (12 ml) all-purpose flour

½ teaspoon (2 ml) salt

1 egg yolk

¾ cup (190 ml) milk

1 tablespoon (15 ml) lemon juice

Pour hot water over dried green beans in a saucepan. Add onion, cover, and cook over low heat for 45 minutes until tender. Drain. Meanwhile, combine mustard, flour, and salt in a saucepan over hot water. In a bowl, combine beaten egg yolk and milk. Add gradually to mustard mixture, stirring well. Cook until thickened, stirring constantly. Add lemon juice and pour over drained, cooked green beans. Serves 4 to 6.

Green Tomatoes

Pick medium-sized tomatoes while still green and firm, before they begin to ripen inside. Trim off core and blossom end and cut into ¼-inch (6-mm) slices.

Dehydrator: Spread slices over dehydrator trays with the slices touching, but not overlapping. Dry for 6 to 8 hours at 120°F (50°C). Turn slices and rotate trays. Dry for another 6 to 8 hours. Cool a few slices and test for dryness. When dry, slices will be crisp, brittle, and almost transparent.

Sun: Spread slices in a single layer on cheesecloth-covered trays. Dry in an area with good air circulation in hot sun, turning slices occasionally and taking trays inside at night. Slices will dry in 2 to 3 days of dry weather.

Oven or Homemade Dryer: Spread slices in a single layer over trays. Dry at 120°F (50°C) until crisp and transparent looking, about 18 to 24 hours. Turn slices and rotate trays once or twice during drying.

To Use: To refresh slices, spread out on a large plate or platter. Spray with warm water and let set for 30 minutes, spraying occasionally. Dip in flour and sauté in butter or margarine or use in cooking as you would fresh green tomatoes.

ITALIAN GREEN TOMATOES

12 green tomato slices

Warm water

1 egg, beaten

3 tablespoons (45 ml) all-purpose flour

½ teaspoon (2 ml) salt

8 tablespoons (120 ml) vegetable oil, heated for frying

¼ pound (100 grams) processed cheese, grated

4 tablespoons (60 ml) minced onion

1 cup (250 ml) tomato sauce

½ teaspoon (2 ml) granulated sugar

¼ teaspoon (1 ml) salt

¼ teaspoon (1 ml) dried oregano

Spray dried tomato slices with warm water. Soak for 30 minutes, spraying or sprinkling with water occasionally. Dip refreshed green tomato slices in beaten egg, then in flour to which salt has been added. Sauté quickly in 6 tablespoons (90 ml) hot oil until golden brown. As they are browned, arrange layers of green tomato slices in a casserole alternately with grated cheese. When all slices are browned, wipe out skillet with a paper towel and add remaining oil. Heat slowly, then sauté minced onion over low heat until transparent, but not browned. Add tomato sauce, sugar, salt, and oregano. Simmer for 5 minutes. Pour over green tomatoes and cheese in casserole. Bake in 350°F (180°C) oven for 20 to 25 minutes, or until cheese has melted. Serves 4 to 6.

DRIED GREEN TOMATOES AND OKRA

2 cups (500 ml) boiling water

12 dried green tomato slices

½ cup (125 ml) sliced or chopped dried onion

1 cup (250 ml) dried tomatoes

12 dried okra pods, sliced

Salt and pepper to taste

2 tablespoons (30 ml) butter or margarine

1 teaspoon (5 ml) dried parsley leaves

Pour boiling water over green tomato slices. Combine in a saucepan with dried onion, dried tomatoes, and dried okra. Simmer for 30 minutes. Season with salt, pepper, and butter or margarine. Sprinkle with parsley. Serves 4 to 6.

Greens

Beet tops, collards, kale, mustard greens, spinach, and Swiss chard can all be successfully, and easily, dried to give you a supply of fresh tasting greens all year long. Trim and wash greens through several waters. Steam blanch for 3 minutes or water blanch for 1½ minutes, or until leaves go limp. Drain well. Chill in cold water. Drain. Chop leaves.

Dehydrator: Spread greens in a thin layer over trays and dry for 12 to 18 hours at 120°F (50°C) until crisp. Stir once or twice during drying and rotate trays once.

Sun: Spread greens in a thin layer over cheesecloth-covered trays. Dry in a well-ventilated area in full sun, stirring several times during the day, and taking trays inside at night. Leaves should be very crisp when dried. Takes 1 to 2 days.

Oven or Homemade Dryer: Spread blanched greens thinly over trays. Dry at 120°F (50°C). Stir occasionally and rotate trays once or twice a day. Greens should be crisp in 18 to 24 hours.

To Use: Pour 1½ cups (375 ml) boiling water over 3 cups (750 ml) greens. Cover and cook for 15 minutes over low heat. Dried greens also may be crumbled and dropped into simmering soup broth and cooked to desired tenderness. A delicious cream of spinach soup may be made by crumbling dried spinach (or other greens) into a cooked, thin white sauce. Stir well, then let set for 30 minutes. Stir well again and reheat.

Clear soup broths can be given a delicious flavor and valuable nutrition by adding 2 teaspoons (10 ml) dried spinach powder, made by crushing dried spinach (or other greens) with a rolling pin or processing in a blender. Three cups yield 1½ cups (375 ml) cooked vegetable.

DRIED GREENS WITH BACON DRESSING

1½ cups (375 ml) boiling water

3 cups (750 ml) dried greens

2 tablespoons (30 ml) chopped dried
   green onions

4 slices bacon

2 tablespoons (30 ml) white vinegar

½ teaspoon (2 ml) dry mustard

1½ teaspoons (7 ml) granulated sugar

Salt and pepper to taste

2 hard-cooked eggs, sliced

Pour boiling water over dried greens and onions in a saucepan. Cover and cook for 5 to 6 minutes, or until greens are tender. Drain and place in a serving dish. Fry bacon until crisp. Drain on paper towels. To bacon fat in skillet, add vinegar, mustard, sugar, salt, and pepper. Stir well. Pour over spinach in serving dish. Top with egg slices and bacon, crumbled. Serves 4.

CREAMED DRIED GREENS

1½ cups (375 ml) boiling water

3 cups (750 ml) dried greens

2 tablespoons (30 ml) butter or margarine

1½ tablespoons (25 ml) all-purpose flour

Dash ground nutmeg

½ cup (125 ml) milk

1 chicken-flavored bouillon cube or 1 teaspoon (5 ml) chicken-flavored broth granules

½ teaspoon (2 ml) minced dried onion

Salt and pepper to taste

Pour boiling water over dried greens in a saucepan. Cover and cook for 15 minutes, or until tender. Drain, reserving cooking liquid for soups. In another saucepan, melt butter or margarine. Stir in flour and nutmeg and gradually stir in milk. Add bouillon, onion, salt, and pepper. Cook, stirring constantly, until smooth and thickened. Add to hot, drained greens. Serves 4.

Kohlrabi

Remove leaves from medium kohlrabi bulbs. Peel bulbs and cut into small cubes or thin slices. Blanch in boiling water for 2 to 3 minutes or in steam for 3 to 4 minutes. Drain. Chill in cold water, drain again. Pat dry with paper towels.

Dehydrator: Spread pieces or slices in a thin layer over trays. Dry at 120°F (50°C) for 18 to 24 hours, or until crisp and dry to center. Stir pieces or turn slices and rotate trays at least once during drying.

Sun: Spread pieces or slices thinly over trays and place in full sun in a well-ventilated area. Dry for 2 to 3 days until crisp and thoroughly dry, stirring occasionally and taking trays inside at night.

Oven or Homemade Dryer: Spread pieces or slices in a thin layer over trays. Dry at 120°F (50°C) for 24 to 36 hours until crisp, stirring occasionally and rotating trays front to back, side to side, and top to bottom once or twice.

To Use: Pour 3 cups (750 ml) boiling water over 1 cup (250 ml) vegetable pieces or slices. Cover and cook for 30 to 45 minutes until tender. Serve hot, seasoned with butter or margarine, salt, and pepper. Garnish with broiled mushrooms or grated nuts. One cup (250 ml) dried yields about 1½ cups (375 ml) cooked vegetable.

DRIED KOHLRABI AU GRATIN

4½ cups (1 litre 125 ml) boiling water

1½ cups (375 ml) dried kohlrabi slices

5 tablespoons (75 ml) butter or margarine

3 tablespoons (45 ml) all-purpose flour

1½ cups (375 ml) milk

Salt and pepper to taste

½ cup (125 ml) dried bread crumbs

½ cup (125 ml) grated cheddar cheese

Pour boiling water over dried kohlrabi slices in a saucepan. Cover and cook over low heat for 30 to 45 minutes, or until tender. Drain, reserving liquid for soups. Place one-half of cooked kohlrabi in a casserole. In a saucepan, melt 3 tablespoons (45 ml) butter or margarine and blend in flour. Gradually add milk and cook, stirring constantly, until smooth and thickened. Season with salt and pepper. Pour one-half of sauce over kohlrabi slices in casserole. Add remaining cooked slices, then remaining sauce. Top with bread crumbs that have been mixed with remaining melted butter or margarine and grated cheddar cheese. Bake in 350°F (180°C) oven for 30 minutes, or until bubbly hot and lightly browned. Serves 6.

DRIED KOHLRABI PATTIES

4½ cups (1 litre 125 ml) boiling water

1½ cups (375 ml) dried kohlrabi pieces

2 tablespoons (30 ml) butter or margarine

Salt and pepper to taste

3 tablespoons (45 ml) all-purpose flour

2 tablespoons (30 ml) vegetable oil, heated for frying

Pour boiling water over dried pieces. Cook for 30 to 35 minutes in a covered saucepan until tender. Drain and mash with a fork or potato masher. Season with 2 tablespoons (30 ml) butter or margarine, salt, and pepper. Form into small patties and dip in flour. Brown in hot oil. Serves 4.

Lettuce

Trim coarse outer leaves and hearts from lettuce heads. Shred or cut into quarters. Blanch until wilted, about 2 to 2½ minutes in steam or 1½ minutes in boiling water. Drain. Chill in cold water. Drain. Pat dry.

Dehydrator: Spread shreds or quarters thinly over trays. Dry at 120°F (50°C) until crisp, about 8 to 12 hours, stirring or turning pieces occasionally and rotating trays once. When dry, cooled pieces should crumble easily when crushed in the hands.

Sun: Spread shreds or place quarters on drying trays in full sun. Dry for 2 to 3 days in a well-ventilated place until crisp, stirring pieces occasionally and taking trays inside at night. To test for dryness, cool a piece, then crush in the hand. It should crumble easily.

Oven or Homemade Dryer: Spread shreds or quarters thinly over trays. Dry at 120°F (50°C) until crisp, about 6 to 8 hours. Stir occasionally and rotate trays once or twice a day.

To Use: While refreshed lettuce does not have the crispness desirable for salads, it is an excellent cooked vegetable and a valuable addition to soups. Pour one cup (250 ml) boiling water over 1 cup (250 ml) dried lettuce, cover and cook over low heat for 20 minutes. Season to taste with butter or margarine, salt, and pepper. Or drop shreds of dried lettuce into simmering soup and cook for 20 to 25 minutes. One cup (250 ml) yields about 1½ cups (375 ml) cooked vegetable.

BRAISED DRIED LETTUCE _____

4 dried lettuce quarters

2 cups (500 ml) boiling water

2 tablespoons (30 ml) butter or
margarine

Salt and pepper to taste

Dash ground nutmeg

1 tablespoon (15 ml) lemon juice

Cook dried lettuce quarters in boiling water for 30 to 35 minutes. Drain, reserving liquid for soups. Melt butter or margarine in a heavy skillet. Add lettuce and cook slowly for 10 to 15 minutes. Add seasonings and lemon juice and stir quickly to blend. Serves 4.

SWEET AND SOUR DRIED LETTUCE _____

3 cups (750 ml) dried lettuce shreds

1 cup (250 ml) dried apple slices

4 cups (1 litre) boiling water

2 tablespoons (30 ml) vegetable oil

2 tablespoons (30 ml)all-purpose flour

3 tablespoons (45 ml) white vinegar

4 tablespoons (60 ml) brown sugar

Salt and pepper to taste

Cover dried lettuce and dried apple slices with boiling water. Cook for 10 minutes in a covered saucepan. Add oil and cook for another 10 to 15 minutes. Sprinkle with flour, vinegar, and sugar. Mix well. Season with salt and pepper. Simmer for 5 minutes more. Serves 6.

Mushrooms

Select only commercially grown varieties or those that you know beyond any doubt are nontoxic. The toxins of poisonous mushrooms are not destroyed by the drying or cooking processes. Wash mushrooms quickly in cold water without soaking or peeling. Trim 1/8 inch (3 mm) off the stem end. Thinly slice or finely chop. Do not blanch.

Dehydrator: Spread slices or pieces thinly over trays. Dry at 120°F (50°C) for 8 to 12 hours, stirring occasionally and rotating trays once or twice. Well-dried mushrooms should be tough and leathery with no sign of moisture in the center when cut.

Sun: Spread slices or pieces over trays and dry in full sun for 1 to 2 days. Choose a drying area with good air circulation and dry until tough and leathery with no sign of moisture in the centers. Take trays inside at night.

Oven or Homemade Dryer: Spread slices or pieces in a thin layer over trays. Dry at 120°F (50°C) for 12 to 18 hours, or until pieces are tough and leathery, stirring occasionally and rotating trays once or twice.

To Use: Pour 1 cup (250 ml) boiling water over 1 cup (250 ml) dried mushrooms. Cook in a covered saucepan for 20 to 30 minutes, or until plump and tender. One cup yields about 1¼ cups (315 ml) cooked mushrooms.

DRIED MUSHROOM CROQUETTES

¾ cup (190 ml) dried mushrooms

¾ cup (190 ml) boiling water

1 tablespoon (15 ml) butter or
  margarine

1 tablespoon (15 ml) all-purpose flour

½ cup (125 ml) milk

½ teaspoon (2 ml) Worcestershire
  sauce

⅛ teaspoon (½ ml) curry powder

1 egg

2 tablespoons (30 ml) dried bread
  crumbs

½ teaspoon (2 ml) salt

½ cup (125 ml) dried bread crumbs

Oil for frying, heated to 360°F (180°C)

Cook dried mushrooms in boiling water for 20 to 30 minutes. Drain, reserving any liquid for soups. In a saucepan, melt butter or margarine and blend in flour. Gradually add milk and cook, stirring constantly, until smooth and thickened. Add mushrooms, Worcestershire sauce, curry powder, egg, 2 tablespoons (30 ml) bread crumbs, and salt. Shape into croquettes and chill thoroughly. Roll in ½ cup (125 ml) bread crumbs and fry until golden brown in deep, hot oil. Serves 4 to 6.

DRIED MUSHROOMS BAKED IN CREAM

1 cup (250 ml) boiling water

1 cup (250 ml) dried mushrooms

2 tablespoons (30 ml) butter or
  margarine

2 tablespoons (30 ml) all-purpose flour

1 cup (250 ml) milk

Salt and pepper to taste

Pour boiling water over dried mushrooms in a saucepan. Cook for 20 to 30 minutes, or until tender. Drain, reserving any liquid for use in soups. Place mushrooms in a 1-quart (1-litre) casserole. Melt butter or margarine in a saucepan. Blend in flour and gradually add milk. Cook, stirring constantly, until smooth and thickened. Season with salt and pepper. Pour sauce over mushrooms and bake in 350°F (180°C) oven for 30 to 35 minutes. Serve over hot toast. Serves 4.

Okra

Select young, tender, 2- to 4-inch (5- to 10-cm) okra pods, which snap easily. Wash well and cut off stem ends. Cut crosswise into ¼-inch (6-mm) slices. Blanching is not necessary.

Dehydrator: Spread slices in a thin layer over trays. Dry for 8 to 12 hours at 120°F (50°C) until very brittle. Stir slices and rotate trays after 4 to 5 hours.

Sun: Spread slices in a thin layer over trays. Dry in hot sun in a well-ventilated place for 1 to 2 days, stirring slices occasionally and taking trays inside at night. Slices should be brittle when dry.

Oven or Homemade Dryer: Spread slices thinly over trays. Dry at 120°F (50°C) for 12 to 18 hours, or until brittle, stirring occasionally and rotating trays once or twice.

To Use: Cook slices for 30 to 45 minutes, using 2 cups (500 ml) boiling water to 1 cup dried okra. One cup (250 ml) yields 1½ cups (375 ml) cooked vegetable.

BAKED DRIED OKRA

3 cups (750 ml) boiling water

1½ cups (375 ml) dried okra slices

¼ cup (65 ml) dried onion slices

2 tablespoons (30 ml) butter or
   margarine, melted

Salt and pepper to taste

1 cup (250 ml) tomato sauce

Pour boiling water over okra and onion slices in a 1½-quart (1½-litre) casserole. Let soak for 3 to 4 hours. Drain. Season with butter or margarine, salt, and pepper. Top with tomato sauce and bake for 30 to 45 minutes in a 350°F (180°C) oven. Serves 4 to 6.

STEWED DRIED OKRA AND RICE

3 cups (750 ml) boiling water

1 cup (250 ml) dried okra slices

1 cup (250 ml) dried tomatoes

¼ cup (65 ml) chopped dried onion

2 tablespoons vegetable oil

3 tablespoons uncooked white rice

½ teaspoon (2 ml) salt

Combine all ingredients in a medium-sized saucepan. Cover and cook over low heat for 30 to 45 minutes, or until rice is cooked and vegetables are tender. Stir occasionally to keep from sticking. Serves 4 to 6.

Onions

Although onions keep well for several months when air-cured 2 to 3 weeks after harvest, chopped, dried onions are a convenience to keep as a quick seasoning on the kitchen shelf or at the vacation cabin. Sliced, dried onions are a must for backpackers or anyone who plans to cook meals outdoors.

In the spring, when winter-stored onions threaten to sprout, they may be saved by slicing or chopping and drying for later use. Peel and cut onions into ⅛-inch (3-mm) slices or finely chop. No blanching is needed. Dry onions separately to prevent a blending of flavors.

Dehydrator: Spread sliced or chopped onions over trays. Dry at 120°F (50°C) until brittle, about 12 to 24 hours, stirring pieces or turning slices after the first 8 hours, and rotating trays once or twice.

Sun: Spread chopped or sliced onions evenly over trays and dry in full sun in a well-ventilated place until papery and brittle, about 2 to 3 days. Stir pieces or turn slices occasionally and take trays inside at night.

Oven or Homemade Dryer: Spread slices or pieces in a thin layer over trays. Dry at 120°F (50°C) for 24 to 36 hours until brittle, stirring occasionally and rotating trays once or twice.

To Use: Dried onions may be used as seasoning in soups, salads, or cooked dishes without refreshing. Simply measure one-half as much dried onion as the fresh onion called for in the recipe. To refresh dried onions, soak for 45 minutes using 2 cups (500 ml) boiling water to 1 cup (250 ml) dried onion. One cup (250 ml) yields about 1⅓ cups (325 ml) refreshed onion.

CREAMED DRIED ONIONS

2 cups (500 ml) boiling water

1 cup (250 ml) dried onion slices

¼ cup (65 ml) dried mushroom slices

4 tablespoons (60 ml) butter or margarine

2 tablespoons (30 ml) all-purpose flour

1 cup (250 ml) milk

½ teaspoon (2 ml) salt

½ cup (125 ml) dried onion slices

2 tablespoons (30 ml) grated dried cheese

Pour boiling water over 1 cup (250 ml) onion slices and mushroom slices. Soak for 45 minutes. Meanwhile, melt 2 tablespoons (30 ml) butter or margarine in a saucepan. Blend in flour and gradually add milk. Add salt. Cook, stirring constantly, until smooth and thickened. Add drained onion and mushroom slices and pour mixture into a casserole. Melt remaining butter or margarine and add ½ cup (125 ml) dried onion slices (not soaked) and grated dried cheese. Sprinkle over top of casserole. Bake in 350°F (180°C) oven until bubbly hot and lightly browned, about 20 to 25 minutes. Serves 6.

DRIED ONION PIE

3 cups (750 ml) boiling water

1½ cups (375 ml) dried onion slices

¼ teaspoon (1 ml) salt

1 cup (250 ml) all-purpose flour

⅓ cup (75 ml) vegetable shortening

¼ cup (65 ml) ice water

6 slices bacon

2 eggs, beaten

1 egg yolk

¾ cup (190 ml) sour cream or yogurt

Salt and pepper to taste

⅛ teaspoon (½ ml) caraway seed

½ teaspoon (2 ml) chopped dried chives

Ground paprika

Pour boiling water over dried onion slices. Soak for 45 minutes. Add salt to flour. Using a pastry blender or two knives, cut shortening into flour until it is the consistency of coarse meal. Add enough ice water to make a stiff dough. Roll out to the size of a 9-inch (22.5-cm) pie pan, making a fluted edge around the rim. Chill.

Fry bacon until crisp. Remove and drain on paper towels. Pour off all but 3 tablespoons (45 ml) bacon fat. Cook refreshed onion slices in fat until yellow, but not browned, stirring often. Crumble bacon into large pieces and add to onion. Add eggs, egg yolk, sour cream, salt, pepper, caraway seed, and chives. Pour into chilled, unbaked pie shell. Sprinkle with paprika. Bake in a 425°F (220°C) oven for 10 minutes. Reduce heat to 350°F (180°C) and bake for 25 to 30 minutes more until set in the center. Serve hot. Serves 6 to 8.

Parsnips

Scrape or peel parsnips, trimming off root and top ends. Cut in ⅛-inch (3-mm) slices or chop into small pieces. Blanching is not necessary for eating dry, but parsnips to be used for cooking should be blanched for 3 minutes in water, 4 minutes in steam. Chill in ice water. Drain. Pat dry.

Dehydrator: Spread slices or pieces thinly over trays. Dry for 8 to 12 hours at 120°F (50°C) until crisp, turning slices or stirring pieces occasionally. Rotate trays at least once.

Sun: Spread slices or pieces in a thin layer over trays and place in hot sun in a well-ventilated area. Dry for 2 to 3 days, stirring once or twice a day and taking trays inside at night. Dry until brittle.

Oven or Homemade Dryer: Spread slices or pieces evenly over trays. Dry at 120°F (50°C) until crisp, about 12 to 18 hours, stirring occasionally and rotating trays once or twice.

To Use: The slices are delicious eaten as a snack alone or with a cheese dip. To cook slices or chopped pieces, pour 2 cups (500 ml) boiling water over 1 cup (250 ml) dried parsnips. Cover and simmer until tender, about 30 to 45 minutes. One cup (250 ml) yields about 1½ cups (375 ml) cooked vegetable.

MASHED DRIED PARSNIPS

3 cups (750 ml) boiling water	½ cup (125 ml) hot milk
1½ cups (375 ml) dried parsnips	Salt and pepper to taste
3 tablespoons (45 ml) butter or margarine	

Pour boiling water over parsnips in a saucepan. Cover and cook over low heat for 30 to 45 minutes, or until tender. Drain well. Mash with a potato masher or electric mixer. Add butter or margarine and beat until melted. Gradually add hot milk, mixing until milk is absorbed and parsnips are fluffy. Season with salt and pepper. Serves 4 to 6.

DRIED PARSNIPS CONTINENTAL

4 cups (1 litre) boiling water

2 cups (500 ml) dried parsnips

¼ cup (65 ml) butter or margarine, melted

1 teaspoon (5 ml) granulated sugar

½ teaspoon (2 ml) salt

3 tablespoons (45 ml) lemon juice

1 cup (250 ml) sour cream

Pour boiling water over dried parsnips in a saucepan. Cover and cook until tender, about 30 to 45 minutes. Drain. In a bowl combine melted butter or margarine, sugar, salt, lemon juice, and sour cream. Pour into a casserole. Pour cooked parsnips over sauce and bake in 350°F (180°C) oven for 20 to 25 minutes. Serves 6.

Peas (Green)

Shell immature green peas within a few hours of picking. Steam blanch for 3 minutes or blanch in boiling water for 2 minutes. Drain. Chill in ice water. Drain. Pat dry.

Dehydrator: Spread blanched peas in a thin layer over trays. Dry for 12 to 18 hours at 120°F (50°C) until wrinkled and hard. Well-dried peas will split in half when tapped with a hammer. Stir occasionally and rotate trays once or twice.

Sun: Spread blanched peas over trays and place in full sun in a well-ventilated area. Dry for 2 to 3 days until wrinkled and hard enough to split when tapped with a hammer. Stir occasionally and take trays inside at night.

Oven or Homemade Dryer: Spread blanched peas in a thin layer over trays. Dry at 120°F (50°C) until hard and brittle, about 18 to 24 hours. Stir peas occasionally and rotate trays once or twice.

To Use: Pour 2 cups (500 ml) boiling water over 1 cup (250 ml) peas and cook for 40 to 45 minutes in a covered saucepan. One cup (250 ml) yields about 2 cups (500 ml) cooked peas.

PUREE OF GREEN PEA SOUP

2 cups (500 ml) boiling water

1 cup (250 ml) dried peas

½ teaspoon (2 ml) salt

2 tablespoons (30 ml) butter or margarine

½ cup (125 ml) cream

Pour boiling water over dried peas. Cover and cook until tender, about 40 to 45 minutes. Add salt. Put peas and cooking water through a food strainer, food mill, or blender. Add butter or margarine and cream. Reheat to simmering. Serves 4 to 6.

BUTTERED DRIED PEAS AND ONIONS _____

1½ cups (375 ml) boiling water

¾ cup (190 ml) dried peas

¼ teaspoon (1 ml) salt

2 tablespoons (30 ml) dried mushroom slices

1 tablespoon (15 ml) minced dried
onion

½ cup (125 ml) boiling water

¼ cup (65 ml) butter or margarine

12 small pearl onions, cooked

Pour boiling water over dried peas in a saucepan. Cover and cook for 40 to 45 minutes. Drain and add salt. Meanwhile, combine dried mushrooms and 1 tablespoon dried onion in a bowl. Cover with boiling water and soak for 15 to 20 minutes. Drain. Melt butter or margarine in a small skillet and add drained, refreshed mushrooms and onion. Stir-fry until golden over low heat. Combine cooked peas and hot, cooked pearl onions in a serving dish and top with sautéed mushrooms and onions. Serves 4 to 6.

Peas
(Black-Eyed, Crowder, and Chick-Peas)

Allow peas to ripen completely and dry as much as possible on the vine. Shell. No blanching is necessary. After drying, place peas in a sealed container in the freezer for 48 hours, or spread peas on a tray in 125°F (50°C) oven for 30 minutes to kill any insect eggs.

Dehydrator: Spread partially dried peas in a single layer over trays. Dry at 120°F (50°C) for 8 to 10 hours, depending on the stage of dryness when picked, stirring occasionally, until a cooled, dried pea splits when tapped with a hammer. Rotate trays once during drying.

Sun: Spread partially dried peas in a thin layer over drying trays and place in a well-ventilated spot in full sun. Dry for 2 to 3 days, or until peas split when tapped with a hammer. Stir occasionally and take trays inside at night.

Oven or Homemade Dryer: Spread partially dried peas thinly over drying trays. Dry at 120°F (50°C) until peas are hard and brittle, about 12 to 15 hours.

To Use: Soak peas in water to cover for 3 to 4 hours or overnight. Drain, add fresh water, and cook over low heat for 2 to 3 hours until tender. One cup (250 ml) yields about 2 cups (500 ml) cooked peas.

FRIED CHICK-PEAS WITH GARLIC _____

1 cup (250 ml) dried chick-peas

3 cups (750 ml) water

½ teaspoon (2 ml) salt

3 tablespoons (45 ml) olive oil

1 clove garlic

Lemon juice

Black pepper

After a thorough washing, soak beans overnight or use the quick-soak method (see page 57). Drain soaking water. Place beans in a kettle with 3 cups (750 ml) fresh water. Add salt. Bring to a boil, reduce heat, cover, and simmer until chick-peas are tender, about 4 hours. Check occasionally to be sure beans are still covered with water and add more water as needed. When beans are tender all the way through (bite into one to test), drain and cool.

Heat oil in a heavy skillet and swirl garlic around in it for a few seconds before adding beans. Keep at medium-high heat and stir chick-peas around in skillet gently for about 10 minutes, or until they form a crispy, brown crust on the outside. Place chick-peas in a serving dish, remove garlic, and season with lemon juice and pepper. Serves 2.

SAVORY DRIED PEAS

4 cups (1 litre) boiling water

2 cups (500 ml) dried peas (black-eyed peas, cowpeas, crowder peas, or chick-peas)

1 teaspoon (5 ml) salt

¼ teaspoon (1 ml) black pepper

2 ounces (50 grams) sliced salt pork

4 small onions, peeled

Pour boiling water over peas. Soak for 3 to 4 hours. Drain. Add fresh water to cover, salt, pepper, pork, and onions. Cover and cook over low heat until tender, about 1 hour. Serves 4 to 6.

SPANISH DRIED PEAS

2 cups (500 ml) boiling water

1 cup (250 ml) dried peas (black-eyed peas, cowpeas, crowder peas, or chick-peas)

1 slice salt pork or ham

1 large onion, sliced

1 mild chili pepper, sliced

2 medium tomatoes, or 1 cup (250 ml) canned tomatoes

1 bouquet garni (see page 114)

3 quarts (3 litres) cold water

Chicken bones (from 1–2 roasted or fried chickens)

Salt and pepper to taste

½ teaspoon (2 ml) crumbled dried mint

Pour boiling water over dried peas. Let soak for 3 to 4 hours. Drain. Place in kettle with salt pork or ham, onion, chili pepper, tomatoes, bouquet garni, water, and chicken bones. Cover and simmer until peas are tender, about 1 to 2 hours. Remove chicken bones and bouquet garni. Put vegetables and broth through a sieve, food mill, or blender. Add salt and pepper. Add mint. Reheat and serve piping hot. Serves 6.

Peppers/Pimientos

Wash, stem, and core thick-walled green or ripe red bell peppers or red ripe pimientos. Remove all inner white membrane. Cut into halves, thin crosswise slices, lengthwise strips, or coarsely chop. Blanching is not necessary.

Dehydrator: Spread halves, slices, or pieces in a thin layer over trays. Dry at 120°F (50°C) until leathery, about 12 to 18 hours for halves, 8 to 12 hours for slices and pieces. Stir occasionally or turn halves. Rotate trays once or twice during drying.

Sun: Spread halves, slices, or pieces thinly over trays. Place trays in full sun in an area with good air circulation. Dry halves for 2 to 3 days and slices and pieces for 1 to 2 days, or until leathery and completely dry. Turn halves, stir pieces occasionally, and take trays inside at night.

Oven or Homemade Dryer: Spread slices or pieces over trays. Dry at 120°F (50°C) for 18 to 24 hours, or until leathery with no moisture inside, stirring occasionally, and rotating trays once. Halves do not dry well in oven.

To Use: Slices and chopped pieces may be used in soups, casseroles, meat loaves, and salads in dry form without refreshing. For each 3 tablespoons (45 ml) fresh green pepper or pimiento called for in a recipe, 2 tablespoons (30 ml) dried pepper or pimiento may be substituted. Green pepper or pimiento halves may be refreshed by soaking in boiling water to cover for 30 to 45 minutes. Use as you would fresh peppers.

See chapter 8, Drying Herbs, for other peppers.

CHEESE-STUFFED DRIED GREEN PEPPERS

2 cups (500 ml) boiling water

6 dried green pepper halves (or pimientos)

2 cups (500 ml) cooked white rice

½ cup (125 ml) milk

1 tablespoon (15 ml) chopped dried pimiento

1 tablespoon (15 ml) chopped dried parsley

1 tablespoon (15 ml) chopped dried onion

½ teaspoon (2 ml) salt

⅛ teaspoon (½ ml) black pepper

2 tablespoons (30 ml) butter or margarine, melted

1 cup (250 ml) grated cheddar cheese

Pour boiling water over pepper halves. Let soak for 30 to 45 minutes. Simmer over low heat for 10 minutes. Drain. Combine cooked rice, milk, dried pimiento, parsley, onion, salt, pepper, melted butter or margarine, and grated cheese. Stuff mixture into green pepper halves. Place peppers in a baking pan into which ½ cup (125 ml) water has been poured. Bake in 350°F (180°C) oven for 30 minutes. Serves 6.

SALMON-STUFFED DRIED PIMIENTOS

2 cups (500 ml) boiling water
12 dried pimiento halves
One 16-ounce (400 gram) can salmon
2 tablespoons (30 ml) dried onion
½ cup (125 ml) dried bread crumbs
¾ cup (190 ml) milk

1 egg, beaten
2 teaspoons (10 ml) lemon juice
¼ cup (65 ml) dried bread crumbs
2 tablespoons (30 ml) grated dried cheese
½ cup (125 ml) hot water

Pour boiling water over dried pimiento halves. Let soak for 30 minutes. Cover and simmer for 10 minutes. Drain. Combine salmon, onion, ½ cup (125 ml) bread crumbs, milk, egg, and lemon juice. Divide mixture among pimiento halves. Top with ¼ cup (65 ml) bread crumbs that have been mixed with grated cheese. Set in baking pan containing ½ cup (125 ml) hot water. Bake in 350°F (180°C) oven for 15 to 20 minutes. Serves 6.

Potatoes

Dried potatoes are convenient for camping and hiking trips or wherever weight is a consideration. They must be watched carefully, however, for any hint of moisture will cause the entire batch to mold. Wash and peel potatoes and cut into ½-inch (12-mm) shoestring strips or ⅛-inch (3-mm) slices. Blanch in steam for 6 to 8 minutes or for 5 to 6 minutes in boiling water. Drain well.

Dehydrator: Spread strips or slices in a single layer over trays. Dry 12 to 18 hours at 120°F (50°C) until brittle and semitransparent. Turn pieces and rotate trays once or twice during drying.

Sun: Spread strips or slices in a single layer over trays. Dry in a well-ventilated place in hot sun 2 to 3 days, until brittle and semitransparent. Turn pieces occasionally and take trays inside at night.

Oven or Homemade Dryer: Spread strips or slices thinly over trays. Dry at 120°F (50°C) until brittle, turning pieces occasionally and rotating trays once or twice. Will dry in 18 to 24 hours.

To Use: Pour 1 cup (250 ml) boiling water over 1 cup (250 ml) potatoes. Cook 45 to 50 minutes for boiled potatoes or hash browns. One cup (250 ml) yields 1 to 1⅓ cups (250 to 325 ml) cooked potatoes.

CHEESY DRIED POTATOES

2 cups (500 ml) boiling water
2 cups (500 ml) dried potato slices
2 tablespoons (30 ml) butter or margarine

2 tablespoons (30 ml) all-purpose flour
½ teaspoon (2 ml) salt
1 cup (250 ml) milk
1 cup (250 ml) sliced processed cheese

Pour boiling water over dried potato slices. Cook for 45 to 50 minutes. Drain and arrange in a baking dish. In a saucepan, melt butter or margarine and blend in flour and salt. Gradually stir in milk and cheese. Cook, stirring constantly, until smooth and thickened. Pour over potatoes and bake in 350°F (180°C) oven for 45 minutes, or until top begins to brown. Serves 6.

TOMATO-POTATO SKILLET

3 cups (750 ml) boiling water

3 cups (750 ml) dried potatoes

¼ cup (65 ml) butter or margarine

1 cup (250 ml) dried onion slices

1 cup (250 ml) dried tomato slices

1 cup (250 ml) water

Salt and pepper to taste

Pour boiling water over dried potatoes. Let soak for 1 to 2 hours. Drain, reserving liquid. In a heavy skillet, melt butter or margarine and add ¼ cup (65 ml) reserved liquid. Arrange soaked potatoes, onions, and tomatoes over bottom of skillet. Add water, cover, and simmer for 45 to 50 minutes. Season with salt and pepper. Serves 4 to 6.

Pumpkin

Any size pumpkin may be used. Cut in half, remove seeds, and core. Cut halves into ¼-inch (6-mm) slices. Peel each slice and cut into 1-inch (25-mm) pieces. Steam blanch for 2½ to 3 minutes or blanch in boiling water for 1½ minutes. Drain. Or cut pumpkin halves into 1-inch (25-mm) slices. Peel each slice and cut into cubes. Cook until tender for 30 to 45 minutes in a steamer, 10 to 12 minutes in a pressure cooker at 15 pounds (7 kilograms) pressure, or 1 hour in 325°F (165°C) oven. Cut cubes into slices. Cooked pumpkin also may be mashed with a potato masher, electric mixer, blender, or food processor.

Dehydrator: Spread pieces or slices in a thin layer over trays. Dry for 12 to 18 hours at 120°F (50°C) until leathery and dry to the center, rotating trays and turning pieces once or twice during drying.

To dry mashed pumpkin, spread thinly over dehydrator trays that have been covered with plastic wrap. Dry for 6 to 8 hours at 120°F (50°C) until pumpkin can be pulled away from plastic. Turn pumpkin over, peel off plastic, and dry until firm and brittle. Break into pieces and reduce to a powder in a blender or by pounding with a pestle. Return to dehydrator for 2 hours.

Sun: Spread pieces or slices in a thin layer over trays and place in a well-ventilated area in full sun. Dry for 2 to 3 days, or until there is no moisture in the center and pieces are hard and brittle. Turn pieces occasionally and take trays inside at night. Process in a blender or food processor to a fine powder, then return to full sun for 2 to 3 more hours.

Oven or Homemade Dryer: Spread pieces over drying trays. Dry at 120°F (50°C) until hard and brittle, about 18 to 24 hours, stirring occasionally and rotating trays. Process in a blender to a powder, then return to oven or dryer for 2 hours.

To Use: Pour ¾ cup (190 ml) boiling water over ¾ cup (190 ml) powdered pumpkin or pumpkin pieces. Let soak for 30 to 45 minutes. Three-fourths cup (190 ml) yields about 1 cup (250 ml) cooked puree, which may be used in puddings, pies, or in baking as you would fresh or canned pumpkin.

DRIED PUMPKIN BREAD

1½ cups (375 ml) boiling water

1½ cups (375 ml) dried pumpkin powder

⅔ cup (150 ml) vegetable shortening

⅔ cup (150 ml) granulated sugar

4 eggs

⅔ cup (150 ml) cold water

3⅓ cups (825 ml) all-purpose flour

2 teaspoons (10 ml) baking soda

1½ teaspoons (7 ml) salt

½ teaspoon (2 ml) baking powder

1 teaspoon (5 ml) ground cinnamon

1 teaspoon (5 ml) ground cloves

⅔ cup (150 ml) coarsely chopped nuts

⅔ cup (150 ml) chopped dried plums

Pour boiling water over dried pumpkin powder. Let soak for 30 to 45 minutes. Meanwhile, in a large mixing bowl, cream shortening and sugar until fluffy. Add eggs, refreshed pumpkin, and ⅔ cup (150 ml) cold water. Beat well. Blend in flour, baking soda, salt, baking powder, and spices. Stir in nuts and chopped dried plums. Pour into two 9 X 5-inch (22.5 X 12.5-cm) well-greased loaf pans. Bake in a 350°F (180°C) oven for about 1 hour and 10 minutes, or until a tester inserted in the center comes out clean. Makes two 9-inch (22.5-cm) loaves.

DRIED PUMPKIN COOKIES

1 cup (250 ml) boiling water

1 cup (250 ml) dried pumpkin powder

½ cup (125 ml) butter or margarine

1 cup (250 ml) granulated sugar

1 egg

1 teaspoon (5 ml) pure vanilla extract

2 cups (500 ml) all-purpose flour

½ teaspoon (2 ml) salt

1 teaspoon (5 ml) baking powder

1 teaspoon (5 ml) baking soda

1 teaspoon (5 ml) ground cinnamon

2 cups (500 ml) chopped dried peaches or apricots

Pour boiling water over dried pumpkin powder. Let soak for 30 to 45 minutes. Meanwhile, cream butter or margarine and sugar until fluffy. Add egg and vanilla and blend well. In another bowl, combine flour, salt, baking powder, baking soda, and cinnamon.

Add chopped dried fruit. Add fruit mixture to creamed mixture, 1 cup (250 ml) at a time, beating well after each addition. Drop by spoonful onto greased cookie sheets and bake in 350°F (180°C) oven for 12 to 15 minutes, or until lightly browned. Makes 4 dozen cookies.

Radishes

Wash firm, fresh, red or white radishes. Trim off root and top ends. Cut into ⅛-inch (3-mm) slices. Do not blanch.

Dehydrator: Spread slices sparsely over trays. Dry at 120°F (50°C) until crisp and dried through, about 8 to 10 hours. Stir slices occasionally and rotate trays once.

Sun: Spread slices in a thin layer over trays and dry in hot sun for 1 to 2 days, stirring occasionally and taking trays inside at night. When dry, slices will be crisp.

Oven or Homemade Dryer: Spread slices thinly over trays. Dry at 120°F (50°C), stirring occasionally and rotating trays once. Dry until crisp, about 10 to 12 hours.

To Use: Eat crisp slices as a snack, alone or with a cheese dip. Add in dry form to gelatin, potato salad, or tossed salads. To serve as a cooked vegetable, simmer for about 20 minutes in an equal amount of boiling water. Season to taste with salt, pepper, butter, or margarine.

Rutabagas

Cut off tops and roots and thinly peel rutabagas. Cut into very thin slices, dice into ⅛-inch (3-mm) cubes, or grate. Blanch in boiling water for 3 minutes or in steam for 4 minutes. Drain well. The tops may be dried as greens (see page 74).

Dehydrator: Spread slices or pieces in a thin layer over trays. Dry at 120°F (50°C) until crisp, about 8 to 12 hours. Stir occasionally or turn slices and rotate trays once or twice.

Sun: Spread slices or pieces over trays in a thin layer. Place in a well-ventilated area in full sun. Dry until crisp, about 1 to 2 days, stirring occasionally and taking trays inside at night.

Oven or Homemade Dryer: Spread slices or pieces over drying trays in a thin layer. Dry at 120°F (50°C) until crisp, about 12 to 18 hours, stirring occasionally and rotating trays once or twice.

To Use: Eat dried slices as a snack alone or with cheese dip, or chop and add in dry form to tossed salads. Chopped pieces also may be dropped into simmering soups. To cook as a vegetable, pour 1 cup (250 ml) boiling water over 1 cup (250 ml) dried rutabaga and cook for 30 to 45 minutes over low heat. Mash or leave in pieces and season to taste with salt, pepper, butter, or margarine. One cup (250 ml) yields about 1 cup (250 ml) cooked vegetable.

DRIED RUTABAGA RING

2 cups (500 ml) boiling water

2 cups (500 ml) dried rutabaga

3 tablespoons (45 ml) butter or margarine

2 tablespoons (30 ml) all-purpose flour

½ cup (125 ml) milk

2 tablespoons (30 ml) brown sugar

½ teaspoon (2 ml) salt

⅛ teaspoon (½ ml) black pepper

3 egg whites, stiffly beaten

Pour boiling water over dried rutabaga. Cover and cook for 30 to 45 minutes, or until tender. Drain. Mash with potato masher, electric mixer, or blender. In another sauce-pan, melt butter or margarine and blend in flour. Gradually add milk and cook over low heat, stirring constantly, until smooth and thickened. Add brown sugar, cooked rutabaga, salt, and pepper. Cool. Fold in stiffly beaten egg whites. Pour into a greased 8-inch (3-mm) ring mold. Set in a pan of hot water and bake in 350°F (180°C) oven for 45 minutes. Unmold and fill center with a hot, cooked vegetable. Serves 6.

CREAMED DRIED CARROTS AND RUTABAGAS

2 cups (500 ml) boiling water

1 cup (250 ml) dried rutabagas

1 cup (250 ml) dried carrots

2 tablespoons (30 ml) butter or margarine

2 tablespoons (30 ml) all-purpose flour

1 cup (250 ml) milk

½ teaspoon (2 ml) salt

1 teaspoon (5 ml) chicken-flavored bouillon granules, or 1 chicken-flavored bouillon cube

Pour boiling water over dried rutabagas and carrots. Cook for 45 to 50 minutes, or until tender. Meanwhile, melt butter or margarine. Stir in flour. Gradually add milk. Cook over low heat, stirring constantly, until smooth and thickened. Stir in salt and chicken-flavored soup broth, granules, or cube. Stir well to dissolve. Pour over mixed carrots and rutabagas in a serving dish. Serves 6.

Salsify

Scrub, scrape, or peel small to medium salsify roots. Cut into ⅛-inch (3-mm) slices. Dip into 1 quart (1 litre) water to which ½ teaspoon (2 ml) salt or 1 table-spoon (15 ml) lemon juice has been added. Or blanch in boiling water for 3 minutes or in a steam blancher for 4 minutes. Drain well.

Dehydrator: Spread slices thinly over trays. Dry at 120°F (50°C) until crisp, about 12 to 18 hours, stirring once or twice and rotating trays.

Sun: Spread slices over trays in a thin layer and place in a well-ventilated area in full sun. Dry until crisp, about 1 to 2 days, stirring occasionally and taking trays inside at night.

Oven or Homemade Dryer: Spread salsify slices thinly over drying trays. Dry at 120°F (50°C) until crisp, about 18 to 24 hours, stirring slices occasionally and rotating trays once or twice.

To Use: Slices are delicious eaten as a snack or mixed with other dried vegetables. Slices are small and may be added in dried form to tossed salads. They may be grated and used as a casserole topping. Drop slices in a simmering soup and cook until tender, or cook alone by simmering in water for 30 to 45 minutes. One cup (250 ml) yields about 1¼ cups (315 ml) cooked vegetable.

MOCK OYSTERS

1¾ (435 ml) cups boiling water

1¾ (435 ml) cups dried salsify

1 egg

½ teaspoon (2 ml) salt

⅛ teaspoon (½ ml) black pepper

1 tablespoon (15 ml) butter or margarine, melted

1 egg, well beaten

Fine dried bread crumbs for coating

Hot oil for frying

Pour boiling water over dried salsify in a saucepan. Cover and cook for 30 to 45 minutes, or until tender. Drain. Mash with a potato masher or electric mixer until fluffy. Add 1 egg, salt, pepper, and butter or margarine. Blend well. Shape into 12 oyster-sized patties. Dip patties into beaten egg, then in crumbs. Fry in hot oil until golden brown on both sides. Serves 4 to 6.

DRIED SALSIFY SOUP

2 cups (500 ml) boiling water

1½ cups (375 ml) dried salsify slices

½ cup (125 ml) dried celery slices

6 tablespoons (90 ml) butter or margarine

6 tablespoons (90 ml) all-purpose flour

1 quart (1 litre) milk

Salt and pepper to taste

Pour boiling water over dried salsify and celery slices in a saucepan. Cover and cook for 30 to 45 minutes, or until tender. Meanwhile, melt butter or margarine in another saucepan. Blend in flour, then gradually add milk. Cook, stirring constantly, until smooth and thickened. Add cooked salsify and celery. Season with salt and pepper. Serves 4 to 6.

Sauerkraut

Make homemade sauerkraut by finely shredding fresh cabbage, then packing down firmly in a crock or earthenware bowl with a wooden pestle or potato masher. Sprinkle each medium head of cabbage with 2 tablespoons (30 ml) flaked salt. Layer cabbage and salt in crock, pressing firmly with each layer until cabbage is covered with juice and all cabbage is used. Top with a plate that just fits the inside of the crock or bowl. Weight down with a stone or a water-filled jar so that juice covers plate. Cover with a clean cloth and keep at 70°F (20°C) for 2 to 3 weeks, or until fermentation stops. Each day remove any film from the top and wash plate.

Dehydrator: Drain sauerkraut well. Spread in a thin layer over trays and dry at 120°F (50°C) until crisp and dried through, about 18 to 24 hours. Stir occasionally and rotate trays once or twice.

Sun: Drain sauerkraut well. Spread in a thin layer over cheesecloth-covered trays. Dry in a well-ventilated area in hot sun for 2 to 3 days, stirring occasionally and taking trays inside at night. Dry until crisp.

Oven or Homemade Dryer: Drain sauerkraut well. Spread thinly over trays and dry at 120°F (50°C). It will take 24 to 36 hours to reach desired crispness.

To Use: Pour 1 cup (250 ml) boiling water over 1 cup (250 ml) dried sauerkraut in a saucepan. Cover and cook for 45 to 50 minutes over low heat. One cup (250 ml) yields about 1½ cups (375 ml) cooked sauerkraut.

TOMATO SAUERKRAUT

2 cups (500 ml) boiling water
2 cups (500 ml) dried sauerkraut
¼ cup (65 ml) dried onion slices
1 tablespoon (15 ml) vegetable oil
1 tablespoon (15 ml) all-purpose flour
1½ cups (375 ml) tomato juice
1 dried bay leaf
1 tablespoon (15 ml) honey

Pour boiling water over dried sauerkraut and onion slices. Set aside. In a large saucepan, place oil. Stir in flour and cook, stirring constantly, until lightly browned. Add sauerkraut, tomato juice, and bay leaf. Cover and cook over low heat for 45 to 50 minutes. Remove bay leaf and add honey. Serves 4 to 6.

DRIED SAUERKRAUT WITH PORK

6 cups (1 litre 500 ml) boiling water
3 cups (750 ml) dried sauerkraut
4 smoked pork hocks (about 3 pounds) (1.5 kilogram)
1 dried bay leaf
8 black peppercorns
¼ cup (65 ml) chopped dried onion
1 large potato, grated
1 cup (250 ml) dried apple slices

Pour boiling water over dried sauerkraut in a large saucepan. Add pork hocks, bay leaf, and peppercorns. Cover and simmer until tender, about 2 to 3 hours. Remove meat and peppercorns. Discard peppercorns and cut meat into serving size pieces. To cooked sauerkraut, add dried onion, potato, and dried apple slices. Arrange meat pieces on top. Cover and simmer for 30 to 45 minutes more. Serves 6 to 8.

Sprouts

Soybean, mung bean, alfalfa, or any favorite variety of sprouts may be dried to create an entirely different tasting vegetable. Since sprouts are flavorful and nutritious when eaten within 3 to 4 days after sprouting, it is a good idea to keep a fresh supply and to dry sprouts more than 4 days old. As the sprouts dry, they take on a delicious, nutlike flavor. Drain well before drying. No pretreatment is necessary.

Dehydrator: Spread drained sprouts thinly over trays. Dry at 120°F (50°C) until crisp and crunchy, about 8 to 12 hours. Stir occasionally and rotate trays front to back, side to side, and top to bottom once or twice.

Sun: Spread drained sprouts in a thin layer over trays and place in a well-ventilated area in full sun. Dry for 1 to 2 days, stirring occasionally and taking trays inside at night. Dry until crisp.

Oven or Homemade Dryer: Spread well-drained sprouts thinly over trays. Dry at 120°F (50°C) for 12 to 18 hours, or until crisp, stirring occasionally and rotating trays once or twice.

To Use: Try without refreshing. Add to meat loaves, breakfast cereals, and vegetables, use as a topping for casseroles, and to add crunch to cookies, cakes, and candies. Dried sprouts add a delicious crispness to tossed salads and scrambled eggs.

TUNA-MUSHROOM CASSEROLE

¾ cup (190 ml) boiling water

¾ cup (190 ml) dried mushrooms

4 tablespoons (60 ml) butter or margarine

4 tablespoons (60 ml) all-purpose flour

2¼ cups (565 ml) milk

Salt and pepper to taste

One 13-ounce (325 gram) can tuna, drained and flaked

2 cups (500 ml) dried sprouts

Pour boiling water over dried mushrooms. Cover and simmer for 30 to 45 minutes. Meanwhile, melt butter or margarine in a saucepan. Stir in flour and gradually add milk and salt and pepper. Cook over low heat, stirring constantly, until smooth and thickened. Combine tuna, 1 cup (250 ml) dried sprouts, and cooked, drained mushrooms. Add to cooked sauce and pour into a greased 1½-quart (1½-litre) casserole. Top with remaining dried sprouts and bake in a 350°F (180°C) oven for 25 to 30 minutes. Serves 6.

Squash

Summer Varieties

Pick summer squash while still immature, before seeds form inside. Wash and cut into ⅛-inch (3-mm) slices without peeling.

Dehydrator: Spread slices over trays without overlapping. Dry at 120°F (50°C) for 6 to 8 hours, or until crisp, turning once.

Sun: Spread slices over trays without overlapping. Dry in full sun for 8 to 10 hours, turning once.

Oven or Homemade Dryer: Spread slices over trays. Dry at 120°F (50°C) until crisp, about 6 to 8 hours.

To Use: Slices are best eaten dried. Eat as a snack with dips or chop and add to salads.

Winter Varieties

Any variety of winter squash can be dried with excellent results. Cut whole squash in half and remove seeds and stem. Bake halves in 350°F (180°C) oven until tender, about 1–1½ hours. Scrape out pulp and mash. Or cut halves in thin slices and peel each slice. Cut slices into small cubes or thin strips. Cook in a small amount of boiling water for 35 to 45 minutes, in a steamer for 45 to 60 minutes, or in a pressure cooker at 15 pounds (7 kilograms) pressure for 12 to 13 minutes. Drain well.

Dehydrator: Line trays with plastic wrap and spread cooked, mashed squash over the wrap in a thin layer. Dry at 120°F (50°C) until squash can be pulled away from the plastic easily. Turn over and peel off plastic and dry other side until dried through, about 8 to 12 hours. Break into pieces and process to a powder in a blender or food processor.

Place cubes and slices of cooked squash directly on trays and dry at 120°F (50°C) until pieces are crisp and hard, about 8 to 12 hours.

Sun: Spread cooked, mashed squash over plastic-covered trays and place in full sun in a well-ventilated area. Dry until top is hard and squash pulls away from the wrap easily. Turn over and pull off plastic. Continue drying until hard enough to break into pieces. Process to a powder in the blender. Drying will take 1 to 2 days.

Spread cubes or slices of cooked squash in a thin layer over drying trays and place in full sun with good air circulation. Dry for 1 to 2 days, stirring pieces occasionally and taking trays inside at night. Dried cubes should be hard and slices crisp.

Oven or Homemade Dryer: Cover trays with plastic wrap and spread cooked, mashed squash in a thin layer over wrap. Dry at 120°F (50°C) until squash is hard on top and can be pulled away from the plastic easily. Invert, pull off plastic, and continue drying on the other side. Dry for 12 to 18 hours until hard enough to break. Process to a powder in a blender.

Spread cooked cubes or slices directly over drying trays and dry at 120°F (50°C). Dry for 12 to 18 hours, stirring occasionally and rotating trays, until hard and dried through.

To Use: Pour 1 cup (250 ml) boiling water over 1 cup (250 ml) powder and let set for 30 to 45 minutes. Use as you would cooked squash in casseroles and pies. Or add 1 cup (250 ml) boiling water to 1 cup (250 ml) dried cubes or slices and cook for 30 minutes over low heat. One cup (250 ml) yields about 1¼ cups (315 ml) cooked squash.

DRIED SQUASH-APPLESAUCE SCALLOP

2 cups (500 ml) boiling water

1 cup (250 ml) dried squash

1 cup (250 ml) chopped dried apples

¼ cup (65 ml) firmly packed brown sugar

Dash ground nutmeg

¼ cup (65 ml) butter or margarine, melted

½ teaspoon (2 ml) salt

½ cup (125 ml) evaporated milk

2 eggs, beaten

2 tablespoons (30 ml) butter or margarine

1 cup (250 ml) dried sprouts

1 cup (250 ml) dried bread crumbs

Pour boiling water over squash and apples. Cover and cook for 35 to 40 minutes over low heat. Place in a blender. Add brown sugar, nutmeg, ¼ cup (65 ml) butter or margarine, salt, milk, and eggs. Process to a smooth puree. Pour into a greased, shallow baking dish. In a small pan, melt 2 tablespoons (30 ml) butter or margarine, stir in sprouts and bread crumbs, and blend. Arrange sprout mixture around edge of top of casserole. Bake in 350°F (180°C) oven for 45 minutes. Serves 6.

GOURMET SQUASH

2 cups (500 ml) boiling water

2 cups (500 ml) powdered dried squash

2 tablespoons (30 ml) butter or margarine

1 cup (250 ml) sour cream

¼ cup (65 ml) dried onions

Salt and pepper to taste

Combine first five ingredients and season with salt and pepper. Pour into an ungreased casserole and bake for 30 to 45 minutes in 350°F (180°C) oven. Serves 6.

Sweet Potatoes

Cook unpeeled sweet potatoes until tender, about 30 to 45 minutes, in 350°F (180°C) oven, 30 to 45 minutes in a steamer, or 8 minutes in a pressure cooker at 15 pounds (6.8 kilograms) pressure. Peel and cut into ⅛-inch (3-mm) slices. Leave in slices or cut into sticks or small cubes.

Dehydrator: Spread slices, sticks, or cubes of sweet potatoes in a single layer over trays. Dry at 120°F (50°C) until hard and brittle, about 12 to 18 hours, stirring occasionally and rotating trays once or twice.

Sun: Spread slices, sticks, or cubes thinly over trays. Dry for 2 to 3 days in hot sun until hard and brittle. Stir occasionally and take trays inside at night.

Oven or Homemade Dryer: Spread slices, sticks, or cubes over trays. Dry at 120°F (50°C) for 18 to 24 hours, turning occasionally and rotating trays once or twice.

To Use: Cook in equal amount of boiling water for 35 to 40 minutes. One cup (250 ml) yields about 1½ cups (375 ml) cooked sweet potatoes.

FRENCH-FRIED SWEET POTATO STICKS

1½ cups (375 ml) boiling water

1½ cups (375 ml) dried sweet potato sticks

1 egg, well beaten

½ cup (125 ml) dried bread crumbs

Oil, heated for frying

Pour boiling water over dried sweet potato sticks. Let soak for 1 hour. Dip sticks in beaten egg, then coat in bread crumbs. Fry in deep hot oil until golden brown. Serves 4.

ORANGE-GLAZED SWEET POTATOES

3 cups (750 ml) boiling water

3 cups (750 ml) dried sweet potato slices

⅔ cup (150 ml) granulated sugar

1 tablespoon (15 ml) cornstarch

½ teaspoon (2 ml) salt

½ teaspoon (2 ml) grated dried orange peel

1 cup (250 ml) orange juice

2 tablespoons (30 ml) butter or margarine

Pour boiling water over sweet potato slices in a saucepan. Cover and cook for 35 to 40 minutes over low heat. Meanwhile, combine sugar, cornstarch, salt, and orange peel. Gradually add orange juice, stirring constantly. Cook over low heat until thickened. Add butter or margarine and boil for 1 minute, stirring constantly. Pour over cooked sweet potatoes in a casserole. Cover and bake for 1 hour in a 350°F (180°C) oven, basting occasionally. Serves 4 to 6.

Tomatoes
(see also Green Tomatoes)

Peel tomatoes by dipping in boiling water for 1 minute, then in cold water for 1 minute. Slip off skins and cut out cores. Cut into ⅛-inch (3-mm) slices or in ¼-inch (6-mm) cubes. Drain well.

Dehydrator: Spread slices or cubes over trays so pieces are not overlapping. Dry for 8 to 10 hours at 120°F (50°C), then turn slices and continue drying for another 6 to 8 hours until brittle.

Sun: Spread slices or cubes in a single layer over trays. Dry in hot sun with good circulation of air until tops are dry. Turn and dry other side. Take trays inside at night. Will dry in 1 to 2 days in good weather. When drying is complete, pieces are brittle.

Oven or Homemade Dryer: Spread slices or cubes over trays. Dry at 120°F (50°C) until hard and crisp, about 18 to 24 hours, turning slices and stirring pieces and rotating trays once or twice.

To Use: Refresh slices by placing on a shallow plate or platter and spraying with warm water. Let soak for 1 hour, spraying with water occasionally. Refresh smaller pieces by soaking in water to cover for 1 hour or more. Add dried slices or cubes without refreshing to salads, soups, and casseroles. One cup (250 ml) yields about 1½ cups (375 ml) refreshed tomatoes.

SPICY PASTA SAUCE

1 cup (250 ml) chopped onion

2 tablespoons (30 ml) olive oil

3 cups (750 ml) boiling water

2 cups (500 ml) dried tomato

2 sliced cloves of garlic

1 teaspoon (5 ml) salt

¼ teaspoon (1 ml) pepper

¾ teaspoon (3 ml) dried parsley

1 teaspoon (5 ml) dried basil

¾ teaspoon (3 ml) dried oregano leaves

2 teaspoons (10 ml) lemon juice

In large skillet over medium heat, sauté onion in oil for 5 minutes. Meanwhile, combine water and tomatoes in bowl; set aside 2 to 3 minutes. With slotted spoon remove and set aside one-third of the tomatoes. With an electric blender or food processor puree the remaining tomato/water mixture and garlic. Add puree and reserved tomato halves to skillet. Bring to boil, reduce heat and simmer for 10 minutes. Stir in remaining ingredients; simmer 1 minute. Remove from heat. Serve over hot cooked pasta. Add grated Parmesan cheese, if desired. Makes 4 to 6 servings.

FRIED TOMATOES SLICES

1 cup (250 ml) boiling water

1½ cups (375 ml) dried tomato slices

4 tablespoons (60 ml) all-purpose flour

4 tablespoons (60 ml) butter or margarine

1 cup (250 ml) milk

Salt and pepper to taste

Spray or pour boiling water over tomato slices spread over a plate or stacked in a water glass. Let soak for 1 hour. Drain and coat refreshed slices with 2 tablespoons (30 ml) flour. Sauté in melted butter or margarine in a heavy skillet, cooking over low heat until lightly browned. Remove half the slices to a serving platter. Sprinkle remaining slices in skillet with remaining flour and blend well. Gradually add milk and cook, stirring constantly, over low heat until thickened. Pour over tomatoes on platter. Add salt and pepper. Serves 4.

LAYERED DRIED TOMATOES

1 cup (250 ml) boiling water

1½ cups (375 ml) dried tomato slices
or cubes

½ teaspoon (2 ml) salt

⅛ teaspoon (½ ml) black pepper

2 tablespoons (30 ml) butter or
margarine, melted

1 cup (250 ml) dried bread crumbs

½ teaspoon (2 ml) dried oregano

½ cup (125 ml) grated dried
American cheese

Spray or pour boiling water over dried tomatoes that are spread over a platter or stacked in a water glass. Let soak for 1 hour or more. Drain and arrange half the tomatoes in a 1-quart (1-litre) casserole. Combine salt, pepper, melted butter or margarine, bread crumbs, oregano, and grated dried cheese. Spread one-half of crumb mixture over tomatoes in casserole. Top with remaining tomatoes and remaining crumb mixture. Bake in 350°F (180°C) oven for 25 to 30 minutes until bubbling hot and lightly browned. Serves 4 to 6.

"SUNDRIED" TOMATO PESTO

2 cups (500 ml) chopped dried
tomatoes

½ cup (125 ml) olive oil

1 large clove garlic

2 cups (500 ml) fresh basil

1 tablespoon (15 ml) dried oregano

¼ cup (65 ml) pine nuts (optional)

Combine ingredients in a blender or food processor and puree. Pack pesto tightly into a glass jar and cover with a thin layer of olive oil. Use as needed and keep refrigerated. Great on pasta, grilled chicken, and vegetables.

"SUNDRIED" TOMATO AND CHEESE PIZZA

2 cups (500 ml) chopped dried
tomatoes

2–3 cloves finely chopped garlic

4 ounces (100 grams) crumbled soft
goat cheese

1 cup (250 ml) grated mozzarella

½ cup (125 ml) grated Parmesan

1 tablespoon (15 ml) olive oil

¼ cup (65 ml) chopped black olives

Prepare dough for one large pizza and place on lightly oiled pizza pan. Coat surface of dough lightly with olive oil. Sprinkle parmesan cheese evenly over dough. Add the dried tomatoes and garlic. Top with goat cheese, mozzarella, Parmesan, and black olives. Bake for 15–20 minutes in a 500°F (260°C) oven or until dough is golden brown and cheese is bubbly. Makes 1 large pizza.

TOMATO SQUASH SOUP

1 butternut squash (about 2 pounds) (800 grams)

1 sliced medium onion

1 tablespoon (15 ml) corn oil

2½ cups (625 ml) water

1 cup (250 ml) dried tomato halves

1 cup (250 ml) half-and-half

1 teaspoon (5 ml) dried basil

Salt, to taste

Cut stem end from squash and halve, lengthwise. Place squash halves, cut sides down, in shallow baking pan. Add ½ inch (15-mm) water. Bake in 400°F (205°C) oven until fork-tender, 45 to 60 minutes. Meanwhile, in 3-quart (3-litre) saucepan over medium heat, sauté onion in oil until limp. Add water and tomatoes. Bring to boil and simmer 5 minutes. Discard squash seeds and scoop out squash pulp into an electric blender or food processor. Add contents of saucepan. Blend until smooth. Return to saucepan. Mix in half-and-half and basil. Simmer 3–5 minutes. Add water if thinner soup desired. Season with salt. Serve hot. Makes 4 to 6 servings.

CHICKEN WITH "SUNDRIED" TOMATOES

4 skinned chicken breast halves

2 tablespoons (30 ml) olive oil

1 chopped medium onion

3 cloves minced garlic

1 red bell pepper, cut into strips

1 cup (250 ml) dried tomato halves

1½ cups (375 ml) dry white wine

⅓ cup (75 ml) sliced pitted ripe olives

1 sliced lemon

1½ teaspoons (7 ml) cinnamon

1 teaspoon (5 ml) honey

Salt and pepper, to taste

Chopped parsley, for garnish

In large skillet over medium heat, sauté chicken breasts in oil about 5 minutes, turning once. Add onion, garlic and red pepper. Sauté, stirring often, about 4 minutes until onion is limp. Stir tomato into skillet with remaining ingredients except parsley. Cover and simmer 15 minutes. Remove cover and cook 5 more minutes until chicken is tender and sauce is reduced slightly. Sprinkle with chopped parsley. Serve as is or over rice. Makes 4 servings.

Tomato Puree

Core and cut up ripe tomatoes without peeling. Simmer for 10 minutes, stirring occasionally to keep from sticking. Cool slightly and force cooked pulp though a food mill, colander, or strainer. In a shallow pan over low heat or in an electric skillet set at 260°F (125°C), cook juice down to a thick puree.

Dehydrator: Cover trays with plastic wrap and spread with ⅛-inch (3-mm) layer of tomato puree. Dry at highest heat setting for 12 to 14 hours, or until firm, top is hard but sticky, and puree can be pulled away from plastic wrap. Turn over, remove plastic and discard. Dry for another 12 to 14 hours, or until hard and dry. Break into pieces and dry for another 3 to 4 hours.

Sun: Spread ⅛-inch (3-mm) layer of tomato puree over cookie sheets or drying trays that have been covered with plastic wrap. Dry in hot sun until hard and brittle, about 2 to 4 days, turning once. Break into pieces and dry for another 6 to 8 hours.

Oven or Homemade Dryer: Spread tomato puree in an ⅛-inch (3-mm) layer over trays lined with plastic wrap. Dry at 150°F (65°C) until firm, then turn over and peel off wrap. Dry for another 12 to 14 hours, or until hard and brittle. Break into pieces and dry for another 3 to 4 hours.

To Make Tomato Powder: Pound pieces of dried tomato puree to a fine powder, using a pestle, grater, blender, or food processor.

To Use: For a tomato puree or paste, add ½–¾ cup (125–190 ml) powder to each cup (250 ml) boiling water. Stir well until dissolved and season to taste. For tomato juice, add 1 tablespoon (15 ml) tomato powder to each cup boiling water. Season with salt and serve hot or cold. Add 1 tablespoon (15 ml) powder to each cup liquid in soups, stews, or sauces.

Turnips

Pull turnips after first hard frost or freeze. Wash, trim off top and root ends, and thinly peel. Cut into thin slices or chop into ¼-inch (6-mm) cubes. Dry without blanching for snacks. For cooking use, blanch for 3 minutes in boiling water or 4 minutes in a steamer. Pat dry with a paper towel.

Dehydrator: Spread raw or blanched slices or cubes thinly over trays. Dry for 12 to 18 hours at 120°F (50°C) until hard and crisp. Stir once or twice and rotate trays once during drying.

Sun: Spread raw or blanched slices or cubes over trays in a thin layer. Dry in full sun where there is good air circulation for 2 to 3 days, or until hard and crisp. Stir occasionally and take trays inside at night.

Oven or Homemade Dryer: Spread raw or blanched slices or cubes in a thin layer over trays. Dry at 120°F (50°C) for 18 to 24 hours, or until crisp, stirring or turning occasionally and rotating trays once or twice.

To Use: Eat slices as a snack alone or with a cheese dip. Add chopped dried turnips to salads. Grind or process in blender and add to meat loaves and casseroles. Drop dried cubes in simmering soup stock for long, slow cooking. To cook as a vegetable, pour 1 cup (250 ml) boiling water over 1 cup (250 ml) dried turnips in a saucepan. Cover and simmer for 35 to 40 minutes, or until tender. One cup (250 ml) yields about 1¼ cups (315 ml) cooked vegetable.

Dried Turnips in a Tossed Salad _____

½ cup (125 ml) French dressing

½ cup (125 ml) dried turnip cubes

½ head lettuce

½ cup (125 ml) chopped tomatoes

Pour French dressing over dried turnip cubes. Keep overnight in refrigerator. At serving time, tear lettuce into bite-sized pieces. Add tomatoes, marinated turnips, and dressing. Toss until lettuce is coated. Serves 4.

Sautéed Turnips _____

1½ cups (375 ml) boiling water

1½ cups (375 ml) dried turnip slices

½ cup (125 ml) all-purpose flour

½ teaspoon (2 ml) salt

6 tablespoons (90 ml) butter or margarine, melted

Pour boiling water over dried turnip slices. Let soak for 3 to 4 hours. Drain and dredge in flour that has been combined with salt. Brown in melted butter or margarine. Serves 6.

Zucchini

Select slender, immature zucchini before seeds form inside. Wash, trim off ends, and cut into ⅛-inch (3-mm) slices. Blanching is not necessary.

Dehydrator: Spread raw slices thinly over trays. Dry at 120°F (50°C) until crisp, about 12 to 18 hours. Turn slices and rotate trays once during drying time.

Sun: Spread slices thinly over trays and dry in hot sun with good air circulation. Dry until crisp, about 1 to 2 days, turning slices occasionally and taking trays inside at night.

Oven or Homemade Dryer: Spread slices thinly over trays. Dry at 120°F (50°C) until crisp, about 18 to 24 hours, turning and rotating trays once or twice.

To Use: Eat slices as a snack, alone or with a cheese dip. Use dry in salads or chop and sprinkle over tops of casseroles. To fry, pour 1 cup (250 ml) boiling water over 1 cup (250 ml) zucchini slices and let set for 3 to 4 hours. Drain, then dredge in flour and sauté in melted butter or margarine.

Zesty Italian Zucchini Slices _____

2 cups (500 ml) boiling water

2 cups (500 ml) dried zucchini slices

1 medium onion, thinly sliced

2 tablespoons (30 ml) butter or margarine

1 cup (250 ml) fresh or canned tomatoes, chopped

Salt and pepper to taste

¼ cup (65 ml) grated dried cheese

Italian seasoning, to taste

Pour boiling water over dried zucchini slices. Let soak for 1 to 2 hours. Drain. Cook onion slices in butter or margarine until transparent. Add drained zucchini slices. Cook and stir for 5 minutes. Add tomatoes and season with salt and pepper. Pour into casserole and top with Italian seasoning and grated dried cheese. Bake in 350°F (180°C) oven for 25 to 30 minutes, or until lightly browned. Serves 4.

CHAPTER EIGHT

Drying Herbs

Herb leaves, seeds, flowers, and roots can add flavor and color to almost any food. Whichever part of the plant is used, except for the seeds, it is most flavorful and best for drying when young and tender. Pick leaves and flowers when flower buds are about half opened. If seeds are being harvested, they should be collected when the seed heads are turning brown — too early means the seeds have not ripened, too late means the seed crop may fall to the ground and be lost.

Pick before noon, as soon as the sun has dried off the dew. If you live in a dusty area or know heavy rains have splattered your herbs with mud, try hosing them off the day before you harvest them. Wash herbs under running water or spray. Shake to remove moisture and pat dry. Inspect leaves for dirt and insects as you move through the process.

Don't try to "pick" herbs as you might daisies. Cut them with pruning shears. Leave 4 inches (10 cm) of stem on leafy annuals. Cut only one-third the growth of leafy perennials. In both cases this permits further growth and further harvesting. The best leaves are the three to four sets from the top.

The delicate flavors of herbs can be spoiled by heat and faded by sun. The flowers and green leaves of herbs should be dried at very low temperatures and away from direct sunlight. Good air circulation is important in order to dry herbs quickly and thus preserve their flavor.

Dry small leaves on the stems. It's easier to strip them off when dry than when green, and it's easier to dry them on the stem. Take larger leaves off the stem, such as sage or basil.

If a commercial dehydrator, oven, or homemade dryer is used, most herbs should be dried separately in order to keep their distinct flavors from blending. This precaution is not necessary, of course, with outdoor drying.

While the methods listed below are ideal for drying herbs, we would be remiss in our treatment of the subject if we didn't point out yet another method, one used for generations. That's to pick and tie small bunches of herbs, then hang them in a room out of the sunlight. They'll be dry in about 2 to 3 weeks, and meantime they will provide a decorative touch to the room.

An alternative to this method is to tie the bunch in a brown paper bag with the stem ends tied with the mouth of the bag, so the bunch hangs down inside the bag. This reduces the light that reaches the herbs, cuts down on possible dust on them, and keeps errant leaves from falling to the floor. The bags should hang in an airy room. Cut a few slits or punch holes in the sides of the bag for good air circulation.

Most herb leaves — the exception is bay leaves — are cooled and crumbled and stored in glass jars. Some, such as sage, oregano, and marjoram, may be coarsely crumbled in the hands. The leaves of rosemary, savory, tarragon, and thyme may be finely crushed with a rolling pin.

Store large batches of herbs in several small glass jars. Small containers will retain the flavors better than large ones, which lose aroma each time the jar is opened. To keep dried herbs at their best, always keep jars tightly covered in a dry, cool, dark place. If there is no dark storage area, jars may be kept in paper bags or in a covered can or box.

Do not store herbs in a cabinet near a stove, radiator, or refrigerator. The heat from them can cause loss of flavor.

Dried herbs are used in the dry state, without refreshing in water. The exception is rosemary, which should be added to the liquid of the dish and allowed to soak for a few minutes just before serving.

The flavor of dried herbs is much more pronounced than fresh herbs, so it is important to use very small amounts at first. To be safe, start with just a pinch. It is easy to add more, but the overpowering flavor of too much can spoil a carefully planned dish.

Microwave Herb Drying

Although herb drying can be accomplished in the microwave, it is not necessarily a safe choice. In fact, some oven manufacturers warn against it, because it removes all of the moisture from the oven, resulting in a no-load situation that can harm the oven's magnetron tube over time. Some ovens, however, have a shielded tube and may be safely used for drying. Check the instruction book of your microwave oven before attempting to use it for drying. To prevent a no-load situation, fill a glass measuring cup with ½ cup (125 ml) cold water and place in the oven during drying. Herbs dried by this method will need further air drying to complete the process.

To Dry: Place a single layer of herb leaves between paper towels. Place the paper towels in a microwave oven and dry for 1 to 2 minutes, depending on the thickness of the leaves. Remove the paper towels. When dry, herbs will crumble in the hands. If not dry, return leaves to the microwave and dry for ½ to 1 minute more. Dry in the microwave at 1 minute intervals as it is easy to overdry leaves causing a burned, charred flavor. Some herbs may actually catch fire.

Conventional Oven Herb Drying

Conventional oven drying may be accomplished by heating the oven to 200°F (95°C), turning it off, and placing a rack of herb leaves in oven for 6 to 8 hours or overnight. This temperature is higher than that used for drying in a dehydrator, because conventional ovens usually cannot be set lower than 200°F (95°C). *Remember to remove the herbs before preheating the oven for baking!*

Anise

Harvest anise seed when it begins to dry on the plant. No preparation is necessary.

Dehydrator: Remove alternate trays in the dehydrator. Spread seed stalks over remaining trays and dry at 110°F (45°C) until stalks and leaves are crisp. Remove seeds, discard stalks, and store. Drying will take 10 to 12 hours total.

Outdoors: Spread seed stalks over trays and stack in a well-ventilated shed or shady area. Or place each one upside down in a brown paper bag and hang in a shady, well-ventilated place. Drying will take several days, but they will need no attention during that time.

Oven or Homemade Dryer: Spread seed stalks over trays. Dry at 110°F (45°C) or less until stalks are brittle and seeds are dried through, about 18 to 24 hours.

To Use: The licorice-flavored seeds are tasty in herb teas, sprinkled on sweet rolls or salads, or added to cookie batter before baking.

Basil

Basil leaves must be dried quickly to prevent mold from forming. Snip leaves from stems of sweet basil as soon as they have developed in the spring. Discard any dirty leaves, spray with water, shake to remove moisture, and pat dry.

Dehydrator: Arrange herbs over dehydrator trays so they do not touch. Dry at no more than 110°F (45°C) until leaves are crisp enough to crumble in the hands, about 8 to 12 hours. Cool, then crumble, discard stems, and store.

Outdoors: Arrange leaves side by side on trays and place in a well-ventilated place out of direct sunlight. Dry until leaves are brittle enough to crumble, about 1 to 2 days. Crumble, discard stems, and store.

Oven or Homemade Dryer: Spread leaves in a thin layer over trays. Leaves will dry to brittle stage at 110°F (45°C) or less in 8 to 12 hours. Cool and crumble, discarding stems before storing.

To Use: Add crumbled leaves to tomato dishes. Use to flavor soups, meat pies, and stews. Garnish peas, squash, and green beans with dried basil. Sprinkle leaves over lamb chops before broiling. Basil is especially good on fish, cheese, or egg dishes.

Bay Leaves

Bay leaves are the shiny green leaves of the evergreen laurel tree, which grows in warm climates. Pluck small mature leaves from the stems. Because bay leaves are one of the herb leaves that are not crumbled, the dried leaves should be handled carefully to keep them whole.

Dehydrator: Spread leaves over trays and dry at no more than 110°F (45°C) until very brittle, about 6 to 8 hours. Cool and store whole.

Outdoors: Spread leaves over trays and place in a well-ventilated area out of direct sunlight. Dry, turning once, until leaves are very brittle, about 10 to 12 hours. Store leaves whole.

Oven or Homemade Dryer: Spread leaves thinly over trays. Dry at 110°F (45°C) or less until crisp, 8 to 12 hours. Cool and store whole.

To Use: Add 2 or 3 dried leaves to soups, stews, and spaghetti sauce. Cook 1 or 2 leaves with beef pot roast and baked fish. Add 1 leaf to the last water when boiling shrimp. Remove bay leaves before serving.

Celery Leaves

Remove leaves from celery stalks or accumulate them in a plastic bag in the refrigerator. Wash and drain dry. Chop or leave whole.

Dehydrator: Spread chopped or whole leaves thinly over trays. Dry at no more than 110°F (45°C) for 6 to 8 hours, or until crisp. Crumble and store.

Outdoors: Spread chopped or whole leaves in a thin layer over trays and place in a well-ventilated, shaded area. Dry for 8 to 12 hours, or until crisp. Crumble, discard stems, and store.

Oven or Homemade Dryer: Spread chopped or whole leaves thinly over trays. Dry at 110°F (45°C) or less until crisp, about 6 to 8 hours.

To Use: Use dried leaves as you would celery, in soups, stews, salads, and cooked dishes.

Chervil

Pick small bunches of chervil in the spring when plants are immature.

Dehydrator: Dry whole bunches by removing alternate dehydrator shelves and arranging bunches thinly over trays. Dry at no more than 110°F (45°C), turning bunches once, until leaves are brittle, about 12 to 18 hours. Cool. Chop or crumble leaves, discarding stems.

Outdoors: Tie stems with string and hang upside down in a well-ventilated, shady place until brittle. Drying will take several days.

Oven or Homemade Dryer: Arrange bunches over trays. Dry at no more than 110°F (45°C) for 12 to 18 hours, with door ajar.

To Use: Use 1 tablespoon (15 ml) to garnish salads. Add 2 or 3 tablespoons (30 or 45 ml) to flavor soups or egg and cheese dishes.

Chili Peppers

Red or yellow chilies may be mild or hot. There are several varieties. Dry whole or cut in half lengthwise or in thin slices. Separate mild and hot peppers, or all the peppers will be hot. Wear rubber gloves when working with hot peppers to prevent burning hands.

Dehydrator: Spread whole, cut, or sliced chili peppers over trays and dry at 120°F (50°C) until hard and brittle, about 12 to 18 hours. Stir once or twice and rotate trays during drying.

Sun: Spread whole, cut, or sliced chili peppers over trays. Dry in a well-ventilated area in full sun until hard and brittle, about 1 to 2 days. Stir occasionally and take trays inside at night.

Oven or Homemade Dryer: Spread whole, cut, or sliced chili peppers over trays. Dry at 120°F (50°C) until hard and brittle, about 18 to 24 hours.

To Use: Add 1 or 2 small, whole, or halved chili peppers — mild or hot — to each jar of dill pickles as they are canned. Drop 3 or 4 slices in soups, stews, and spaghetti sauce. Grind to use in chili powder (see recipe on page 113). Use hot varieties carefully until you are accustomed to them.

Chives

Betty E.M. Jacobs, author of *Profitable Herb Growing at Home*, has advice on drying chives: Don't. She believes too much of the flavor is lost, and a pot of chives is easy to keep inside and productive all winter.

If you don't agree, try this: With scissors, cut chive tops from the plant before flowers form. Chop into ¼-inch (6-mm) pieces. Do not wash, but discard any dirty pieces.

Dehydrator: Spread chives in a thin layer over trays and dry at no more than 110°F (45°C) until brittle, about 4 to 6 hours.

Outdoors: Spread chives in a thin layer over trays. Dry in a well-ventilated area out of sunlight for 8 to 10 hours.

Oven or Homemade Dryer: Spread chives in a thin layer over trays. Dry at not more than 110°F (45°C) for 4 to 6 hours until crisp, keeping door ajar.

To Use: Dried chives add a mild onion flavor to salads and casseroles. Sprinkle 1 tablespoon (15 ml) dried chives over an omelet before cooking or into 2 eggs to be scrambled. Add 1 tablespoon (15 ml) with each cup of milk in a white sauce to add flavor and color.

Cumin

Allow cumin seeds to dry as much as possible on the plant, but pluck pods before they burst and scatter seeds.

Dehydrator: Spread seeds over trays. If tray mesh is too large, cover with cheesecloth. Dry at 120°F (50°C) until seeds are hard and completely dry.

Sun: Spread seeds evenly over trays and place in a well-ventilated area in hot sun. Dry, stirring occasionally, until seeds are hard and dry, about 1 day.

Oven or Homemade Dryer: Spread seeds over trays. Dry at 120°F (50°C) until seeds are hard, about 6 to 8 hours.

To Use: Blend 1 teaspoon (5 ml) seed into 2 cups (500 ml) cheese or cheese spread. Add 1 teaspoon (5 ml) dried seed to each 2 cups (500 ml) liquid when baking bread. Grind it to add flavoring to sausage and game meats. Ground cumin is an ingredient of chili powder (see recipe on page 113).

Dill

Cut dill heads as soon as flower buds form, but before all the buds are open. Chop, discarding stems. For milder flavor, snip off green sprigs and finely chop with scissors. Dill seed may be partially dried on the plant and gathered before pods burst and scatter seeds.

Dehydrator: Spread flowers or leaves or partially dried seeds over trays. Dry flowers and leaves for 6 to 8 hours and seeds for 4 to 6 hours at 120°F (50°C).

Outdoors: Flower heads or sprigs may be dried whole by hanging by the stem in an airy, shaded place. Dry under shelter for 3 to 4 days, or until crisp. Crumble and store.

Spread seeds over trays and place in hot sun. Dry for 4 to 8 hours.

Oven or Homemade Dryer: Spread dill flowers or leaves over trays. Dry at 110°F (45°C) for 6 to 8 hours, or until crisp.

Spread seeds over trays and dry for 4 to 6 hours at 120°F (50°C).

To Use: Add 1 tablespoon (15 ml) dill flowers or leaves to mashed potatoes or stew. Sprinkle 1 teaspoon (5 ml) over fish or apple pie. Stir ½ teaspoon (2 ml) into each cup (250 ml) of salad dressing. Sprinkle dill seeds over sauerkraut or cabbage. Add ¼ teaspoon (1 ml) or more dill seed to every quart (1 litre) of dill pickles. Use to garnish coleslaw and cooked vegetables. Make dill vinegar by steeping 1 teaspoon (5 ml) dill seeds in 1 pint (475 ml) of plain cider vinegar.

Fennel

Pluck immature fennel leaves in morning after dew has dried off. Discard any dirty leaves, wash others with a spray, shake to remove moisture, and pat dry. Fennel seed is harvested after it has dried somewhat in the pod, but before the pods burst and scatter the seed.

Dehydrator: Spread leaves or seeds over trays. If tray mesh is too large, cover with a layer of cheesecloth. Dry leaves for 6 to 8 hours at no more than 110°F (43.3°C) and seeds for 4 to 8 hours at 120°F (50°C).

Outdoors: Spread leaves over trays and place in a well-ventilated, shaded area. Dry for 8 to 10 hours, or until crisp.

Spread seeds over trays that are covered with cheesecloth, if necessary. Dry in full sun for 6 to 8 hours, stirring occasionally.

Oven or Homemade Dryer: Spread leaves or seeds in an even layer over trays. Dry leaves for 6 to 8 hours at no more than 110°F (45°C) and seeds for 4 to 6 hours at 120°F (50°C), or until leaves are crisp, and seeds are dried through.

To Use: Add ½ teaspoon (2 ml) leaves to simmering soup and casseroles before cooking. Dried fennel seeds add a mild licorice flavor to candies, pastry, rolls, and cookies. Use ¼ teaspoon (1 ml) for each cup of batter.

Filé Powder

Pick tender young leaves of the sassafras tree in the spring.

Dehydrator: Spread leaves thinly over trays. Dry at not more than 110°F (45°C) until leaves are crisp, about 6 to 8 hours.

Outdoors: Spread leaves over trays and place in a well-ventilated, shady place. Dry for 8 to 12 hours, or until leaves are crisp.

Oven or Homemade Dryer: Spread leaves in a thin layer over trays. Dry at 110°F (45°C) until leaves are crisp, about 8 to 12 hours.

To Use: Make a fine powder of dried sassafras leaves by processing in a blender or pounding with a pestle. Use filé powder as an ingredient in recipes for gumbo and other Creole dishes. Do not cook filé powder in the dishes, but add just before serving.

Garlic

Peel and finely chop garlic bulbs. No other pretreatment is necessary.

Dehydrator: Spread chopped garlic over trays. If mesh in trays is too large, cover with cheesecloth. Dry at 120°F (50°C) until crisp, about 6 to 8 hours.

Outdoors: Spread chopped garlic in a thin layer over trays and place in a well-ventilated area out of direct sunlight. Dry for 6 to 8 hours, or until crisp.

Oven or Homemade Dryer: Spread chopped garlic thinly over trays. Dry at 120°F (50°C) for 6 to 8 hours, or until garlic is crisp.

To Use: Store garlic chopped, pound with a pestle, or process in a blender to a fine powder. Add sparingly to salads or use in Italian foods, omelets, and chili. Sprinkle over roast beef or add to salad dressings. Mix powdered garlic with salt to make garlic salt.

Green Onions

Pull green onions or scallions before the bulbs have developed fully. Wash throughly, separate the white bulbs from the green tops, and finely chop tops with scissors. Using a knife, cut bulbs into thin slices.

Dehydrator: Spread green and white parts separately over trays. Dry green tops at not more than 110°F (45°C) for 6 to 8 hours, or until crisp. Dry white bulb slices at 120°F (50°C) for 8 to 12 hours, or until crisp. Stir occasionally.

Outdoors: Spread tops in a thin layer over trays and dry in a well-ventilated shady area until crisp, about 8 to 10 hours. Spread sliced white bulbs in sun until crisp, about 8 to 12 hours.

Oven or Homemade Dryer: Spread green tops thinly over trays. Dry for 6 to 8 hours at not more than 110°F (45°C) until crisp.

Spread chopped green onion bulbs thinly over trays. Dry at 120°F (50°C) until crisp, about 12 to 18 hours.

To Use: Add tops to salads, soups, and casseroles. Use bulbs as you would dried onions (see chapter 7). Either may be pulverized to a powder and added to salt to make onion salt.

Marjoram

Pick the gray-green leaves at maturity. Do not wash, but discard any soiled leaves. Do not pretreat.

Dehydrator: Spread leaves thinly over trays and dry at 110°F (45°C) until crisp enough to crumble in the hands, about 6 to 8 hours.

Outdoors: Spread leaves in a thin layer over trays. Place in a well-ventilated area out of direct sunlight. Dry for 8 to 12 hours, or until crisp.

Oven or Homemade Dryer: Spread leaves thinly over trays. Dry at 110°F (45°C) until crisp, about 6 to 8 hours.

To Use: Crumble leaves, discarding stems. Sprinkle over leg of lamb or beef before roasting. Use to season sausage and to add zest to stews and gravies. Sprinkle fine crumblings over hot lima beans, peas, and green beans.

Mint

Pick the leaves of peppermint or spearmint plants in early summer, when leaves are most fragrant and before the plant flowers.

Dehydrator: Spread leaves in a thin layer over trays and dry at not more than 110°F (45°C) until crisp, about 6 to 8 hours.

Outdoors: Spread leaves thinly over trays and place in a well-ventilated, shady place. Dry until crisp, about 8 to 12 hours.

Oven or Homemade Dryer: Spread leaves thinly over trays. Dry at 110°F (45°C) or less until crisp, about 6 to 8 hours.

To Use: Cool, then crumble leaves, discarding stems. Use mint for making jelly and to add flavor to lemonade or tea. Sprinkle crumbled leaves over roast lamb or cooked vegetables.

Oregano

Pick oregano flowers and the outer leaves just as the flower begins to open. Dry quickly to preserve the flavor.

Dehydrator: Spread over trays in a thin layer. Dry at no more than 110°F (45°C) until crisp, about 4 to 8 hours.

Outdoors: Spread in a thin layer over trays. Place in an area with good air circulation out of direct sunlight. Dry for 8 to 12 hours, or until crisp.

Oven or Homemade Dryer: Spread leaves and petals over trays. Dry at 110°F (45°C) or less until crisp, about 6 to 8 hours.

To Use: Cool dried leaves and petals, then finely crumble before storing. Add 1 teaspoon (5 ml) crumbled leaves to tomato dishes, especially spaghetti sauce, pizza, and lasagna. Sprinkle ½ teaspoon (2 ml) over pork roast, beef stew, and omelets. Oregano is especially good with wild game.

Parsley

Cut parsley tops with scissors as soon as new leaves have formed. Parsley can be cut throughout the growing season. Dry whole sprigs cut from the stem or finely chop with scissors for quicker drying.

Dehydrator: Place sprigs or spread chopped parsley leaves over trays. Dry at not more than 110°F (45°C) until crisp. Sprigs will take 8 to 12 hours and chopped leaves will dry in 6 to 8 hours.

Outdoors: Spread chopped leaves over trays. Drying whole sprigs outdoors is not recommended. Place trays in a well-ventilated, shady area. Dry until crisp, about 8 to 12 hours.

Oven or Homemade Dryer: Spread tops over drying trays in a thin layer. Dry at 110°F (45°C) until crisp, about 8 to 10 hours.

To Use: Just before serving, sprinkle flakes over soups, salads, and sauces. Add to dumpling batter and egg dishes. Use as a garnish for cooked vegetables.

Rosemary

Pick young, tender leaves of the rosemary plant as soon as their aroma has developed. Discard any that are soiled. Do not wash.

Dehydrator: Spread leaves in a thin layer over trays. Dry at no more than 110°F (45°C) until crisp, about 6 to 8 hours.

Outdoors: Spread leaves thinly over trays and place in a well-ventilated area out of direct sunlight. Dry until crisp, about 8 to 10 hours.

Oven or Homemade Dryer: Spread leaves in a thin layer over trays. Dry until crisp, about 8 to 12 hours, at no more than 110°F (45°C).

To Use: Dried rosemary should not be cooked, but needs to soak a few minutes in liquid to revive its flavor. Add ½ teaspoon (2 ml) dried rosemary to the cooking liquid of potatoes, cauliflower, green beans, or peas a few minutes before serving. Add ¼ teaspoon (1 ml) rosemary to ½ cup (125 ml) salad dressing or vinegar and let set a few minutes before tossing a salad. Rosemary is especially suited to lamb dishes.

Sage

Pick gray-green sage leaves in midsummer, when their flavor is fully developed. Discard any soiled leaves and spray others lightly with water. Shake to remove moisture and pat dry with a paper towel.

Dehydrator: Spread leaves in a thin layer over trays. Dry at no more than 110°F (45°C) until crisp, about 8 to 12 hours.

Outdoors: Spread leaves thinly over trays. Dry in a well-ventilated, shady area. Dry until crisp, about 10 to 14 hours, stirring occasionally and taking trays inside at night, if necessary.

Oven or Homemade Dryer: Spread leaves thinly over trays. Dry at 110°F (45°C) for 10 to 12 hours, or until crisp.

To Use: Coarsely crumble leaves and discard any stems. Sage is a longtime favorite for sausage seasoning. Dried sage also adds flavor to cheese, poultry, omelets, and meat loaf. Sage dressing is a good accompaniment to pork.

Savory

Pluck the leaves of winter savory or summer savory as they develop full flavor. Young, tender leaves are best. Discard any soiled leaves, spray with water, shake to remove moisture, and pat dry.

Dehydrator: Spread leaves in a thin layer over trays. Dry at 110°F (45°C) until leaves are brittle, about 6 to 8 hours.

Outdoors: Spread savory leaves in a thin layer over trays and place in a shady area with good cross-ventilation. Dry until brittle, about 8 to 12 hours.

Oven or Homemade Dryer: Spread savory leaves thinly over trays. Dry at 110°F (45°C) until crisp, about 6 to 8 hours.

To Use: Cool, then crumble leaves, discarding any stems. Dried savory improves almost any bean dish. Add up to ½ teaspoon (2 ml) leaves for every cup of beans before cooking. Add ¼ teaspoon (1 ml) to bread dressings and sprinkle a small amount over pork or lamb before roasting.

Tarragon

Cut the leaves and tops of young tarragon plants early in the day, as soon as the sun has dried the dew off the leaves.

Dehydrator: Spread leaves and tops over trays, removing every other tray. Dry at 110°F (45°C) until brittle, about 6 to 8 hours.

Outdoors: Spread leaves thinly over trays and place in an airy, shady area. Let dry until crisp, about 8 to 12 hours, stirring occasionally.

Oven or Homemade Dryer: Spread leaves in a thin layer over trays. Dry at 110°F (45°C) until crisp, about 8 to 12 hours or overnight.

To Use: Cool dried leaves and tops, then finely crumble. Add a pinch of dried tarragon to tomato juice or to any dish made with tomatoes. A recipe for tarragon vinegar — a favorite dressing for salads — can be found on page 119.

Thyme

Pick thyme leaves when plants first begin to flower. Discard any soiled leaves. Spray with water, shake to remove moisture, and pat dry.

Dehydrator: Spread leaves in a thin layer over trays. Dry at 110°F (45°C) until leaves are crisp, about 6 to 8 hours.

Outdoors: Spread leaves in a thin layer over trays and place in a well-ventilated area out of direct sunlight. Dry until leaves are crisp, about 8 to 12 hours. Take trays inside at night, if necessary.

Oven or Homemade Dryer: Spread leaves thinly over trays. Dry at 110°F (45°C) until crisp, about 6 to 8 hours or overnight.

To Use: Cool and crumble dried thyme leaves before storing. The strong, distinctive flavor of thyme adds character to meat loaf, onion soup, or lamb in any form. Add a pinch to Italian dishes, stew, or wild game.

Herb Mixtures

The flavors of some dried herbs are so compatible they have become traditional companions in certain dishes. The following are some of the favorite herb blends:

CHILI POWDER

1 tablespoon (15 ml) chopped dried mild chili peppers

1 teaspoon (5 ml) dried cumin seeds

1 teaspoon (5 ml) dried oregano leaves

¼ teaspoon (1 ml) chopped dried hot chili peppers

½ teaspoon (2 ml) dried garlic

1 teaspoon (5 ml) salt

Combine all herbs and pulverize to a coarse powder with a pestle or in a blender. Use for chili, barbecue sauce, bean dishes, or meat loaf.

BOUQUET GARNI

6 tablespoons (90 ml) dried parsley

3 tablespoons (45 ml) dried celery
  leaves

3 tablespoons (45 ml) chopped dried onion

3 tablespoons (45 ml) dried thyme

Tie all herbs in a small piece of cheesecloth and immerse in a pot of simmering soup or stew. Remove and discard before serving.

Fines Herbes

Fines Herbes is a French term for a combination of herbs used for specific dishes. They are finely chopped, mixed, and added to dishes just before serving. The following are some Fines Herbes combinations:

FOR PORK DISHES

1 teaspoon (5 ml) dried sage

1 teaspoon (5 ml) dried basil

1 teaspoon (5 ml) dried savory

FOR BEEF DISHES

1 teaspoon (5 ml) dried rosemary

1 teaspoon (5 ml) dried parsley

¼ teaspoon (1 ml) dried garlic

FOR POULTRY DISHES

1 teaspoon (5 ml) dried sage

1 teaspoon (5 ml) dried savory

1 teaspoon (5 ml) dried parsley

FOR LAMB DISHES

1 teaspoon (5 ml) dried parsley

1 teaspoon (5 ml) dried rosemary

1 teaspoon (5 ml) dried marjoram

FOR FISH DISHES

1 teaspoon (5 ml) dried chervil

1 teaspoon (5 ml) dried parsley

1 teaspoon (5 ml) dried savory

FOR BEAN DISHES

1 teaspoon (5 ml) dried savory

1 teaspoon (5 ml) dried onion

1 teaspoon (5 ml) dried parsley

POULTRY SEASONING

This mixture of herbs is used in stuffings for veal and pork. It is a "must" for adding flavor to poultry.

1 tablespoon (15 ml) dried sage

1 tablespoon (15 ml) dried thyme

1 tablespoon (15 ml) dried marjoram

1 tablespoon (15 ml) dried savory

1 tablespoon (15 ml) dried rosemary

Add 1 or 2 teaspoons (5 or 10 ml) of mixture to any stuffing recipe.

Herb Teas

Teas made from the dried leaves of herbs can be soothing or invigorating, spicy or mellow, served hot or cold. It all depends on which herbs you select. Most herb teas are made by steeping the dried leaves in boiling water for 5 minutes. The steeping should be timed carefully because too little steeping will leave the tea tasteless, and tea that is steeped too long can be bitter.

Camomile

Pick the daisylike flower heads of the camomile plant as soon as they open fully.

Dehydrator: Spread heads in a single layer over trays. Dry at 110°F (45°C) until crisp, about 4 to 6 hours.

Outdoors: Spread heads over trays and place in a well-ventilated, shady area. Dry until crisp, about 6 to 8 hours.

Oven or Homemade Dryer: Spread heads in a thin layer over trays. Dry until crisp at 110°F (45°C) for 8 to 12 hours.

To Use: In making tea, pour 1 quart (1 litre) boiling water over ⅓ cup (75 ml) heads and place in a warm teapot. Let steep for 5 minutes. Strain. Drink hot or cold, plain, or sweetened with sugar or honey.

Catnip

Pick young catnip leaves in early summer, before flower blossoms open.

Dehydrator: Spread leaves thinly over trays and dry at 110°F (45°C) until leaves are crisp enough to crumble, about 6 to 8 hours.

Outdoors: Spread leaves in a thin layer over trays and dry in a well-ventilated, shady area. Dry until crisp enough to crumble, about 8 to 10 hours.

Oven or Homemade Dryer: Spread leaves thinly over trays. Dry at 110°F (45°C) until crisp, about 6 to 8 hours.

To Use: Crumble leaves and store in small glass jars. Place ⅓ cup (75 ml) leaves in a heated teapot. Cover with 1 quart (1 litre) boiling water and steep for 5 minutes. Drink hot or cold, plain or sweetened.

Horehound

Cut a few woody branches of the horehound plant in midsummer, when plants are covered with bud clusters. Cut or break branches into 3- to 4-inch (7.5- to 10-cm) pieces.

Dehydrator: Spread pieces thinly over trays and dry for 18 to 24 hours at 115°F (47.5°C) until dried through. Store whole branches in glass jars.

Sun: Spread broken branches over trays and place in a well-ventilated area in sun. Dry until branches snap easily in the hands, about 2 to 3 days. Store whole pieces in glass jars.

Oven or Homemade Dryer: Spread broken pieces over trays. Dry at 115°F (47.5°C) for 18 to 24 hours, or until brittle. Store pieces in glass jars.

To Use: Break up three 4-inch (10-cm) pieces for each quart of water. Cover with cold water in a saucepan and slowly bring to a boil over low heat. Turn off heat and let steep for 10 minutes. Dilute to taste. Serve hot, sweetened with honey.

Lemon Balm

Cut sprigs of the lemon balm plant when blossoms begin to form. Chop lemon-scented leaves and stems into ½-inch (12-mm) pieces.

Dehydrator: Spread chopped leaves and stems over trays in a thin layer. Dry at 110°F (45°C) until crisp, about 6 to 8 hours. Crumble and store in glass jars.

Outdoors: Tie a few sprigs together with string at the stem end and hang upside down or spread chopped pieces over trays. Place in a shady area with good circulation and dry until crisp, about 8 to 12 hours for chopped pieces, 2 to 3 days for sprigs. Store in glass jars. Take trays inside at night, if necessary.

Oven or Homemade Dryer: Spread chopped pieces over trays in a thin layer. Dry at 110°F (45°C) until crisp, about 6 to 8 hours. Crumble and store in glass jars.

To Use: In a heated teapot, steep ⅓ cup (75 ml) leaves in 1 quart (1 litre) boiling water for 5 minutes. Drink hot or cold, sweetened or plain.

Lemongrass

Cut long blades from the cactuslike lemongrass plant. Wash and drain well. With a pair of scissors, cut into ½-inch (12-mm) pieces.

Dehydrator: Spread blades thinly over trays. Dry at 110°F (45°C) until crisp enough to crumble in the hands, about 6 to 8 hours. Cool and crumble before storing.

Outdoors: Spread blades in a thin layer over trays and place in a well-ventilated, shady area. Dry, stirring occasionally, until crisp, about 8 to 10 hours. Crumble after cooling.

Oven or Homemade Dryer: Spread blades thinly over trays. Dry at 110°F (45°C) until crisp, about 6 to 8 hours. Cool and crumble before storing in glass jars.

To Use: Measure ⅓ cup (75 ml) blades in a saucepan. Cover with 1 quart (1 litre) cold water. Bring to a boil, turn off heat, and let steep for 10 to 15 minutes. Serve as a hot or cold beverage, plain or sweetened with honey or sugar.

Rose Hips

In late fall, after the leaves have dropped, cut partially dried, orange-red rose hips from rose bushes. Cut off and discard both ends and cut remainder into thin slices.

Dehydrator: Spread slices thinly over trays and dry at 110°F (45°C), stirring occasionally. Dry for 12 to 18 hours, or until crisp and hard.

Outdoors: Spread slices over trays in a thin layer and dry in a well-ventilated, shady area for 2 or 3 days, until crisp and hard. Take trays inside at night.

Oven or Homemade Dryer: Spread slices thinly over trays. Dry at 110°F (45°C) until crisp, about 18 to 24 hours, stirring occasionally.

To Use: Although rose hips have little flavor, they are rich in vitamin C and are a good winter source of that vitamin. Rose hip tea benefits from the addition of other herbs, such as lemon balm or mint. To make rose hip tea, cover ⅓ cup (75 ml) dried rose hips with 1 quart (1 litre) cold water. Cover and slowly bring to a boil. Simmer over low heat for 15 minutes. Strain liquid, mashing the hips with a fork to extract all the vitamin-rich juice. Drink hot or cold with a spoonful of lemon juice and honey or sugar.

Sassafras

Harvest the bark or root of the sassafras tree in early fall. Cut into thin shavings, finely chop or grind.

Dehydrator: Spread bark or root thinly over trays and dry at 115°F (47.5°C) for 8 to 12 hours. Cool and store.

Sun: Spread bark or root in a thin layer over trays and place in sun. Dry for 1 to 2 days, stirring occasionally and taking inside at night. Cool and store.

Oven or Homemade Dryer: Spread bark or root thinly over trays. Dry at 115°F (47.5°C) for 8 to 12 hours, or until crisp. Cool and store.

To Use: Place ⅓ cup (75 ml) in a saucepan. Cover with 1 quart (1 litre) cold water. Place over low heat and slowly bring to a boil. Remove from heat and let set for 10 minutes.

Solar Tea

Most herb teas may be made this energy- and vitamin-saving way. Just place ½ cup (125 ml) dried herbs in a 2-quart (2-litre) clear glass jar. Fill with cold water to within 1 inch (25 mm) of top. Screw lid on tightly and shake well. Place in sun for 5 to 6 hours. Strain off liquid and add sugar or honey. Chill before serving.

Herb Tea Blends

For variety and delicious blending of flavors, try these combinations of dried herb leaves:

ROSE HIP SPARKLE

2 tablespoons (30 ml) dried rose hip slices

3 tablespoons (45 ml) crumbled dried peppermint leaves

2 tablespoons (30 ml) crumbled dried orange blossoms

To Use: Simmer dried rose hips in 1½ quarts (1½ litres) water for 15 minutes. Remove from heat. Add peppermint leaves and dried orange blossoms and let steep for 5 minutes.

PEPPERMINT PLEASURE

2 tablespoons (30 ml) dried peppermint leaves

2 tablespoons (30 ml) dried rosemary leaves

To Use: Steep in 1 quart (1 litre) of boiling water for 5 minutes.

CAMOMILE CALMER

3 tablespoons (45 ml) dried camomile flowers

3 tablespoons (45 ml) dried lemon balm leaves

To Use: Steep for 5 minutes in 1 quart (1 litre) boiling water.

COMMERCIAL TEAS

Add interest and flavor to commercial teas by adding ¼ teaspoon (1 ml) dried peppermint, spearmint, lemon balm, or thyme to a pot of steeping tea.

Herb Butters

Add 1 teaspoon (5 ml) dried dill, chives, chervil, fennel, marjoram, or tarragon to ½ cup (125 ml) butter or margarine. Blend well. Cover and leave at room temperature for 2 hours to blend flavors.

Herb butter may be stored for several days in the refrigerator. To use, spread over fried or broiled meat or fish. Just before serving, add to scrambled eggs or spread on bread when making sandwiches.

Herbal Vinegars

Herb-flavored vinegars are an expensive delicacy in gourmet food shops. They add piquancy and zest to salads and cooked vegetables. Herbal vinegars should be stored in sterilized bottles that are either capped or corked.

DRIED BASIL VINEGAR

1 quart (1 litre) red wine vinegar

1½ tablespoons (25 ml) crumbled dried basil leaves

Bring vinegar to a boil. Remove from heat, add basil leaves, and let stand for 48 hours. Strain. Makes 1 quart (1 litre).

TARRAGON VINEGAR

1 quart (1 litre) red wine
1 pint (475 ml) cider vinegar
¼ teaspoon (1 ml) dried garlic

2 tablespoons (30 ml) crumbled dried tarragon leaves
2 whole cloves

Combine all ingredients in an enameled saucepan. Let stand for 2 hours. Simmer for 15 minutes over low heat. Strain and chill before using. Makes 1½ quarts (1½ litres).

HERBAL WINE VINEGAR

1 quart (1 litre) white vinegar
1 quart (1 litre) dry red or white wine
1 teaspoon (5 ml) crumbled dried tarragon leaves
4 whole cloves

2 teaspoons (10 ml) crumbled dried lemon balm leaves
6 dried bay leaves
¼ teaspoon (1 ml) minced dried garlic

Combine all ingredients in a kettle and place over low heat. Bring slowly to a boil, cover, and simmer for 10 minutes. Strain through filter paper or double thickness of cheesecloth. Cool. Store in tightly covered, sterilized bottles. Makes 2 quarts (2 litres).

SAGE VINEGAR _____

1 quart (1 litre) white wine vinegar   1 tablespoon (15 ml) crumbled dried
                                              sage leaves

*Heat vinegar to boiling point. Turn off heat and add sage leaves. Let stand for 24 hours
before using. Strain. Makes 1 quart (1 litre).*

Drying Meats

Anglers and hunters take notice: Here's a time-honored method of preserving and storing your catch or take.

A time-honored method? Of course. American Indians were using it in this country centuries before our explorers set out to "spread learning" and wound up learning a thing or two themselves.

Spanish explorers were among the early discoverers of this method of saving a bit of today's meat for tomorrow's meal. As they pushed through Mexico, Central America, and the southwestern part of this country, they found Indians cutting meat into long strips and drying it in the wind and sun. The Indians called this *charqui*, pronounced "sharky." As English explorers moved in, they picked up that name for dried meat, and it gradually changed to "jerky" or "jerked beef."

Most North American Indian tribes used some method of drying meat, refining the system used. One advancement was to pound the dried meat with a rock, pound it and pound it, and gradually mix it with fat, dried fruits, and vegetables. The result was "pemmican." That dish and today's variations of it provided ideal food, concentrated and energy packed, for the trail, be it the Long Trail or the war trail.

Another variation was probably originated on a cool, rainy day when meat that was hanging in the sun was suddenly hanging in the rain. The long strips of meat were then carried into the tepee and hung there. It was a day when the fire was smoking and the tepee ventilation system needed servicing. The result was a new dish, smoked jerky, with a finer flavor and possibly longer lasting powers.

Today's hunters and anglers can use these same historic methods for preserving food, and if they take care in their work, the results will be more than edible, they will be eaten with relish.

Meats may be dried in much the same way vegetables and fruits are dried. There are, however, a few more precautions to take when drying meats than when drying fruits and vegetables. Meat is made up of both lean and fat portions, and while the lean keeps well when dried, the fat portion will soon turn rancid. To avoid this, only the leanest meat should be dried, and all possible fat should be removed before drying.

Select only very fresh, lean beef, venison, poultry, lamb, and fish for long-term storage. Very lean dried meats may be stored a year or more. Most cuts of pork do not dry well because of the high-fat content, but lean portions of ham may be dried and stored for several months.

With one exception, meats to be dried should be fully cooked, which makes drying an ideal way of preserving leftover roast turkey or pot roast. The exception to using cooked meat is jerky. Information on jerky can be found on pages 127 to 129.

Beef and Venison

Select a tender roasting cut with as little fat as possible and trim off any bits of fat. Steam, braise, or simmer in a small amount of water until tender, about 2 hours, or cook in a pressure cooker for 35 minutes. Remove from heat, drain and cool. Cut into ½-inch (12-mm) cubes, keeping cubes as uniform in size as possible for even drying.

Dehydrator: Spread cubes sparingly over trays. Dry at 140°F (60°C), stirring occasionally, for 6 hours. Reduce heat to 130°F (55°C) and continue drying until cubes are hard and dried through. Test for dryness by cooling a cube and trying to cut through the center. Well-dried meat should be too hard to cut easily and should have no moisture in the center.

Sun: Spread cooked cubes in a thin layer over trays and place in a well-ventilated place in full sun. Dry until hard, stirring occasionally. Drying time will depend on the weather and the moisture in the meat, but should be from 2 to 3 days. Take trays inside at night.

Oven or Homemade Dryer: Spread cooked cubes in a thin layer over trays. Dry at 140°F (60°C) for 6 hours, then stir cubes and rotate trays. Lower temperature to 130°F (55°C) and continue drying until hard. Keep door of oven or dryer ajar.

To Use: Pour 1 cup (250 ml) boiling water over 1 cup (250 ml) meat cubes. Soak for 3 to 4 hours, or until water is absorbed. Use in any recipe calling for cooked meat. Or pour boiling water over meat and simmer over low heat for 45 to 50 minutes, then use.

DRIED MEAT-VEGETABLE STEW

3 cups (750 ml) boiling water

1½ cups (375 ml) dried meat cubes

½ cup (125 ml) dried carrot slices

½ cup (125 ml) dried peas

½ cup (125 ml) dried green beans

½ cup (125 ml) dried celery slices

½ cup (125 ml) dried parsnip slices

1 tablespoon (15 ml) chopped dried onion

¼ cup (65 ml) all-purpose flour

¼ cup water

Salt and pepper to taste

Pour boiling water over dried beef or venison cubes in a large stewing kettle. Simmer for 1 hour, or until meat is tender. Add all dried vegetables and simmer for another 30 to 45 minutes. Blend flour and water in a cup. Gradually stir into cooked mixture and cook, stirring constantly, until gravy is thickened. Season with salt and pepper. Serves 6 to 8.

Ham

Select very lean, well-cured ham. Trim off all fat. Because it is a cured meat, ham may be dried without cooking, but it is more tender if it is cooked before drying. Cut into uniform-sized pieces about ¼-inch (65-mm) square or in very thin slices, then cut into pieces about 2 inches (5 cm) wide.

Dehydrator: Spread pieces or slices one layer deep over trays. Dry for 4 hours at 140°F (60°C). Lower temperature to 130°F (54.4°C) and dry until pieces are hard and dried through. Stir pieces occasionally and rotate trays once or twice during drying.

Sun: Spread pieces or slices in a thin layer over trays and place in a well-ventilated area in full sun. Dry until hard, stirring or turning pieces occasionally. Take trays inside at night. Drying will take 2 to 3 days.

Oven or Homemade Dryer: Spread pieces or slices in a single layer over trays. Dry for 5 hours at 140°F (60°C) or until hard and dried through, stirring or turning pieces occasionally.

To Use: Pour 1 cup (250 ml) boiling water over 1 cup (250 ml) pieces or slices in a saucepan. Cover and cook over low heat for about 1 hour, or until tender. Use in any cooked dish or casserole calling for cooked ham. Dried ham should be used within 3 months.

DRIED HAM IN RICE

½ cup (125 ml) dried ham pieces

1 quart (1 litre) boiling water

1 cup (250 ml) uncooked white rice

2 tablespoons (30 ml) grated dried carrot

2 tablespoons (30 ml) chopped dried celery

1 tablespoon (15 ml) butter or margarine

2 teaspoons (10 ml) chicken-flavored bouillon granules, or 2 chicken-flavored bouillon cubes

½ cup (125 ml) boiling water

1 teaspoon (5 ml) soy sauce

1 tablespoon (15 ml) chopped chives or dried green onion tops

Simmer dried ham in 1 quart (1 litre) boiling water for 1 hour over low heat, or until tender. Add water to make 3 cups (750 ml). Bring to a boil, then add rice, dried carrot, dried celery, and butter or margarine. Bring again to boil, reduce heat, cover, and cook for 20 minutes without lifting lid. Dissolve chicken granules or bouillon cube in ½ cup (125 ml) boiling water. Stir in soy sauce and add to cooked rice mixture. Mix lightly. Place in a serving dish and top with chopped dried chives or dried green onion tops. Serves 6 to 8.

DRIED HAM AND APPLE DUMPLINGS_____

½ cup dried ham pieces

2 quarts (2 litres) boiling water

1 cup (250 ml) dried apple slices

2 tablespoons (30 ml) brown sugar

1 cup (250 ml) all-purpose flour

1 teaspoon (5 ml) baking powder

¼ teaspoon (1 ml) salt

1 egg

2 tablespoons (30 ml) butter or margarine

½ cup (125 ml) milk

Cover ham with boiling water in a heavy kettle. Bring to a boil. Simmer for 1 hour, or until tender. Add dried apples and simmer for another 30 to 45 minutes. Add brown sugar. Meanwhile, in a mixing bowl, sift together flour, baking powder, and salt. Add butter, egg, and enough milk to make a stiff batter. Drop batter by spoonful into simmering liquid in pot. Cover and steam for 15 to 20 minutes. Serves 6 to 8.

Poultry

Select very fresh chicken or turkey. Duck and goose meat is too fat for drying. Steam or simmer until tender. Cool. Remove skin and any fat. Cut meat into uniform-sized pieces ¼ to ½ inch (5 to 15 mm) square.

Dehydrator: Spread cooked cubes in a thin layer over trays. Dry at 140°F (60°C) for 4 hours, then lower temperature to 130°F (55°C) and dry until cubes are hard and dried through. Stir occasionally and rotate trays once or twice.

Sun: Spread cooked cubes thinly over trays and place in a well-ventilated area in full sun. Dry until hard, stirring occasionally. Take trays inside at night. Test for dryness by trying to cut with a knife. Well-dried poultry should be too hard to cut easily. Drying time will vary, but should take 2 to 3 days.

Oven or Homemade Dryer: Spread cooked cubes in a thin layer over trays. Dry at 140°F (60°C) for 6 hours, keeping door ajar, then stir cubes and rotate trays. Lower temperature to 130°F (55°C) and continue drying until hard and dried through.

To Use: Pour 1 cup (250 ml) boiling water over 1 cup (250 ml) cubes in a saucepan. Cover and cook over low heat for 45 to 50 minutes, or until tender. Use in any cooked dish or casserole calling for cooked poultry.

DRIED CHICKEN-NOODLE CASSEROLE _____

4 cups (4 litres) boiling water

2 cups (500 ml) dried chicken cubes

¼ cup (65 ml) dried celery slices

1 tablespoon (15 ml) minced dried onion

2 cups (500 ml) dried noodles

2 chicken-flavored bouillon cubes, or 2 teaspoons (10 ml) chicken-flavored bouillon granules

½ teaspoon (2 ml) salt

2 tablespoons (30 ml) dried parsley flakes

Pour boiling water over dried chicken cubes in a stewing kettle. Cover and simmer for 45 to 50 minutes, or until tender. Add dried celery, onion, and noodles and simmer for another 30 minutes or more, or until noodles are tender. Add bouillon and salt. Sprinkle parsley flakes over top. Serves 6.

Lamb

Select a lean roasting cut of young lamb. Trim off any fat. Steam until tender or cook in a pressure cooker for 20 minutes at 15 pounds (6.8 kilograms) pressure. Cool and cut into ½-inch (15-mm) cubes.

Dehydrator: Spread cooked cubes thinly over trays. Dry at 140°F (60°C) for 4 to 6 hours. Stir well, rotate trays, and lower temperature to 130°F (55°C). Continue drying until cubes are hard and dried through.

Sun: Spread cooked cubes thinly over trays and place in a well-ventilated area in full sun. Dry until hard and dried through, about 2 to 3 days, stirring occasionally. Take trays inside at night.

Oven or Homemade Dryer: Spread cooked cubes in a thin layer over trays. Dry at 140°F (60°C) for 4 to 6 hours, keeping door ajar, then stir cubes and rotate trays. Lower temperature to 130°F (55°C) and continue drying until cubes are hard and dried through.

To Use: Pour 1 cup (250 ml) boiling water over 1 cup (250 ml) cubes in a saucepan and simmer for 45 to 50 minutes, or until tender. One cup (250 ml) yields about 1½ cups (375 ml) cooked meat.

HERBED DRIED LAMB

1½ cups (375 ml) dried lamb cubes

½ teaspoon (2 ml) chopped dried garlic

¼ cup (65 ml) chopped dried green onion

1 dried bay leaf

½ teaspoon (2 ml) dried basil

½ teaspoon (2 ml) dried oregano

¼ teaspoon (1 ml) dried rosemary

6 black peppercorns

4 cups (1 litre) boiling water

1 cup (250 ml) dried carrots

1 cup (250 ml) dried onion slices

1 cup (250 ml) dried celery slices

½ cup (125 ml) dried tomato slices

½ cup (125 ml) dried peas

6 medium potatoes, cut into 1-inch (25-mm) cubes

½ cup (125 ml) white wine

¼ cup (65 ml) cornstarch

¼ cup (65 ml) water

Salt to taste

Combine the first nine ingredients in a large pot. Cover and simmer over low heat for 1 hour, or until lamb is tender. Add dried vegetables and cook for 30 minutes more. Add potatoes and wine and cook for 20 minutes more, or until potatoes are tender. Remove bay leaf and peppercorns. Combine cornstarch and ¼ cup (62.5 ml) water in a cup. Remove meat and vegetables to a serving dish with a slotted spoon. Add corn-starch and water mixture to liquid in pot and cook, stirring constantly, until thickened. Season with salt and pour over meat and vegetables. Serves 6.

Fish

Clean and scale fish. Soak for 30 minutes in a solution of ¼ cup (65 ml) flake salt dissolved in 1 quart (1 litre) water. Drain, remove skin, and cut meat into small, uniform-sized pieces. Or clean and scale fish and leave small fish whole. Fillet large fish or cut crosswise into steaks. Steam pieces or fillets for 10 minutes and whole fish and steaks for 15 to 20 minutes, or until flaky. Remove skins and cut meat into pieces or flake with a fork, keeping pieces uniform in size.

Dehydrator: Spread pieces of fish sparsely over trays. Dry at 140°F (60°C) for 2 hours, stirring pieces occasionally and rotating trays. Lower temperature to 130°F (55°C) and dry until hard. Do not dry fish with other foods.

Leave fillets, steaks, or very small fish whole. Remove skins and dry at 140°F (60°C) for 4 to 6 hours. Lower temperature to 130°F (55°C), turn fish, and rotate trays. Continue drying for another 4 to 6 hours before testing for dryness.

Sun: Lay pieces of cooked fish over trays and place in a well-ventilated area in full sun. Dry for 1 to 3 days, depending on size of pieces. Turn or stir pieces occasionally and take trays inside at night.

Oven or Homemade Dryer: Spread pieces over trays. Dry at 140°F (60°C) for 4 to 6 hours. Turn pieces, rotate trays, and lower temperature to 130°F (55°C). Continue drying until dried through. Do not dry fish with other foods.

To Use: Soak fish in boiling water to cover. If fish is salted, discard any remaining soaking water and add 1 cup (250 ml) fresh water for steaming. If not salted, use soaking water to steam fish for 10 to 15 minutes. Use as you would cooked fish. One cup (250 ml) yields about 1¼ cups (315 ml) cooked fish.

DRIED FISH-VEGETABLE PIE

2 cups (500 ml) boiling water

2 cups (500 ml) dried fish

4 tablespoons (60 ml) butter or margarine

6 tablespoons (90 ml) all-purpose flour

¼ teaspoon (1 ml) black pepper

3 cups (750 ml) milk

½ cup (125 ml) dried peas

1 tablespoon (15 ml) chopped dried onion

½ cup (125 ml) dried celery slices

½ cup (125 ml) dried carrot slices

1½ cups (375 ml) boiling water

Salt to taste

3½ cups (875 ml) seasoned mashed-potatoes

Pour 2 cups (500 ml) boiling water over dried fish. Let soak for 30 minutes. If fish was soaked in salt water before drying, drain off water and add fresh. If not, use soaking water to simmer fish until tender, about 10 to 15 minutes. Meanwhile, melt butter or margarine in a small saucepan over low heat. Stir in flour and pepper and gradually add milk. Cook, stirring constantly, until thickened. Set aside. Cook dried vegetables in 1½ cups (375 ml) boiling water until tender, about 30 to 35 minutes. Drain. Combine cooked fish, white sauce, and cooked vegetables in a 1½-quart (1½-litre) casserole. Season with salt and top with a border of mashed potatoes. Bake in 350°F (180°C) oven for 30 to 45 minutes, or until lightly browned. Serves 6.

Jerky

There are many methods for making jerky. In the past, the simplest — but hardly the safest — was to cut the meat into strips and hang them in the sun.

Oceanside North American Indian tribes improved on this by soaking the strips in seawater before drying them. That idea is still used by those who soak the strips in brine before drying.

Another Indian method was to hang the strips over a slow-burning fire of hardwood, or even an aromatic wood. The strips weren't near enough to the fire to cook, but were near enough to hasten drying and to keep off flies.

Another step forward was taken when pepper was pounded into the meat, adding flavor. The next step was a logical one — to soak the meat in a marinade. We find this the best way to produce a jerky that is tasty as well as nourishing.

Don't consider jerky an all-purpose food. It is, of course, high in protein, but it lacks both fat and vitamin C. It's fine for a few meals on the trail, since it can be eaten cold, requiring vigorous chewing, or it can be the basis for many a recipe for stew.

Delicious, nourishing jerky can be made inexpensively of strips of almost any lean meat marinated in soy or Worcestershire sauce, brushed with liquid smoke, or sprinkled with garlic powder or seasoned salt. There are many ways to add flavor to jerky.

No matter how well you make jerky, consider its shelf life short. Keep it in plastic bags or glass jars, so it will not absorb moisture, and store the containers in the refrigerator or freezer for maximum safe storage. Eat the jerky within 6 months.

BEEF JERKY

2 pounds (800 grams) very lean beef (chuck or round)

¼ cup (65 ml) Worcestershire sauce

¼ cup (65 ml) soy sauce

1 tablespoon (15 ml) tomato sauce

1 tablespoon (15 ml) white vinegar

1 teaspoon (5 ml) granulated sugar

¼ teaspoon (1 ml) chopped dried garlic

¼ teaspoon (1 ml) chopped dried onion

1 teaspoon (5 ml) salt

Trim off all traces of fat from meat. Freeze until firm and solid enough to slice easily. Cut across the grain into very thin, ⅛-inch (3-mm) slices, then cut slices into strips 1 to 1½ inches (25 to 35 mm) wide. Meanwhile, combine remaining ingredients in a blender or shaker jar. Pour over meat strips that have been arranged in rows in a shallow baking pan. Refrigerate overnight, then drain strips.

Dehydrator: Cover trays with strips without overlapping. Dry for 4 hours at 140°F (60°C). Turn strips and rotate trays. Dry for another 6 to 8 hours. Well-dried jerky should be dark and fibrous looking and brittle enough to splinter when bent in half.

Sun: Drying jerky in the sun is not recommended in most climates.

Oven or Homemade Dryer: Lay strips of marinated meat in rows over trays, being careful not to overlap strips. Dry at 140°F (60°C) until strips will splinter on the edges when bent in half, about 18 to 24 hours.

VENISON, TURKEY, OR CHICKEN JERKY

4 pounds (2 kilogram) venison, turkey, or chicken

1 cup (250 ml) barbecue sauce

2 tablespoons (30 ml) liquid smoke

1 teaspoon (5 ml) chili powder

1 tablespoon (15 ml) Worcestershire sauce

Dash cayenne pepper

Freeze meat until firm and solid enough to slice easily. Cut into ⅛-inch (3-mm) slices with a sharp knife or slicer, then cut slices into strips 1½ inches (40 mm) wide. Meanwhile, blend remaining ingredients and pour over meat strips that have been arranged in rows in a shallow baking pan. Marinate overnight in refrigerator. Drain well. Dry venison, turkey, or chicken following the same guideline given for Beef Jerky, above.

HAMBURGER JERKY

1 pound (400 grams) very lean ground beef

1 tablespoon (15 ml) Worcestershire sauce

1 teaspoon (5 ml) seasoned salt

¼ teaspoon (1 ml) minced dried onion

For the leanest ground beef that will keep well in storage, buy ground beef with as little fat as possible or select a lean chuck roast and have it ground. Combine meat with remaining ingredients, mixing well. Cut a piece of plastic wrap the size of your drying tray. Put seasoned ground beef on plastic wrap and, using a moistened rolling pin, roll ground beef to ⅛-inch (3-mm) thick, spreading meat over entire area of tray.

Dehydrator: Place meat-covered plastic wrap on tray and dry at 140°F (60°C). Dry for 4 to 6 hours. Remove tray, plastic wrap-side up. Peel off wrap and discard.

Roll paper towels over top with a rolling pin to remove melted fat. Invert meat onto another tray, plastic wrap-side up. Peel off wrap and discard. Return meat to dehydrator and dry for another 4 to 6 hours. Top with paper towels and roll again to absorb fat. Dry until jerky is hard and leathery. Cut into strips before storing.

Sun: Drying jerky in the sun is not recommended in most climates.

Oven or Homemade Dryer: Lay meat-covered plastic wrap on tray and dry at 140°F (60°C). Dry for 4 to 6 hours with door ajar. Remove tray to countertop and cover with a layer of paper towels. Roll gently with a rolling pin to remove any melted fat. Invert meat onto another tray. Peel off plastic wrap and discard. Return meat to oven or dryer for another 4 to 6 hours. Cover top with paper towels and roll to remove fat again. Test for dryness before cutting into strips. Dried jerky should be hard and leathery.

Drying Dairy Products

Cheese

Cheese with high-fat content will not keep long in storage, but may be refrigerated or frozen. Grate Parmesan cheese or shred any variety of dry cheese.

Dehydrator: Cover trays with paper towels. Spread grated or shredded cheese over top. Dry at 120°F (50°C) until hard. Stir cheese occasionally, rotate trays, and change paper towels at least once as the melted fat accumulates. Drying will take 6 to 8 hours.

Sun: Cover trays with paper towels and spread grated or shredded cheese over the towels. Dry in full sun in a well-ventilated place until hard and dry, stirring cheese occasionally and replacing paper towels at least once. Will dry in 1 to 2 days. Take trays inside at night.

Oven or Homemade Dryer: Cover trays with paper towels. Spread cheese over towels and dry at 120°F (50°C). Stir occasionally, rotate trays once or twice, and replace paper towels at least once. Dry for 6 to 8 hours.

To Use: Use in cheese sauces, over meat sauce, or to top casseroles.

Milk

Drying milk is a time-consuming process and not as satisfactory as buying the inexpensive dry milk powders available in the supermarket. It also has a shorter storage life, because any cream in the milk has a tendency to turn rancid. If you have, however, a surplus of pasteurized milk (directions for pasteurization follow) and would like to try it, here's how:

Remove as much cream as possible from the milk by skimming or running through a separator. Pour a thin (about ⅛-inch) (3-mm) layer of the skimmed pasteurized milk on trays that have been lined with plastic wrap or aluminum foil.

Dehydrator, Oven, or Homemade Dryer: Dry for 36 to 48 hours at 120°F (50°C) until milk flakes. Powder by pounding with a pestle or running through a blender.

Sun: Drying milk in the sun is not recommended.

To Use: This powder *must be* used dry in baked or cooked foods. Add ⅓ cup (75 ml) powder to dry ingredients and ⅔ cup (150 ml) water in place of 1 cup (250 ml) milk called for in recipe. To make 1 cup (250 ml) liquid milk, measure ⅓ cup (75 ml) powder in a measuring cup and add water to fill. Combine in a blender or shaker. It is more difficult to dissolve than the instant dry milk granules made commercially.

To pasteurize milk: Fill sterilized, heat-tempered jars 1 to 2 inches (25 to 50 mm) from the top with milk. Place jars on a rack in a deep kettle. Add water to come up to the level of the milk. Put a sterile dairy thermometer in one of the jars. Heat the water. When the thermometer registers 145°F (65°C), hold the heat at that temperature for 30 minutes. Cool the milk rapidly by placing the jars in cold water until the milk reaches 50° to 40°F (10 to 5°C). Refrigerate any milk you do not dry.

Eggs

Only the use of commercially dried pasturized egg powder is recommended due to the possible contamination of eggs by bacteria.

To Use: Use in baked goods, such as muffins, pancakes, and cookies or in egg dishes calling for beaten eggs. For each egg needed, combine 1½ tablespoons (25 ml) egg powder with 1½ tablespoons (25 ml) water.

CHAPTER ELEVEN

Drying Grains

Freshly harvested grains often must be dried before being stored in airtight containers. Grain dryers are used for crops grown for commercial use, but grains grown and stored for home use may be dried in small batches in the kitchen (or outside the kitchen door).

Grains, such as wheat, barley, oats, and rye are harvested when the stalks are dry and yellow, but before the seeds scatter. Corn is dried on the stalk as long as the weather allows.

Ideally, grains should have a moisture content of about 10 to 12 percent to prevent mold and spoilage during storage. If you have access to a commercial tester, this is easily measured. If you do not, it is possible to estimate moisture content. The smaller grains are dry when they have a hard, crunchy texture and a pleasant nutty taste when chewed. Well-dried corn kernels have a shriveled appearance or a dimpled end, depending on the variety.

Unless the grain is harvested in very dry weather, it should be dried to some extent before storage.

Grains

Dehydrator: Spread trays with a ½-inch (15-mm) layer of wheat, barley, rye, oats, or buckwheat that has been partially dried on the stalk. Dry at 115°F (48°C) for 12 to 18 hours or more, stirring occasionally.

Sun: Dry small batches of wheat, barley, rye, oats, or buckwheat spread thinly on trays in full sun. Large batches may be spread out on sheets of plastic in the sun. Dry for 1 to 2 days, stirring occasionally and taking trays inside at night. Grain dried in the sun should be placed in 125°F (50°C) oven for 1 to 2 hours or stored in freezer for 2 to 3 days to destroy any insect eggs deposited during drying.

Oven or Homemade Dryer: Spread small grains in a thin layer over trays. Dry at 115°F (48°C) for 18 to 24 hours, stirring occasionally.

Corn

Dehydrator: Spread shelled corn over trays in a single layer. Dry at 115°F (48°C), stirring occasionally and rotating trays once or twice. Drying time will vary from 12 to 18 hours.

Sun: Spread corn kernels thinly over trays and dry in hot sun where there is good air circulation. Stir once or twice a day and take trays inside at night. Drying time will vary from 2 to 3 days.

Oven or Homemade Dryer: Spread shelled corn in a thin layer over trays. Dry at 115°F (48°C), stirring occasionally and rotating trays until kernels are hard and dried through, about 18 to 24 hours.

To Use Grains: Grind in an electric grain mill or hand grinder. If grinder is adjustable, set it at medium-coarse grind for corn, at fine grind for smaller grains. An electric blender may be used to grind small amounts. Grind only enough grain to be used at one time. Ground grains lose flavor and vitamins in storage and are likely to turn rancid. Grains dried at the temperatures recommended may be used for seed. One cup (250 ml) dried small grains yields about 1½ cups (375 ml) flour. One cup (250 ml) dried corn yields about ¾ cup (190 ml) cornmeal.

BOSTON BROWN BREAD

1 cup (250 ml) finely ground dried wheat

1 cup (250 ml) finely ground dried rye

1 cup (250 ml) medium-ground dried corn

1½ teaspoons (7 ml) baking soda

1½ teaspoons (7 ml) salt

¾ cup (190 ml) molasses

2 cups (500 ml) buttermilk

Combine all dry ingredients. Add molasses and buttermilk. Fill a greased 2-quart (2-litre) mold two-thirds full and cover loosely with aluminum foil. Set mold on a rack in a large kettle. Pour boiling water around the outside, half way to the top of mold. Cover kettle tightly and steam over medium heat for 3½ hours, keeping water boiling around the mold the entire time. Add boiling water as needed. Remove mold from water, take off foil, and run a spatula around the inside of mold to loosen bread. Invert mold. Serve hot.

Breakfast Cereals

Homemade breakfast cereals are delicious and far more nutritious than many commercially made ready-to-eat cereals. Try these for whole-grain goodness:

WHOLE WHEAT FLAKES

2 cups (500 ml) finely ground dried wheat (approximately)

1 teaspoon (5 ml) ground cinnamon

1 teaspoon (5 ml) ground nutmeg

½ teaspoon (2 ml) salt

½ teaspoon (2 ml) baking soda

¼ cup (65 ml) warm water

½ cup (125 ml) molasses

Combine 1 cup (250 ml) ground dried wheat with spices and salt. Dissolve baking soda in water and stir quickly into molasses. Add the flour mixture, then enough of the ground wheat to make a very stiff dough. Roll very thin and cut into strips. Serves 10 after drying.

Dehydrator: Lay strips on trays without overlapping. Dry at highest setting until crisp, about 4 to 6 hours. Remove and cool. Crumble into small, flaky pieces. Spread over trays again and dry at highest setting for another 2 hours, or until very crisp.

Sun: Lay strips over trays and dry in full sun where there is good air circulation. Dry until crisp, about 6 to 8 hours, turning once. Crumble into small pieces and spread over trays. Continue drying for another 2 to 4 hours, stirring occasionally. Take trays inside at night, if necessary.

Oven or Homemade Dryer: Lay strips on trays. Dry at 150°F (65°C) for 4 to 6 hours with door ajar until crisp. Remove from oven or dryer and crumble, then return to trays and dry for another 2 to 4 hours, or until very crisp.

To Use: Store in an airtight container or in several small containers. Serve with sugar and milk as a ready-to-eat cereal.

GRANOLA CEREAL

3 cups (750 ml) uncooked rolled oats

½ cup (125 ml) toasted ground soy beans

1 cup (250 ml) coarsely shredded coconut

½ cup (125 ml) sunflower seeds

½ teaspoon (2 ml) salt

½ cup (125 ml) honey

1 teaspoon (5 ml) pure vanilla extract

Combine oats, soybeans, coconut, sunflower seeds, and salt in a bowl. In a cup, combine honey and vanilla. Drizzle honey mixture over dry ingredients and mix well. Serves 10 after drying.

Dehydrator: Cover fine mesh trays with a thin layer of granola. (Coarse mesh trays must first be covered with cheesecloth or plastic wrap, which will lengthen drying time.) Dry at highest dehydrator setting, stirring occasionally and rotating trays once. Dry until crisp, about 6 to 8 hours.

Sun: Spread granola over cookie sheets and dry in full sun until crisp, about 8 to 10 hours. Stir occasionally and take cookie sheets in at night.

Oven or Homemade Dryer: Spread granola over trays (or cookie sheets if mesh is too large). Dry at 150°F (65°C) until crisp, stirring occasionally.

To Use: Store in small batches in tightly closed containers. The oil usually used in granola is omitted for better storage. Serve as a snack or as a ready-to-eat cereal with milk.

OAT CRISPS

2½ cups (625 ml) uncooked rolled oats

½ cup (125 ml) honey

2 eggs (use commercially dried pasteurized eggs)

½ teaspoon (2 ml) salt

2 teaspoons (10 ml) baking powder

1 teaspoon (5 ml) pure vanilla extract

Put all ingredients in a blender jar. Blend, adding just enough water to make a thick batter.

Dehydrator: Spread batter thinly (about ⅛-inch (3-mm) thick) over plastic-covered trays. Dry at highest heat setting until firm and dry on top. Flip over and peel off plastic wrap. Discard wrap and dry for another 3 to 4 hours, or until crisp. Crumble with the hands and return to dehydrator. Dry for another 3 to 4 hours, or until very crisp.

Sun: Spread batter thinly over plastic-covered trays or cookie sheets. Dry in full sun until firm and dry on top. Flip over and dry for another 5 to 6 hours, or until dried through. Finely crumble and return to trays. Dry until crisp.

Oven or Homemade Dryer: Spread batter thinly over plastic-covered trays. Dry at 150°F (65°C) until firm and dry on top. Flip over and peel off plastic wrap. Dry for another 3 to 4 hours, or until crisp. Crumble and return to oven or dryer. Dry for another 3 or 4 hours, or until crisp.

To Use: Store in small batches in tightly closed containers. Serve as a snack or as a ready-to-eat cereal with milk.

COCONUT CRISPS

2 cups (500 ml) grated coconut

½ cup (125 ml) packed brown sugar

1 egg (use commercially dried pasteurized egg or egg substitute)

1½ cups (375 ml) whole-wheat flour

1¼ cup (315 ml) uncooked rolled oats

¼ teaspoon (1 ml) salt

2 teaspoons (10 ml) baking powder

1 teaspoon (5 ml) pure vanilla extract

Combine all ingredients well. Add 1–2 tablespoons (15–30 ml) water if dough is too stiff to work. Roll out very thin. Cut into 3-inch (7.5-cm) strips. Serves 15 after drying.

Dehydrator: Lay strips on trays without overlapping. Dry at highest setting until crisp, about 4 to 6 hours. Remove and cool. Crumble with the hands and spread over trays again. Dry at highest setting for another 2 hours, or until crisp.

Sun: Lay strips over trays and dry in full sun until crisp, about 6 to 8 hours, turning once. Crumble into small pieces and spread pieces over trays. Dry for another 2 to 3 hours, stirring occasionally.

Oven or Homemade Dryer: Lay strips on trays. Dry at 120°F (50°C) for 4 to 6 hours with door ajar. Crumble, then return to trays and dry for another 2 to 4 hours, or until very crisp.

To Use: Eat as a snack or with milk or cream as a ready-to-eat breakfast cereal.

CARROT CEREAL

½ cup (125 ml) firmly packed brown sugar

1 egg (use commercially dried pasteurized egg)

1 cup (250 ml) cooked, mashed, and cooled carrots

¾ cup (190 ml) uncooked rolled oats

2 cups (500 ml) finely ground dried wheat

½ teaspoon (2 ml) salt

1½ teaspoons (7 ml) baking powder

1 teaspoon (5 ml) pure vanilla extract

Combine all ingredients. Beat well. Cover trays with plastic wrap and thinly spread batter over plastic. Serves 10 after drying.

Dehydrator: Spread batter on plastic-covered trays and dry at highest setting for 4 to 6 hours, or until top is firm and batter can be peeled away from plastic easily. Invert onto another tray and peel off and discard plastic wrap. Continue drying batter until hard and crisp, about 6 to 8 hours. Cool and crumble, then spread over trays again and dry until very crisp, about 2 to 3 hours.

Sun: Spread batter on plastic-covered trays and dry in full sun in a well-ventilated area. Dry for 4 to 6 hours, or until batter can be pulled away from plastic. Invert onto another tray and peel off and discard plastic. Dry batter until hard, about 4 to 6 hours. Take trays inside at night. In the morning, crumble and spread over trays to dry until very crisp, about 3 to 4 hours or more.

Oven or Homemade Dryer: Spread batter on plastic-covered trays. Dry at 150°F (65°C) for 6 to 8 hours with door ajar, or until batter can be peeled away from plastic. Invert onto another tray, peel off plastic and discard. Return batter to oven or dryer and dry until hard, about 6 to 8 hours. Crumble and spread flakes over uncovered trays. Dry for another 3 to 4 hours, or until very crisp.

To Use: Store in small batches in tightly closed containers. Serve as a snack or as a ready-to-eat cereal with milk.

WHEAT GERM CEREAL

2 tablespoons (30 ml) honey

3 eggs, well beaten

1 teaspoon (5 ml) salt

1 teaspoon (5 ml) pure vanilla extract

2 cups (500 ml) wheat germ

1½ cups (375 ml) whole-wheat flour

1 cup (250 ml) chopped dried plums

Combine all ingredients and mix well. Thinly spread over greased jelly-roll pans and bake in 300°F (150°C) oven for 20 to 30 minutes, or until lightly browned. Cool well, then run through a food grinder, using a coarse blade.

Dehydrator: Spread crumbs over trays covered with plastic wrap or aluminum foil. Dry at highest heat setting until crisp, stirring occasionally.

Sun: Spread crumbs over trays covered with plastic or over cookie sheets. Cover with a layer of cheesecloth and dry in full sun until crisp, about 8 to 10 hours or longer.

Oven or Homemade Dryer: Spread crumbs over trays covered with plastic wrap or aluminum foil. Dry at 120°F (50°C) for 6 to 8 hours, or until crisp.

To Use: Store in small batches in tightly closed containers. Serve as a snack or as a ready-to-eat cereal with milk.

GROUND NUTS CEREAL

1 cup (250 ml) buttermilk

½ cup (125 ml) dark corn syrup

½ teaspoon (2 ml) salt

1 teaspoon (5 ml) pure vanilla extract

½ teaspoon (2 ml) pure maple extract

1 teaspoon (5 ml) baking soda

¼ cup (65 ml) hot water

3 cups (750 ml) whole-wheat flour

1 cup (250 ml) chopped nutmeats

Combine buttermilk and corn syrup. Add salt, extracts, and baking soda dissolved in hot water. Mix well. Add flour and nutmeats. Mixture should resemble cake batter. Pour into three greased cake pans and bake for 40 minutes in 350°F (180°C) oven. Cool on rack for 10 minutes. Remove from pans and wrap in a damp dish towel until cold. Cut into chunks and grind in a meat grinder, using a coarse blade.

Dehydrator: Cover trays with plastic wrap or aluminum foil. Spread crumbs over covered trays and dry at highest heat setting for 6 to 8 hours, or until very crisp.

Sun: Spread crumbs over trays covered with plastic wrap or aluminum foil, or on cookie sheets. Dry in full sun for 8 to 10 hours or more, or until crisp. Protect from insects or birds with cheesecloth.

Oven or Homemade Dryer: Spread crumbs over trays covered with aluminum foil. Dry at 120°F (50°C) for 6 to 8 hours, or until crisp.

To Use: Store in small batches in tightly closed containers. Serve as a snack or as a ready-to-eat cereal with milk.

Crackers

Crackers dried in a dehydrator, the sun, oven, or homemade dryer are not intended for long storage, although they may be kept for a few weeks if tightly sealed in a jar or can when stored. They may be recrisped in the dehydrator or oven, if necessary. These crackers are a healthful, lightweight form of bread to take on camping or backpacking trips. Here are two recipes to get you started.

DRIED BRAN SNACKS

½ cup (125 ml) chunk-style peanut butter

½ cup (125 ml) honey

3 tablespoons (45 ml) butter or margarine

2 cups (500 ml) bran cereal

½ cup (125 ml) whole-wheat flour

½ cup (125 ml) dry milk powder

3 tablespoons (45 ml) sesame seeds

3 tablespoons (45 ml) sunflower seeds

¼ cup (65 ml) chopped dried apricots

Melt peanut butter, honey, and butter or margarine over low heat, stirring well to blend. Add remaining ingredients and stir well. Press firmly in the bottom of a 9 X 12-inch (22.5 X 30-cm) baking pan. Cool and cut into squares. No baking is necessary.

Dehydrator: Spread cut squares over trays, removing every other tray. Dry at 110°F (45°C) for 4 to 6 hours, or until crisp and no longer sticky.

Sun: Spread cut squares over trays and place in full sun, covering with cheesecloth to protect from insects and birds. Dry for 6 to 8 hours, or until crisp.

Oven or Homemade Dryer: Spread cut squares over trays. Dry at 110°F (45°C) for 4 to 6 hours.

To Use: Store in an air-tight container. Serve as ready-to-eat snack.

CORN CRISPS

1 teaspoon (5 ml) salt

2½ cups (625 ml) boiling water

½ cup (125 ml) yellow cornmeal

½ cup (125 ml) cold water

Add salt to boiling water over medium heat. Meanwhile, combine cornmeal and cold water in a small mixing bowl. Gradually add to boiling water, stirring constantly. Cook, stirring frequently, until thick. Cover and cook over very low heat for 20 to 30 minutes, stirring occasionally.

Cover trays with plastic wrap. Drop a scant teaspoonful of cornmeal mixture on plastic wrap. Using the back of a spoon dipped in water, spread very thinly. Continue procedure with remaining mixture over plastic wrap without overlapping crisps.

Dehydrator: Place trays in dehydrator set at 145°F (65°C). Dry until crisps will peel away from plastic wrap easily. Peel off, discarding plastic, and place crisps, inverted, directly on trays. Dry until crisp, about 4 to 6 hours.

Sun: Place trays in full sun. Dry for 6 to 8 hours, or until plastic can be peeled away. Place crisps directly on trays and dry for another 6 to 8 hours, or until crisp.

Oven or Homemade Dryer: Place trays in oven or homemade dryer. Dry at 145°F (65°C) until firm, then peel off plastic sheet and place directly on trays, upside down. Dry for another 4 to 6 hours, or until crisp.

SESAME-OAT CRACKERS

3 cups (750 ml) uncooked rolled oats

1 cup (250 ml) finely ground dried wheat flour

1 cup (250 ml) all-purpose flour

1 cup (250 ml) wheat germ

¾ cup (190 ml) honey

1 teaspoon (5 ml) salt

¾ cup (190 ml) vegetable oil

1 cup (250 ml) water

1 cup (250 ml) egg white, slightly beaten (use dry egg white, reconstituted, for safety)

Sesame seeds

Combine oats, both flours, wheat germ, honey, and salt. Pour oil and water into a well in the center and stir until mixture forms a dough that leaves the sides of the bowl. Divide into four parts. Roll each part out to a thickness of ⅛-inch (3-mm) and cut into cracker-sized squares. Sprinkle tops with sesame seeds. Makes 8 dozen crackers.

CHEDDAR CRACKERS

1 cup (250 ml) finely ground dried wheat flour

½ teaspoon (2 ml) salt

⅓ cup (75 ml) butter or margarine, at room temperature

1½ cups (375 ml) grated sharp cheddar cheese

½ cup (125 ml) finely chopped walnuts

¼ cup (65 ml) minced onion

Dash cayenne pepper

Combine flour and salt. Cut in butter and cheese, using two knives or a pastry blender. Stir in walnuts, onion, and cayenne. Press dough into a square mold. Chill in the refrigerator or freezer for 3 to 4 hours. Thinly slice into ¼-inch (6-mm) wafers. Makes 4 dozen crackers.

Dehydrator: Spread crackers over trays in a single layer without overlapping. Dry at highest setting until tops are dry, about 4 to 6 hours. Turn and dry for another 4 to 6 hours, or until crisp.

Sun: Spread crackers over trays without overlapping and place in full sun. Dry for 6 to 8 hours, then turn and dry on other side until crisp.

Oven or Homemade Dryer: Spread crackers in a single layer over trays. Dry at 150°F (65°C) for 4 to 6 hours, then turn and continue drying until crisp.

Bread Crumbs

Drying bread crumbs is a good way to make nutritious toppings for casseroles or coatings for meats from leftover biscuits, rolls, and stale bread. Stale crackers also may be recycled in this way. Cut bread, biscuits, or rolls into slices before drying.

Dehydrator: Lay slices over trays. Dry at 145°F (65°C) for 4 to 6 hours, or until bread is dry enough to crumble. Grind through a food chopper, using a fine blade. Spread over trays again and dry for another 2 hours, or until crisp.

Sun: Lay slices over trays and dry in full sun for 6 to 8 hours. Grind through the fine blade of a food chopper and return to trays. Dry for another 2 to 4 hours, or until crisp.

Oven or Homemade Dryer: Lay slices over trays. Dry at 145°F (65°C) with door ajar for 4 to 6 hours. Crumble and grind in food chopper and spread crumbs over trays. Dry for another 2 to 4 hours, or until crisp.

Croutons

To make these delicious accompaniments for soups and salads, dice stale bread into small cubes and sprinkle with dried marjoram, onion salt, or garlic salt. If no fat is used in seasoning them, well-dried croutons will keep for several months tightly sealed.

Dehydrator: Spread thinly over trays and dry at 145°F (65°C) for 4 to 6 hours, or until crisp.

Sun: Spread thinly over trays and place in full sun. Cover lightly with cheese-cloth to protect from birds, if necessary. Dry for 6 to 8 hours, or until crisp, stirring occasionally.

Oven or Homemade Dryer: Spread thinly over trays. Dry at 145°F (65°C) for 4 to 6 hours, or until crisp.

Noodles and Pasta

The growing popularity of pasta machines has made it easier than ever to have fresh pasta and noodles anytime. Most pasta recipes are meant to be eaten immediately, but if you want to stockpile your favorites, the following drying methods will do the trick. And for those of you without the convenience of a pasta machine, this pasta recipe is quick and easy to make by hand.

EGG NOODLES

2 eggs (use commercially pasteurized dried egg or egg substitute for safety)

1 teaspoon (5 ml) salt

2 cups (500 ml) all-purpose flour (approximately)

Beat eggs and salt with a fork. Gradually stir in as much flour as possible, ½ cup (125 ml) at a time, then work in more flour by hand until dough is very stiff. Cut dough in half and roll out paper thin. Let set for 10 minutes. Sprinkle with flour, roll up as a jelly roll, and cut into thin crosswise slices. Repeat with other half of dough. Makes 3 cups (750 ml) noodles.

Dehydrator: Spread slices in a thin layer over trays and dry at 145°F (65°C) until crisp, stirring occasionally. Noodles will dry in 4 to 6 hours.

Sun: Spread slices in a thin layer over trays and place in a well-ventilated area in full sun. Dry until crisp, about 6 to 8 hours, stirring occasionally.

Oven or Homemade Dryer: Spread slices in a thin layer over trays. Dry at 150°F (65°C) until crisp, stirring occasionally.

Leathers

Leathers have almost as many names as they have uses. The first settlers in the Old West made leathers to preserve the goodness of fruits and vegetables that would otherwise have gone to waste. They called them "papers," because of their paper-thinness, or "fruit leathers," because of their pliable, leathery texture. Today they are often called fruit rolls or fruit taffy, because of their delicious candy-like taste.

Leathers usually are rolled in wax paper or plastic wrap and eaten (with relish!) with the hands. Children love them, and they're a wonderful substitute for candy. They also may be dissolved in water and used as a pie filling, as a dessert topping for ice cream or pudding or as a flavoring for yogurt.

Any fruit or vegetable or combination of them can be made into leather. They are an excellent way to use slightly overripe fruits. Almost-brown bananas have more banana flavor. Peaches that have ripened to the soft, juicy stage taste more "peachy." Both make better tasting leathers than the just-ripe fruit.

Leathers are made from the puree of raw or cooked fruits or vegetables, although the fresh flavor is preferred by many. Cooked leathers will appear bright and shiny, uncooked leathers will appear dull.

To make a puree, strain cooked or thoroughly ripened raw fruit or vegetables through a food mill or liquify in a blender. Blend or stir the fruits or vegetables and flavorings to a smooth puree, adding enough liquid (juice or water) to make the mixture thin enough to pour. Use 2 cups (500 ml) puree on a 10½ X 15½-inch (25 X 340-cm) standard rimmed cookie sheet to obtain the appropriate depth.

To convert this puree into leather, line a drying tray with plastic wrap or brown wrapping paper. Some dehydrator manufacturers offer a reusable sheet for making fruit leathers.

Pour a small amount of the puree onto the plastic wrap or wrapping paper and tilt the tray until the puree is spread about ⅛ inch (6 mm) deep almost to the edges of the wrap or paper.

Use your imagination in making leathers. Try different fruits and vegetables and different combinations, and vary the sweetening, seasoning, and spicing to find what you like best. Remember, though, that fruits become more concentrated and therefore sweeter as they dry.

The times for drying will vary according to the amount of moisture in the puree and the depth of the layer you pour onto the trays. Drying should continue until leather is pliable, but no longer sticky.

Dehydrator: Spread puree thinly over covered trays and dry at 120°F (50°C) for 6 to 8 hours, or until leather can be pulled easily from wrap or paper. Invert, pull off plastic or paper, and continue drying for another 4 to 6 hours.

Sun: Spread puree thinly over covered trays or cookie sheets and place in a well-ventilated area in sun. Dry for 1 day, or until leather pulls away from plastic easily. Invert and dry directly on tray or cookie sheet for 1 more day.

Oven or Homemade Dryer: Spread puree over covered trays. Dry at 120°F (50°C) for 6 to 8 hours, or until leather can be pulled away from wrap or paper. Invert onto another drying tray, peel off wrap or paper and dry for another 6 to 8 hours.

To Store: For storing up to 6 weeks, roll up in wax paper or plastic wrap, close and twist ends, and store in refrigerator. For longer storage, roll each strip in wax paper or plastic wrap and seal in glass jars. Cut rolls to fit, if necessary. Leathers may also be stored flat separated by sheets of wax paper, brown wrapping paper, or plastic wrap. Place layers in a cardboard box or metal box. Cover and seal with masking tape. Store jars or boxes in a dark, constantly cool place. Well-dried, well-protected leathers will keep 1 to 2 years.

RAW APPLE LEATHER

2 cups (500 ml) peeled, cored, and chopped apples

½ cup (125 ml) apple cider

¼ teaspoon (1 ml) ground cinnamon

Puree all ingredients in a blender. Dry.

COOKED APPLE LEATHER

4 medium apples

½ cup (125 ml) water

¼ cup (65 ml) honey

Core and cut up apples without peeling. Add water and cook over medium heat for 15 to 20 minutes, or until tender. Force through a sieve or colander and stir in honey. Dry.

APPLE-APRICOT LEATHER

For a tasty flavor combination add a jar of pureed baby food apricots to a 32-ounce (800 gram) jar of applesauce. Fresh fruits can be used when in season. Dry.

RAW APRICOT LEATHER

Immerse ripe apricots in boiling water for 2 minutes, then in cold water. Slip off skins and cut in half. Remove seeds and drop into blender. Process until pureed. Dry.

COOKED APRICOT LEATHER

Cut apricots in half without peeling. Remove seeds. To every 2 cups (500 ml) of halves, add ½ cup (125 ml) water. Cover and cook over low heat until soft. Force through a sieve or colander and dry.

BANANA LEATHER

Select ripe or overripe bananas. Mash well or puree. Spread on plastic- or paper-covered trays and sprinkle with finely chopped pecans or walnuts and dry. For long storage, omit nuts, as the fat in the nuts tend to go rancid.

CHERRY LEATHER

2 cups (500 ml) pitted tart cherries   ½ cup (125 ml) granulated sugar

Combine cherries and sugar in blender. Process until sugar is dissolved and cherries are pureed, then dry.

RAW PEACH LEATHER

Select ripe or slightly overripe peaches. Peel and cut into halves, removing seeds. Puree in blender and dry.

COOKED PEACH LEATHER

Slice peaches without peeling and add ½ cup (125 ml) water and ½ cup (125 ml) granulated sugar for every 2 cups (500 ml) sliced peaches. Cover and cook over low heat until peaches are soft. Force through sieve or colander and add ¼ teaspoon (1 ml) ground cinnamon or nutmeg. Stir well and dry.

PINEAPPLE LEATHER

Cut whole pineapple into ½-inch (15-mm) slices. Core and peel each slice. Cut into pieces and shred or puree in blender, then dry.

PUMPKIN LEATHER

2 cups (500 ml) canned pumpkin, or 2 cups (500 ml) cooked pureed fresh pumpkin

½ cup (125 ml) honey

¼ teaspoon (1 ml) ground cinnamon

⅛ teaspoon (½ ml) ground nutmeg

⅛ teaspoon (½ ml) ground cloves

Blend ingredients well and dry.

PRUNE LEATHER

Soak 1 cup (250 ml) dried prunes overnight in 2 cups (500 ml) boiling water in a covered saucepan. Cook over low heat, without draining, for 15 to 20 minutes, or until prunes are tender. Force through a sieve or colander. Add ¼ cup (62.5 ml) lemon juice, stir well, and dry.

STRAWBERRY-RHUBARB LEATHER

1 cup (250 ml) unpeeled red rhubarb stalks, cut into 1-inch (25-mm) pieces

1 cup (250 ml) sliced strawberries

1 cup (250 ml) granulated sugar

Combine all ingredients in a covered saucepan. Stir well to dissolve sugar. Cook over low heat for 10 to 15 minutes. Pour into blender and puree. Dry.

MIXED VEGETABLE LEATHER

2 cups (500 ml) chopped tomatoes

1 small onion, chopped

¼ cup (65 ml) chopped celery

Salt to taste

Cook all ingredients over low heat in a covered saucepan for 15 to 20 minutes. Puree, or force through a sieve or colander. Cook in electric skillet or shallow pan until thickened. Dry.

TOMATO LEATHER

Core ripe tomatoes and cut into quarters. Cook over low heat in a covered saucepan 15 to 20 minutes. Puree, or force through a sieve or colander. Pour into electric skillet or shallow pan. Add salt to taste and cook over low heat until thickened. Dry.

CHAPTER THIRTEEN

Dried Soup Mixes

Dried vegetable mixtures are convenient for making soups at home or on camping trips. Their light weight makes them especially practical for hiking trips, and they may be stored for long periods in vacation cottages.

Because of the differences in drying times of different vegetables, dried soup mixtures are made most easily by drying each ingredient separately and combining them. They should be stored in recipe-sized batches and kept sealed until used.

To use these dried soup mixes, add the mixes to boiling water and simmer for 20 to 30 minutes, or until vegetables are tender. For a low-cost soup, simmer mixed dried vegetables in boiling water and flavor to taste with beef or chicken-flavored bouillon cubes or granules.

A delicious instant soup may be made from dried vegetables that have been powdered by forcing through a food grinder or processing with a blender. Add boiling water and cook for a few minutes. Some vegetables that make excellent instant soups are tomatoes, peas, squash, spinach, carrots, and almost any combination of favorite vegetables.

The following dried soup mixes are convenient for hiking and camping trips and will save you time and money in the kitchen. Salt may be eliminated or reduced for low-sodium diets.

CREAMED PEA (OR BROCCOLI) SOUP MIX

2 cups (500 ml) dried green peas or dried broccoli

½ cup (125 ml) minced dried onion

½ cup (125 ml) dried celery slices

½ cup (125 ml) dry milk powder

1 tablespoon (30 ml) dried parsley flakes

½ teaspoon (2 ml) salt

⅛ teaspoon (½ ml) black pepper

Combine all ingredients and store in a sealable plastic bag, glass jar, or any tightly sealed container. To use, add to 3 quarts water. Cover and simmer until peas are tender, about 45 to 50 minutes. A ham bone or three or four bacon slices may be added, if desired. Serves 6 to 8.

MUSHROOM-BARLEY SOUP MIX

½ cup (125 ml) dried barley

¼ cup (65 ml) dried mushroom slices

2 tablespoons (30 ml) minced dried onions

¼ cup (65 ml) dried carrot slices

2 tablespoons (30 ml) dried parsley flakes

2 tablespoons (30 ml) dried dill

2 bay leaves

2 beef-flavored bouillon cubes, or 2 teaspoons (10 ml) beef-flavored bouillon granules

Combine all ingredients in a sealable plastic bag, glass jar, or any tightly sealed container. Store in a dark, cool place. To use, add to 1 quart (1 litre) boiling water and simmer until barley is tender. Remove bay leaves before serving. Serves 4 to 6.

CREAM OF TOMATO SOUP MIX

3 cups (750 ml) dried tomato slices

½ cup (125 ml) dry milk powder

1 tablespoon (15 ml) granulated sugar

½ teaspoon (2 ml) salt

¼ teaspoon (1 ml) ground cinnamon

Powder dried tomato slices in a blender or with a pestle. Add remaining ingredients. To use, add to 1½ quarts (1½ litres) boiling water and simmer for 10 minutes. Add 1 teaspoon (5 ml) butter or margarine after cooking, if desired. Serves 4 to 6.

BEAN-PEA SOUP MIX

½ cup (125 ml) dried pinto beans

½ cup (125 ml) dried navy beans

1 cup (250 ml) dried green peas

¼ cup (65 ml) dried celery slices

2 tablespoons (30 ml) chopped dried onions

¼ cup (65 ml) dried carrot slices

4 black peppercorns

¼ teaspoon (1 ml) dry mustard

½ teaspoon (2 ml) salt

Combine all ingredients and store in a tightly sealed container. To use, add to 2 quarts (2 litres) boiling water. Stir well. Boil for 2 minutes. Turn off heat and let stand for 1 hour. Cover and simmer for 2 hours, or until beans and peas are tender. Remove peppercorns before serving. Serves 6 to 8.

FISH CHOWDER MIX

2 cups (500 ml) chopped dried fish

1 cup (250 ml) chopped dried
potatoes

½ cup (125 ml) dried carrots

½ cup (125 ml) chopped dried onions

2 tablespoons (30 ml) all-purpose flour

½ cup (125 ml) dry milk powder

½ teaspoon (2 ml) salt

⅛ teaspoon (½ ml) black pepper

Combine all ingredients. Store in a tightly sealed container. To use, add to 1½ quarts (1½ litres) boiling water. Stir well and simmer for 30 to 40 minutes. Serves 6.

VEGETABLE SOUP MIX

4 beef-flavored bouillon cubes, or 4
teaspoons (20 ml) beef-flavored
bouillon granules

½ cup (125 ml) dried carrot slices

¼ cup (65 ml) dried barley

¼ cup (65 ml) dried celery slices

½ cup (125 ml) dried green beans

¼ cup (65 ml) dried corn

½ cup (125 ml) dried green peas

½ cup (125 ml) dried tomatoes

1 bay leaf

6 black peppercorns

1 teaspoon (5 ml) salt

Combine all ingredients and store in a tightly sealed container. To use, add to 2 quarts (2 litres) boiling water. Cover and simmer for 30 to 40 minutes. Serves 6 to 8.

CREAM OF MUSHROOM SOUP MIX

1 cup (250 ml) dried mushrooms

½ teaspoon (2 ml) dried onions

½ teaspoon (2 ml) grated dried lemon
rind

3 tablespoons (45 ml) all-purpose flour

1 teaspoon (5 ml) salt

⅛ teaspoon (½ ml) black pepper

1 cup (250 ml) dry milk powder

Combine all ingredients and store in a tightly sealed container. To use, add to 1½ quarts (1½ litres) boiling water. Cook, stirring constantly, until smooth and thickened. Cover and cook over very low heat for 20 to 30 minutes. Serves 4 to 6.

TOMATO-NOODLE SOUP MIX

4 cups (1 litre) dried tomatoes

½ teaspoon (2 ml) salt

2 tablespoons (30 ml) chopped dried
onions

1 teaspoon (5 ml) sugar

½ cup (125 ml) dried noodles

Powder dried tomatoes with a pestle or in a blender. Combine tomato powder with remaining ingredients and store in a tightly sealed container. To use, add to 1½ quarts (1½ litres) boiling water, stirring well. Simmer for 20 to 30 minutes. Serves 6.

CREAM OF CELERY SOUP MIX

1½ cups (375 ml) dried celery slices

¼ cup (65 ml) chopped dried onions

2 tablespoons (30 ml) all-purpose flour

½ teaspoon (2 ml) salt

½ cup (125 ml) dry milk powder

2 chicken-flavored bouillon cubes or 2 teaspoons (10 ml) chicken-flavored bouillon granules

Combine all ingredients and store in a tightly sealed container. To use, add to 1½ quarts (1½ litres) boiling water. Cook over low heat, stirring constantly, until thickened. Cover and simmer for 20 to 30 minutes more. Serves 6. (To make cream of onion soup, use 1 cup (250 ml) dried onion and ½ cup (125 ml) dried celery. Dried carrot — ½ cup (125 ml) — is a nice addition to this recipe.)

CAMPFIRE MINESTRONE

4 beef-flavored bouillon cubes, or 4 teaspoons (20 ml) beef-flavored bouillon granules

½ cup (125 ml) chopped dried onions

½ teaspoon (2 ml) minced dried garlic

½ cup (125 ml) dried navy beans

½ teaspoon (2 ml) dried oregano

2 bay leaves

6 black peppercorns

1 cup (250 ml) sliced or chopped dried tomatoes

1 cup (250 ml) dried celery slices

1 cup (250 ml) dried carrot slices

2 cups (500 ml) dried green beans

2 tablespoons (30 ml) dried green pepper

1 teaspoon (5 ml) salt

Combine all ingredients and store in tightly sealed container. To use, add to 4 quarts (4 litres) boiling water and simmer over low heat for 2 to 3 hours, or until beans are tender. Remove bay leaves and peppercorns before serving. Serves 8 to 10.

CHICKEN-NOODLE SOUP MIX

½ cup (125 ml) dried chicken cubes

½ cup (125 ml) dried noodles

¼ cup (65 ml) chopped dried carrots

¼ cup (65 ml) chopped dried celery

¼ cup (65 ml) dried green peas

1 tablespoon (15 ml) chopped dried onions

2 tablespoons (30 ml) chicken-flavored bouillon granules, or 6 chicken-flavored bouillon cubes

Combine all ingredients and mix well. Store in a sealable plastic freezer bag. To serve, simmer over a campfire or camp stove in 2 quarts (2 litres) boiling water until vegetables and meat are tender, about 1 hour. Stir occasionally and add water as necessary. Season to taste with salt and pepper. Serves 4.

CHAPTER FOURTEEN

Drying Foods For Hiking and Camping

Almost every well-stocked sporting goods store has a display of packaged, dehydrated foods developed especially for the hunter, the camper, and the backpacker. It's an appetizing array: vegetable-beef stew, chicken noodle soup, peach cobbler, scrambled eggs and bacon, and potato soup. These meal-sized packages are convenient for camping trips where there is no refrigeration and where keeping fresh foods is a problem. They are small enough for canoeing trips where there is little space for supplies and are light enough in weight for backpacking.

But those convenient little packages are expensive. A package containing the ingredients for a main dish of beef and noodles or vegetable-beef stew to serve four persons costs $12 to $15. A scrambled egg breakfast with biscuits costs $10 to $12 for four people. At these prices, a weekend supply of dried foods for a camping trip for a family of four could cost $100 to $120 for four people.

But the same supply of camping foods can be dried and packaged at home for $10 or less. If the fruits and vegetables are harvested from your garden, the cost may be almost nothing.

Some of the dried foods that would fit well in a backpack for hiking trips where cooking facilities are not available are:

Beef, venison, and hamburger jerky, granola cereal, crackers, instant soups (powdered dried green peas, tomatoes, or asparagus), any dried fruits, fruit and vegetable leathers, and any dried vegetables you enjoy eating, such as zucchini, parsnips, or sprouts.

For camping trips where dried foods may be cooked over a campfire or a commercial camping stove, a complete menu of nourishing meals can be created from a supply of home-dried foods, supplemented by a few staples from your grocer's shelves.

The following sample menu for a weekend camping trip can be made using foods dried at home:

Saturday Breakfast:
    Rehydrated apricot halves or slices
    Scrambled eggs (commercially
      dried and pasteurized)
    Whole-grain biscuits
    Hot chocolate

Saturday Lunch:
    Chicken-noodle soup
    Cheese-topped crackers
    Milk
    Whole-grain cookies

Saturday Dinner:
    Hot tomato broth
    Campfire stew
    Blueberry biscuits
    Banana chip pudding
    Milk
    Herb tea

Sunday Breakfast:
    Tomato juice
    Whole-grain pancakes
    Milk

Sunday Lunch:
    Beef and Potatoes in foil
    Green beans and tomatoes
    Cherry cobbler
    Milk
    Herb tea

Sunday Dinner:
    Campfire beans and ham
    Corn bread
    Cooked apples
    Milk
    Herb tea

If you wish to use this menu to feed two adults and two children for a weekend, you'll need the following home-dried foods. Recipes follow.

Chicken-Noodle Soup Mix
Campfire Stew Mix
Beef and Potatoes in Foil
Campfire Beans and Ham
Scrambled Egg Mix
½ cup (125 ml) dried cheese
½ cup (125 ml) commercially dried
pasteurized egg powder
1 cup (250 ml) dried apple slices
1¼ cups (315 ml) dried apricot
    halves or slices
½ cup (125 ml) dried banana chips
¼ cup (65 ml) dried blueberries
1 cup (250 ml) dried cherries
¼ cup (65 ml) dried plums
12 cups (3 litres) Whole-Grain
    Baking Mix
Crackers (see chapter 11, Drying Grains)

1 cup (250 ml) dried green beans
½ cup (125 ml) dried tomatoes
¾ cup (190 ml) dried tomato powder
Herb tea mixture

Other foods needed:
Butter or margarine
Pancake syrup
Salt and pepper
Instant coffee
Instant cocoa mix
1 large box powdered milk
⅔ cup (150 ml) brown sugar
1 cup (250 ml) granulated sugar
1 package vanilla-flavored instant
    pudding

Recipes for Camping Dishes

CHICKEN-NOODLE SOUP MIX

½ cup (125 ml) dried chicken cubes

½ cup (125 ml) dried noodles

¼ cup (65 ml) chopped dried carrots

¼ cup (65 ml) chopped dried celery

¼ cup (65 ml) dried green peas

1 tablespoon (15 ml) chopped dried onions

2 tablespoons (30 ml) chicken-flavored bouillon granules, or 6 chicken-flavored bouillon cubes

Combine all ingredients and mix well. Store in a sealable plastic freezer bag. To serve, simmer over a campfire or camp stove in 2 quarts (2 litres) boiling water until vegetables and meat are tender, about 1 hour. Stir occasionally and add water as necessary. Season to taste with salt and pepper. Serves 4.

REHYDRATING DRIED FRUITS

To prepare dried fruits for camp meals, place 1 cup (250 ml) dried fruit in a 1-quart (1-litre) glass jar or plastic container. Cover with hot or cold water, shake a little, and cap with a lid. Let set in hot sun for 4 to 6 hours or soak overnight. Serve without cooking, or simmer for 5 to 10 minutes over a campfire.

SCRAMBLED EGG MIX

1 cup (250 ml) commercially dried pasteurized egg powder

¼ cup (65 ml) dry milk powder

¼ cup (65 ml) imitation bacon bits

1 tablespoon (15 ml) finely chopped dried onion

1 tablespoon (15 ml) finely chopped dried green pepper

Combine all ingredients and store in a sealable, plastic freezer bag. To serve, blend with ½ cup (125 ml) water. Let set for 10 minutes. Beat with a fork and cook over hot coals in a skillet in which 1 tablespoon (15 ml) butter or margarine has been melted. Serves 4.

CHEESE-TOPPED CRACKERS

Combine ¼ cup (65 ml) dried cheese with ¼ cup (65 ml) softened butter or margarine. Spread over homemade crackers (see chapter 11, Drying Grains). Heat in Dutch oven or reflector oven.

Hot Tomato Broth

Place 3 tablespoons (45 ml) powdered tomato puree in a cup. Fill cup with boiling water and stir well. Season to taste with salt. Serve hot or cold.

Campfire Stew

1 cup (250 ml) dried beef cubes
½ cup (125 ml) dried potato slices
½ cup (125 ml) carrot slices
½ cup (125 ml) dried onion slices
2 tablespoons (30 ml) all-purpose flour

1 tablespoon (15 ml) beef-flavored bouillon granules, or 3 beef-flavored bouillon cubes

Salt and pepper to taste

Combine all ingredients and store in a sealable, plastic freezer bag. To serve, add to 2 quarts (2 litres) water in a stewing kettle. Simmer over hot coals or on a camp stove over low heat for 1 to 1½ hours, or until dried foods are tender. Season with salt and pepper.

Banana Chip Pudding

½ cup (125 ml) dried banana chips
½ cup (125 ml) dry milk powder

1 package vanilla-flavored instant pudding

Mix ingredients well. Store in a sealable, plastic freezer bag. To serve, stir in water according to directions on pudding package. Beat with a fork. Divide into four dishes. Let set for 10 minutes.

Campfire Beans and Ham

1½ cups (375 ml) dried beans (great northern, navy, pinto, etc.)
½ cup (125 ml) chopped dried ham
¼ cup (65 ml) chopped dried onions
2 tablespoons (30 ml) dried green pepper

¼ cup (65 ml) grated dried carrots
1 tablespoon (15 ml) chicken-flavored bouillon granules, or 3 chicken-flavored bouillon cubes
1 teaspoon (5 ml) salt
⅛ teaspoon (½ ml) black pepper

Store beans separately from other ingredients in sealable, plastic freezer bags. Soak beans in 3 quarts (3 litres) of water for 1 hour. Add remaining ingredients. Simmer over hot coals or medium heat on camp stove for 2 to 3 hours, or until beans are tender, stirring occasionally and adding water, if necessary.

DRUGSTORE WRAP FOLD

Freezing can be an effective means of preserving the original flavor and quality of foods. Proper wrapping is key. A popular style of wrapping is called the "drugstore wrap fold." This wrap effectively seals the food and prevents moisture from getting in or out.

To wrap foods drugstore style, place the food in the center of a large sheet of the freezer wrap (shiny side up). Be sure to allow plenty of extra wrap on the edges for folding. Next, pull two opposite edges up to meet evenly over the food and begin folding down in one-inch increments until the wrap is snug against the food. Close open ends gift wrap style being extra sure to force out as much air as possible. Seal with tape and note the contents and date on the outside of the package.

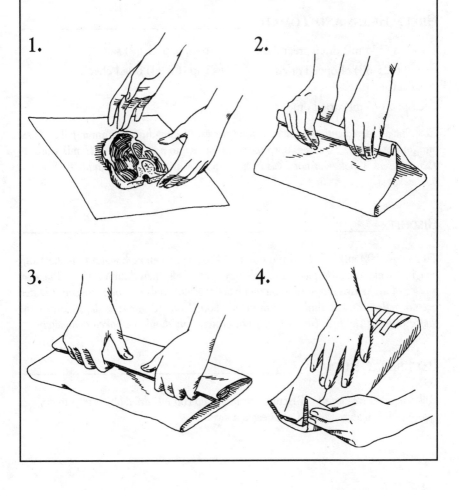

1.

2.

3.

4.

BEEF AND POTATOES IN FOIL

2 cups (500 ml) dried beef cubes

2 cups (500 ml) dried potato slices

½ cup (125 ml) dried peas

1 tablespoon (15 ml) dried onions

1 tablespoon (15 ml) beef broth powder

⅛ teaspoon (½ ml) dried garlic

Salt and pepper to taste

Combine all ingredients well, except salt and pepper. Divide onto four pieces of heavy-duty aluminum foil. Seal foil squares, using drugstore wrap folds (see page 155). To serve, open each foil package just enough to add 1 cup (250 ml) water to each. Season with salt and pepper and reseal tightly. Cook over hot coals or in a camp oven for 1 to 2 hours. Serve in foil packages.

GREEN BEANS AND TOMATOES

1½ cups (375 ml) dried green beans

½ cup (125 ml) chopped dried tomatoes

1 teaspoon (5 ml) dried onions

¼ teaspoon (1 ml) salt

¼ cup (65 ml) dried cheese

Combine all ingredients. Divide onto four pieces of heavy-duty aluminum foil and seal into four packages. To serve, open packages enough to add ½ cup (125 ml) water to each. Reseal. Cook over hot coals or in a camp oven for 30 to 45 minutes. Serve in foil packages.

BISCUITS

To 2 cups (500 ml) Whole-Grain Baking Mix, add just enough water to make a stiff dough. Divide into eight pieces and roll each into a ball, then flatten slightly. Place on a piece of ungreased aluminum foil and bake over hot coals or camp stove in a Dutch oven or reflector oven until baked through, about 15 to 30 minutes, depending on the temperature of the fire. Biscuits may not brown, but should be baked completely.

BLUEBERRY BISCUITS

Following the directions for Biscuits, stir in ¼ cup (65 ml) dried blueberries to dry mix before adding water. Proceed as directed above.

WHOLE-GRAIN BAKING MIX

3 cups (750 ml) whole-wheat flour

3 cups (750 ml) unbleached all-purpose white flour

1 cup (250 ml) wheat germ

4 cups (1 litre) uncooked rolled oats

2 cups (500 ml) dry milk powder

4 tablespoons (60 ml) baking powder

1 tablespoon (15 ml) salt

1½ pounds (600 grams) margarine or vegetable shortening

Combine dry ingredients. Using a pastry blender or electric mixer, cut in margarine to the consistency of fine meal. Spread over dehydrator trays covered with plastic wrap and dry for 2 hours at lowest heat setting. Cool, then divide into eight sealable plastic freezer bags and seal.

Because of the margarine or shortening, this mix will turn rancid in long-term storage at room temperature. It may be stored in the freezer, or it will keep well, unrefrigerated, for a camping trip of 1 week or more. For longer storage without refrigeration, omit margarine or shortening and add ¼ cup (65 ml) shortening to each cup (250 ml) dry mix just before using.

To Use Whole-Grain Baking Mix: Follow the recipes below.

WHOLE-GRAIN PANCAKES

1 tablespoon (15 ml) commercially dried pasteurized egg powder, or

1 egg

1 tablespoon (15 ml) granulated sugar

3 cups (750 ml) Whole-Grain Baking Mix

1 cup (250 ml) water

Combine all ingredients. Stir until dry ingredients are moistened. Add water, if needed, to make a thin batter. Drop by spoonsful on a hot, greased griddle. Turn once to brown on both sides. Serve immediately with butter or margarine and syrup.

WHOLE-GRAIN COOKIES

1 tablespoon (15 ml) commercially dried pasteurized egg powder, or

1 egg

2 cups (500 ml) Whole-Grain Baking Mix

⅔ cup (150 ml) packed brown sugar

⅓ cup (75 ml) water

¼ cup (65 ml) chopped dried plums

¼ cup (65 ml) chopped dried apricots

Blend all ingredients well. Drop by spoonsful on a greased, doubled sheet of aluminum foil, spreading slightly with the back of a spoon. Bake in a Dutch oven or reflector oven over hot coals for 10 to 20 minutes. Makes 2 dozen cookies.

WHOLE-GRAIN CORN BREAD

1½ cups (375 ml) Whole-Grain
Baking Mix

1 tablespoon (15 ml) commercially
dried pasteurized egg powder, or
1 egg

¾ cup (185 ml) ground dried corn

½ cup (125 ml) water (approximately)

Combine all ingredients. Stir just until blended. Pour into a well-greased, 8-inch (20-cm) square baking pan, or a pan made by folding a doubled thickness of heavy-duty aluminum foil into a pan shape, then greasing well. Bake in a camp stove oven over medium heat or in a Dutch oven or reflector oven over hot coals. Bake until a straw inserted in the middle comes out clean. Baking time depends on the temperature of the fire.

CHERRY CRISP

1 cup (250 ml) dried cherries

½ cup (125 ml) granulated sugar

1½ cups (375 ml) water

2 tablespoons (30 ml) butter or
margarine

2 cups (500 ml) Whole-Grain Baking
Mix

½ cup (125 ml) water

Combine first four ingredients and cook over campfire for 30 minutes in an iron skillet or Dutch oven. Meanwhile, mix together remaining ingredients in a bowl. Spread over top of hot cherry mixture. Bake in reflector oven or camp stove oven for 20 to 30 minutes, or cover Dutch oven with a lid and cook for 20 to 30 minutes over hot coals.

Recipes for other dried foods suitable for outdoor cooking can be found in chapter 13.

CHAPTER FIFTEEN

Drying Flowers for Potpourri

Through the magic of drying, the fragrance of flower blossoms can be captured outdoors in summer, stored away in sealed containers, and enjoyed indoors in winter.

Dried flower petals may be used in potpourri jars, sprinkled over lingerie in dresser drawers, crushed and added to bath water, or sewed into tiny cloth sachets and tucked between the sheets and towels in the linen closet. Wherever they are used, their fragrance will spread and linger in a delightful way.

Dry any fragrant blossoms available. Some of the best are roses — especially the wild varieties — apple blossoms, geraniums, lavender, marigolds, nasturtiums, and honeysuckle.

Dehydrator: Pluck the petals of just-opened flowers early in the day, as soon as the dew has been dried by the sun. Spread in a thin layer over trays and dry at 110°F (45°C) until brittle, about 6 to 8 hours.

Outdoors: Tie three or four flowers together with a string around the stems. Hang upside down in a well-ventilated, shady place until crisp, about 3 to 4 days. Pluck petals from flowers.

Oven or Homemade Dryer: Pluck petals from flowers and spread thinly over trays. Dry at 110°F (45°C) for 6 to 8 hours, or until brittle.

To Use Dried Blossoms: On a warm summer day, prepare dried blossoms in a potpourri — a combination of fragrances sealed in glass jars. Then some cold winter day, when the house is closed and stuffy and spring seems far away, open the jar for an hour or two and suddenly the room will be filled with instant summer. Or make several potpourri jars, enough so that you can keep one open all the time.

Make potpourri mixtures from any flowers, herbs, and spices available to you. The only necessary expense is for a small bottle of scent fixative, which you can buy in most drugstores. Ask for gum benzoin or powdered orrisroot. Although it isn't absolutely necessary, the fixative retards evaporation of the oils that give the petals their fragrance.

POTPOURRI METHOD

To make potpourris, combine all ingredients listed in a large roasting pan or mixing bowl. Toss gently, but thoroughly. Store in several tightly sealed glass jars in a cool, dark place for 5 to 6 weeks to allow the fragrance to develop.

To make sachets, sew the fragrant petals and petal mixtures inside small pieces of brightly colored material. Sachets usually are 2 to 3 inches (5 to 7.5 cm) square, but shapes and materials may vary from plain cotton to embroidered silks and needlepoint. Seal several sachets in a glass jar for a few weeks to blend aromas. Place them in closets and dresser drawers to lend their fragrance to stored clothes and linens.

Here are some recipes for potpourris. Once you get started, you'll be creating your own.

ROSE-GERANIUM POTPOURRI

2 quarts (2 litres) dried rose petals

1 quart (1 litre) dried geranium petals

1 cup (250 ml) dried peppermint
   leaves

½ cup (125 ml) lavender petals

8 whole cloves

1 tablespoon (15 ml) grated nutmeg

2 ounces (50 grams) gum benzoin or
   powdered orrisroot

LAVENDER POTPOURRI

3 quarts (3 litres) dried lavender
   blossoms

2 quarts (2 litres) dried rose petals

1 ounce (25 grams) gum benzoin or
   powdered orrisroot

1 quart (1 litre) dried nasturtium
   petals

2 quarts (2 litres) dried rose petals

1 ounce (25 grams) gum benzoin or
   powdered orrisroot

APPLE BLOSSOM POTPOURRI

2 quarts (2 litres) dried apple
   blossoms

1 quart (1 litre) dried honeysuckle
   blossoms

2 cups (500 ml) dried rose petals

Two 4-inch (10-cm) sticks cinnamon,
   broken into small pieces

1 ounce gum (25 grams) benzoin or
   powdered orrisroot

Herb Potpourri

1 quart (1 litre) dried sage leaves
1 quart (1 litre) dried rosemary leaves
2 cups (500 ml) dried thyme
1 cup (250 ml) dried oregano

1 cup (250 ml) dried basil
1½ ounces (40 grams) gum benzoin
or powdered orrisroot

Pine Potpourri

2 quarts (2 litres) pine, fir, or spruce needles
1 quart (1 litre) dried juniper berries
1 cup (250 ml) dried sage leaves

1 cup (250 ml) dried parsley
2 tablespoons (30 ml) dried basil
1 ounce gum (25 grams) benzoin or powdered orrisroot

Geranium Potpourri

2 quarts (2 litres) dried geranium leaves
2 cups (500 ml) dried geranium flower petals
1½ ounces (40 grams) gum benzoin or powdered orrisroot

1 cup (250 ml) dried spearmint leaves
1 tablespoon (15 ml) ground dried cardamom seeds
1 tablespoon (15 ml) ground dried coriander seeds

CHAPTER SIXTEEN

Other Uses For Drying Equipment

O nce it has become part of the household equipment, a commercial dehydrator or a homemade dryer can prove to be a very convenient appliance. You'll find their low, warm temperatures ideal for:

- **Bread raising.** Remove trays and preheat dehydrator or homemade dryer to 120°F (50°C). Turn off heat and place a shallow pan of hot water on the bottom shelf. Place covered bowl of bread dough on shelf directly above hot water. Let rise for 1 hour, or until doubled in bulk. Punch down and place in greased bread pans. Return to dehydrator until loaves are light. Bake.
- **Making yogurt.** Preheat dehydrator or homemade dryer to 110°F (45°C). Meanwhile, scald 1 quart (1 litre) of milk. Cool to 110°F (45°C) and add 1 tablespoon (15 ml) yogurt culture or ¼ cup (65 ml) yogurt containing live culture. Blend thoroughly. Divide into cups or containers and place on dehydrator shelves. Keep in dehydrator at 110°F (43°C) until set, about 4 to 8 hours.
- **Making cheese.** The low temperature of a dehydrator is ideal for ripening milk to be made into cheese. To 1 gallon (4 litres) cooled, scalded milk, add ½ cup (125 ml) buttermilk or yogurt. Stir well and place in a dehydrator preheated to 90°F (35°C). Let set for 12 to 24 hours, or until flavor has developed. Add 1 teaspoon (5 ml) liquid rennet or 1 rennet tablet dissolved in 1 teaspoon (5 ml) warm water and stir well. Let set for 1 to 2 hours, or until curdled. Cut the curd into small cubes and stir gently. Return to dehydrator

and increase temperature to 110°F (45°C). Hold at this temperature until curd is firm, about 30 to 45 minutes. Drain and press according to individual cheese recipe.

• **Recrisping crackers and cereal.** Crackers and cereal that have lost their crispness may be rejuvenated by spreading on drying trays and placing in the dehydrator or homemade dryer heated to 145°F (65°C). Dry for 30 to 45 minutes, or until crisp.

•**Drying seeds.** Seeds for the home garden may be dried without harm in a dehydrator or homemade dryer, if the temperature is kept at 100°F (40°C) or less.

•**Curing nuts.** Walnuts, hickory nuts, peanuts, and pecans may be cured in days instead of weeks by drying them at 110°F (45°C) in a dehydrator or homemade dryer.

•**Decrystalizing honey.** When a jar of honey crystallizes into a solid mass, as all honey eventually does, slip the jar into the dehydrator or homemade dryer. Keep the heat at 110°F (45°C) for a few hours and you'll have liquid honey again without any loss of nutrients or natural goodness.

•**Drying crafts.** Whether you're into ceramics, painting, or dough art, you'll find the dust-free warmth of a dehydrator or homemade dryer ideal for drying.

There are other uses for this convenient appliance. The more you use it, the more uses you'll find.

Building an Electric Food Dehydrator

Editor's Note: We studied diagrams and plans for several electric food dehydrators before selecting this one, which appeared to be best because of its design and its size. We built it at Garden Way Publishing, tested its operation, then shipped it to the author of this book, Phyllis Hobson, for her to test.

The following information was written by three persons. The first article, describing the construction of the dehydrator, was written by Dale E. Kirk, agricultural engineer at Oregon State University, as published in the USDA Home and Garden Bulletin 217.

The next section was written by Roger Cota, a former Garden Way staff member, who built and tested this dehydrator.

Finally, the results of the food tests were written by author Phyllis Hobson.

Plans For a Dehydrator

By Dale E. Kirk

A small dehydrator can be used in the home to preserve many types of fruits, blanched vegetables, meats, and nuts and to make specialty confections from fresh, natural products.

This dehydrator provides 8½ square feet of tray surface, which can accommodate approximately eighteen pounds of fresh, moist product. The necessary heat for evaporating the moisture is supplied by standard household light bulbs, which are efficient and relatively safe heating elements. An 8-inch household electric fan can be used for air circulation, or a 6-or 8-inch-diameter air-duct circulating fan may be purchased from an electrical supply house.

The dehydrator box described here is easy to build. It requires only two forms of wood building materials: ½-inch plywood and ¾-inch square wood strips. Construction can be done with a handsaw, coping saw or compass saw, drill, countersink, screwdriver, and knife. A square or tape is needed for measurements.

The drying trays may be built of wooden slats or metal mesh. We recommend, however, that you purchase prefabricated aluminum window screens for use as trays. They are lightweight, sturdy, easily cleaned, and relieve the builder of much of the more difficult construction. Sometimes under heavy use, however, screening tends to pull out of aluminum frames with the weight of the food.

Construction Materials. You'll need these materials to build the dehydrator described:

1 sheet of ½-inch, 4 X 8-foot , A-C exterior plywood

9 – 4-foot pieces of 1 X 1-inch nominal (¾ X ¾-inch actual) wood strips

1 – 8-inch household electric fan

1 set of 5 aluminum screens for trays. *16¾ X 20, 16¾ X 19, 16¾ X 17¾, 16¾ X 16¾, and 16¾ X 15½ inches

1 pair of 2-inch metal butt hinges

1 ball chain or equivalent door latch

9 porcelain surface-mount sockets

9 – 75-watt light bulbs

15 feet of S.F. #14 copper wire

6 feet of #14 wire extension cord with male plug

1 – 36-inch length of heavy-duty household aluminum foil

116 – 1-inch No. 8 flathead wood screws (nails and glue may be used instead)

18 – ⅝-inch No. 7 roundhead wood or sheet-metal screws

1 – 10-amp-capacity thermostat, 100°–160°F approximate range (a baseboard heater thermostat may be used)

1 – 4-inch electrical surface utility box with blank cover

2 – ½-inch utility box compression fittings

2 wire nuts

---

*Fiberglass treated with nylon or teflon or wood trays may be substituted for aluminum. Do not use galvanized screening material.

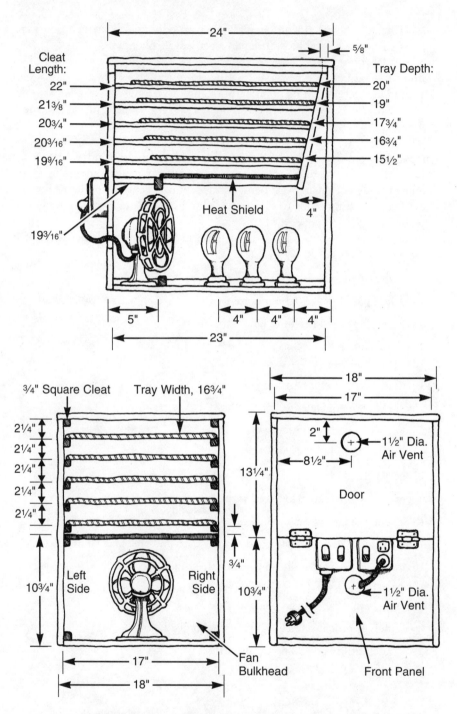

Front and two section views of dehydrator construction.

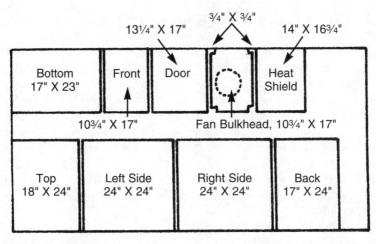

13¼" X 17"   ¾" X ¾"   14" X 16¾"

| Bottom 17" X 23" | Front | Door | | Heat Shield |

10¾" X 17"   Fan Bulkhead, 10¾" X 17"

| Top 18" X 24" | Left Side 24" X 24" | Right Side 24" X 24" | Back 17" X 24" |

Cutting plan to obtain the necessary plywood parts with a minimum of saw cuts.

Cutting and Assembly. The cutting diagram shows how all of the ½-inch plywood pieces can be cut from the single 4 X 8-foot sheet. It is usually most satisfactory to measure from the factory-cut edges as shown. Allowances for saw kerfs must be made between adjacent pieces.

Cut the plywood sections to size and the 1 X 4-foot strips to the lengths shown. Then assemble the side panels as shown in the illustration.

Next, lay out the porcelain sockets and fasten to the base, as shown. Fasten the S.F. wire to the porcelain sockets. Connect the wire that goes to the yellow screws on the sockets to the thermostat, mounted near the rear on the left side panel. (The yellow screws on the sockets connect to the center pole, rather than the threaded wall of the socket.) Connect the wire that goes to the white screws to the white wire in the extension cord. The third wire (green) in the extension cord should be connected directly to the junction box, mounted on the front panel.

If you use a household electric fan with the base left attached, fasten it in place on the dehydrator base and cut the hole in the fan bulkhead to fit. If you use a duct-type fan, cut the necessary size hole (approximately 8½ inches in diameter for an 8-inch fan or approximately 6½ inches in diameter for a 6-inch fan) in the bulkhead and fasten the fan mounting frame directly to the bulkhead. Now set the bulkhead in place (approximately 5 to 5½ inches from the front panel) and fasten it temporarily in position by two screws through the left side panel as shown. Center the 1½-inch-diameter air vent hole in the front panel directly in front of the fan motor, approximately 1 inch away from the motor. This will allow the cold air to enter and pass over the motor to cool it.

Next, fasten the right side, back, and top in place.

Cover the heat shield with heavy-duty household aluminum foil. This provides a reflective surface to protect the plywood heat shield and also provides a smooth surface on the top of the shield for easier removal of juices that may drip from the drying trays.

You could build the drying trays, but we suggest you purchase aluminum window screens made to the sizes listed. You can order these through your local lumber or building supply dealer. If they do not have a ready source of supply, further information about suppliers may be obtained through your local county Extension office. If you prefer to build the trays, we suggest you make a light, wooden frame and aluminum screen. Most plastic screens will sag badly under load and heat. Black metal screens will rust and leave stains on the food product.

You'll need some type of adjustable latch to hold the door in a partially opened position during the early stages of drying, when the moisture is being removed rapidly.

As a check on the thermostat setting, some type of thermometer capable of service in the 100° to 160°F (38° to 71°C) temperature range should be avail-

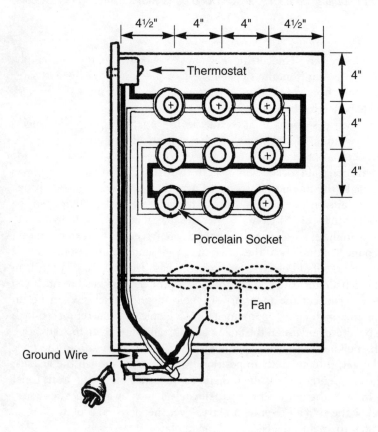

Layout of socket locations and wiring plan.

able. The dial type should be rugged and easily read. A kitchen meat thermometer also will serve. The sensing part of the thermometer should project through the box into the space above the trays for accurate indication of the drying temperature. Placing the sensing element in the heating chamber with the light bulbs will give a misleading, high reading.

Operation. For most moist fruits and blanched vegetables, the trays may be loaded at the rate of 1 to 2 pounds (400 to 800 grams) of fresh product per square foot of tray surface. The door may be kept closed for the first 30 to 60 minutes to bring the product and the dehydrator box up to the desired drying temperature. Once this temperature is reached, the door should be opened about ½ to ¾ inch at the top to allow easier escape of the moisture-laden air. The moist air will exhaust at the top, and additional fresh air will be taken in along the sides of the partially opened door.

Test to see when the first high-moisture stage is over. Hold your hand at the opening at the top of the door.

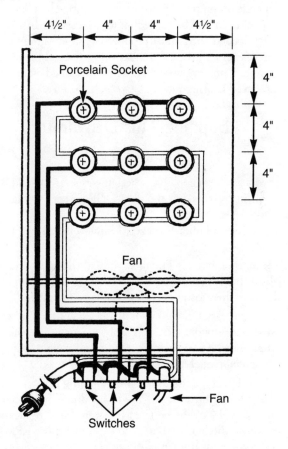

Socket location and wiring plan for use with three-switch control.

When moisture no longer tends to condense on your hand or on your metal watch band, close the door. The air exchange provided by the two 1½-inch-diameter vents should be enough to complete the drying process.

Maintenance. The electric fan motor is supplied by a stream of fresh air from the lower vent, positioned in front of the motor, but it will still operate at a higher temperature than in normal, open-room service. Lubricate the motor bearings with 30-weight engine oil. Lighter grade household or sewing machine oil may tend to gum and stall the fan motor after extended service.

Wash trays with hot water and a detergent when they become soiled with dried-on juices. If you purchased the recommended aluminum window screens with an aluminum wedge strip to hold the screen in place, you can put them in a dishwasher without damage.

Alternate Construction and Operation. The dehydrator can be built without a thermostat. Temperature can be controlled by the use of switches to operate various numbers of light bulbs. The diagram shows such a unit, with three separate switches, each controlling three bulbs in the heating chamber.

All three switches should be turned on for at least the first hour or two when the dehydrator is loaded with moist product. As soon as the temperature comes up to the desired level and the extra heat is not needed to warm large amounts of incoming fresh air, one or two switches may be turned off and the drying completed at the reduced heating rate.

Building This Dehydrator

By Roger Cota

I like this dehydrator. It's a good basic design — easier to build than I thought it would be when I first glanced at the plans. The directions plus the illustrations are easy to follow.

Before you decide to build, however, let me tell you two things you should consider:

1. *Parts may be difficult to find.* The most difficult thing to find was the thermostat. Usually a thermostat is available from an electrical supply company. A baseboard heater thermostat may be possible to mount in the dehydrator.

2. *The parts are not cheap.* I bought everything except the bulbs. You could cut costs if you scrounge parts, such as the plywood, the fan, the thermometer, or any of the others. If you value your time and have to buy all of the materials, a commercial model might be a good buy for you.

And here are a few thoughts I had while building this:

The fan that I found turns at 3,000 RPM. I don't think that speed is necessary. About 1,700 RPM might be fine. If I were building again, I might even mount a rheostat on the fan, so that I could control those RPM.

We had a surprise with the fan motor. On the first test everything was going smoothly — until the fan quit. We waited. The bulbs, of course, heated the box quickly, and the thermostat shut them off. Within a minute, the fan kicked back in, cooled the box, and the lights came on again. The cycle was repeated a few minutes later. That's when we learned that this motor (and most of the electric motors built today) turns itself off when it shows signs of overheating. This temperature level was reached only when the thermostat was turned to give the hottest conditions in the box. It seemed to make no difference in the functioning of the dehydrator — our test apple dried at just about the same speed as the one in a commercial dryer.

We added one refinement to our dehydrator — a piece of the tray screen tacked above the fan at the level of the heat shield. You'll see in the illustrations that there's a space there. Food might drop down from a tray being moved and hit the fan, or a finger might stray down and get spanked by the fan.

The thermostat we bought came without a box. We had to fashion a utility box to hold it.

The door on ours fits very smoothly (he said with some pride), but you might want to add a magnetic catch to yours to hold it in place. They're available at most hardware stores.

Finally, I painted a polyurethene coating over the exterior of the box to give it a protective coating.

If I were going to build another, I wouldn't build the trays. They can be built of wood, as mine were, but any repair shop that handles screen doors and windows can quickly turn out five aluminum trays that would be dandy — and maybe easier to clean than the ones with wooden sides.

Dale Kirk did a fine job on this design. A lot of thought went into it to produce a workable dehydrator that even the person with little experience can build.

Tests of This Dehydrator

By Phyllis Hobson

This dehydrator was larger and heavier than any commercial models I've tested. But it did fit nicely on a low table in a well-ventilated utility room, which I had already decided was a better location than the kitchen for an electric dehydrator. I liked this dryer, because it has two features — deep, sturdy trays and a snug-fitting door. These are two of the most consistent problems I've encountered in commercial models.

This dryer performed beautifully. On as dry a day as you're likely to find in Indiana in early spring, apple slices and banana chips were crisp in 5 hours. Without any pretreatment, there was no darkening of pear slices and no loss of flavor in grapes. Unlike many of the commercial dehydrators, it was not necessary to turn the fruit or rotate the trays. All areas of every tray dried evenly.

With the dial set on low and the trays empty, the interior temperature reached 100°F (38°C) in 10 minutes. With the dial turned to the 110° (43°C) mark, it reached precisely 110°F (43°C) in another 10 minutes. It took 10 minutes more to reach 120°F (49°C).

With the trays filled, it took longer to reach maximum temperature, but the thermostat worked well, adjusting the temperature by turning the lights off, then on again.

I especially liked the trays. With almost 1 inch of depth, they were easy to handle, even when fully loaded. But I had some problems with the open-weave wire mesh, because the rough surface made it difficult to remove sticky foods at almost any stage of drying. Not only were the dried foods hard to peel off, but the trays were hard to clean and almost impossible to soak.

In spite of that, I still would use the open-weave wire mesh, because it allows for better circulation of air and quicker drying of foods than fine screen. Not only are the trays sturdier than those made of screen, but they will last longer. Those are the reasons I would vote against using aluminum window screens as suggested, even though it would be a lot easier on the builder than making wood-framed trays. Under heavy use, screening tends to pull out of aluminum frames with the weight of the food.

I would suggest one change in the trays. Roger Cota followed the directions faithfully for the test model and graduated the length of the trays to fit the sloping tray slots. With every tray ½ inch longer than the tray below it, inserting five different lengths of trays into five different lengths of slots can be a shell game when you have five full trays to load at once. I'm sure the slope is necessary for air circulation, and it is possible to mark the trays, but it would simplify construction and use to make all the trays the shorter length.

OTHER GARDEN WAY PUBLISHING BOOKS YOU WILL ENJOY

Keeping the Harvest, by Nancy Chioffi and Gretchen Mead

Enjoy your abundant harvest of garden-fresh fruits and vegetables throughout the year by following the simple, satisfying home-preserving techniques found in this popular book. A reliable easy-to-use reference for gardeners and cooks, this up-to-date book covers that latest techniques, equipment, and USDA guidelines for home preserving in the 90's. 208 pages.

The Harvest Gardener, by Susan McClure

This useful handbook shows you how to plant, harvest, and store your crops for maximum yield, freshness, and flavor. A true encyclopedia, it's packed with field-tested recommendations and specific growth and harvest characteristics of all popular garden vegetables. 298 pages.

The Joy of Gardening, by Dick Raymond

Written by Garden Way's own master gardener Dick Raymond, this classic, comprehensive reference book is packed with how-to advice and information that will show anyone, anywhere how to turn a patch of ground into a lush, bountiful vegetable garden. Color photographs and illustrations throughout. Over 600,000 copies sold! 365 pages.

Successful Small Food Gardens, by Louise Riotte

Best-selling author Riotte shows you how to grow vegetables even if you live in the city, a condominium, or a mobile home. Learn about raised beds, container and hanging gardens, water and drainage techniques, improving soil quality, dwarf fruits and vegetables, landscaping tricks, companion plants and succession planting, edible flowers, herbs and shrubs, and more. 196 pages.

Fruits and Berries for the Home Garden, by Lewis Hill

This classic guide has been completely revised and updated by this "north country" grower. Lewis says "if you can grow them in northern Vermont, you can grow them anywhere!" Covers improved fruit varieties, earth-sound fertilizing, pest and disease control methods, and cultivar recommendations. Dozens of helpful lists and charts for "what to use when." 288 pages.

The Big Book of Gardening Skills,
by the Editors of Garden Way Publishing

When the title say big, it means BIG — 336 oversized pages packed with information on virtually every aspect of growing vegetables, fruits and berries, flowers, herbs, and shrubs. Clearly organized by topic with charts, tables, and over 450 illustrations, this book will help you plan, plant, and maintain beautiful, healthy, and productive gardens. 336 page.

The Organic Gardener's Home Reference, by Tanya Denckla

You'll save countless hours with this plant-by-plant reference book. It's packed with all the essential information you need to grow vegetables, fruits, nuts, and herbs organically. Discover which plants may help or hinder each other. Learn easy and environmentally safe ways to controls diseases and pests. Find out how to grow more than 60 of the most popular plants. Learn when to harvest for best size and quality. With this well-organized, convenient guide, you'll find yourself reading less and growing more! 273 pages.

Growing and Using Herbs Successfully, by Betty M. Jacobs

In helpful, easy-to-understand language, Betty Jacobs shows you how to get the best results with 64 herbs. You learn how to start herbs indoors and out, how to harvest and store herbs for maximum flavor, and more. 240 pages.

The Herbal Tea Garden, by Marietta Marshall Marcin

This complete handbook reveals everything you need to know about selecting, growing, blending, brewing, and enjoying over 70 herbal tea blends. Includes detailed information on reported medicinal and beneficial qualities of dozens of herb teas, and a source list of herb tea suppliers. 224 pages.

These books are available at your bookstore, lawn and garden center, or may be ordered directly from Garden Way Publishing, Department WM, Schoolhouse Road, Pownal, VT 05261. To order toll-free, call 1-800-441-5700.

Index

Pages in **bold** type indicate that instructions for drying are included.